TO FLY
AMONG
THE STARS

TO FLY AMONG THE STARS

The Hidden Story of the Fight for Women Astronauts

REBECCA SIEGEL

SCHOLASTIC
FOCUS

NEW YORK

Library of Congress Cataloging-in-Publication Data

Names: Rissman, Rebecca, author.
Title: To fly among the stars : the hidden story of the fight for women astronauts / Rebecca Siegel.
Description: New York, NY : Scholastic Focus, [2020] | Audience: Ages 8-12.
Identifiers: LCCN 2018055439 (print) | LCCN 2018058595 (ebook) |
    ISBN 9781338290172 (Ebook) | ISBN 9781338290158 (hardcover : alk. paper)
Subjects: LCSH: United States. National Aeronautics and Space
    Administration—History—Juvenile literature. | Space race—History—Juvenile
    literature. | Astronauts—Training of—United States—Juvenile literature. |
    Astronautics—United States—History—Juvenile literature. | Women in
    astronautics—History—Juvenile literature.
Classification: LCC TL793 (ebook) | LCC TL793 .R5448 2020 (print) | DDC
629.4500973—dc23 | LC record available at https://lccn.loc.gov/2018055439

10 9 8 7 6 5 4 3 2 1   20 21 22 23 24

Printed in the U.S.A.   23
First edition, March 2020
Book design by Abby Dening

TABLE OF CONTENTS

PREFACE vii

PROLOGUE: February 20, 1960 ix

CHAPTER 1: Flight Dreams 1

CHAPTER 2: The Sky Belonged to Men 13

CHAPTER 3: Lightning Fast and Always Lovely 24

CHAPTER 4: The Jet Age 38

CHAPTER 5: "A Man's Work" 49

CHAPTER 6: The Test Pilot Years 60

CHAPTER 7: Setting Records, *Sputnik*, and

                the Start of the Space Race 75

CHAPTER 8: Astronaut Testing and Selection 85

CHAPTER 9: Female, Unit 1: Testing Begins 97

CHAPTER 10: Dedication 114

CHAPTER 11: Going Public 127

CHAPTER 12: Money, Monkeys, and Men 142

CHAPTER 13: Testing More Women.. 158

CHAPTER 14: Corvettes and Parties...................................... 170

CHAPTER 15: The Women Who Fought for Flight............. 183

CHAPTER 16: A Test Pilot Questioned...................................193

CHAPTER 17: Phase III Testing and a Telegram................. 206

CHAPTER 18: Race to the Finish...222

CHAPTER 19: The Fight Goes to Washington 237

CHAPTER 20: Of Course, No Women.................................... 253

CHAPTER 21: After Mercury 260

CHAPTER 22: Picking Up the Pieces 266

EPILOGUE: The Ultimate Glass Ceiling................................. 280

A NOTE ABOUT THE WOMEN'S TEST SCORES.....................283

GLOSSARY 285

BIBLIOGRAPHY..287

PHOTO CREDITS..303

INDEX 305

ACKNOWLEDGMENTS... 337

ABOUT THE AUTHOR..341

PREFACE

R eady?" asked my flight instructor, Pete, his voice almost impossible to hear over the roar of our engine.

His warnings rattled through my mind: *Go easy on the podals. Don't overcompensate. Keep the plane's nose centered. Maintain control.*

I nodded weakly and stared straight ahead.

Here goes nothing.

Pete released the brakes and we thundered forward. Our speed increased. When the dotted line down the center of the runway began to blur, I cautiously pulled back on the yoke. I felt the nose grow light and begin to lift. I gave the yoke another tiny tug. And just like that, I pulled an airplane into the sky.

You see, I'll do just about anything for research.

When I first stumbled upon the story inside this book, I didn't anticipate how incredibly inspired I'd be by it all. And I never could have guessed that I would find myself at the controls of a single-engine airplane. But research takes you on funny journeys, and I think it's my job as a nonfiction author to embrace each bump and turn.

To Fly Among the Stars is a true story. The details come from a variety of sources, including memoirs, interviews, flight plans, newspaper articles, airplane manuals, photos, videos, and letters. Anything that appears between quotation marks comes from one of my sources and reflects the exact words of these very real people.

To put this story in context, I worked with military pilots, commercial pilots, and private pilots. I researched the history of aviation in general, and got a little hands-on experience as well.

I've done my very best to re-create these exciting moments in history for you, my reader, so that you might feel the energy and suspense and yes, frustration, of this iconic American era. It was a time when aviation technology advanced at a breakneck pace, while gender rules remained stubbornly old-fashioned.

I was moved by both groups of pilots in this tale. The men were talented aviators who bravely jumped at the chance to explore space. The women were outstanding pilots who fought valiantly for the same opportunity. I hope that you find this story compelling, and that it encourages you to follow your dreams, whatever they may be.

Wishing you blue skies and tailwinds,
Rebecca Siegel

PROLOGUE

FEBRUARY 20, 1960

ick, tick, tick, tick.

Somewhere behind her, a metronome clicked a
relentless beat. Jerrie Cobb pumped her legs furiously on
the stationary bike, straining to match the rhythm. Sweat
ran down her back.

Inhale. Exhale.

Thick plastic straps held a mask over her mouth and nose.
A long black tube snaked from the mask through a grid of
metal scaffolding in front of the bike. Cobb could hear her
breath filling the tube. Each exhale pushed it farther away.
Her exhales would be tested. Everything would be tested.

Keep pedaling.

The mask held Cobb's face in place. She sensed someone
approach her bike from the rear. He slid something against
the back wheel. The resistance suddenly increased, and her
muscles screamed with effort. Her legs seared with pain as
she pushed forward. She would not slow down. She would
match that metronome.

A cluster of scientists stood at the edges of the room, observing her and scribbling notes. Occasionally, one would step forward to adjust a piece of her equipment or check an instrument's reading before retreating to his watchful perch.

Jerrie's lungs burned. Sweat stung her eyes. Her breath was ragged now.

Off to her left, she saw a gray-haired physician give her a quick nod. It was a tiny gesture of encouragement. Jerrie knew what it meant: *Keep pedaling.*

This was a test. It was the same test that the Mercury 7 astronauts had taken just a year earlier. If Cobb did well enough, maybe she could become an astronaut, too. Her heart pounded as she fought the temptation to quit. "I had to go on—that I knew," she said in later years. "If riding a bicycle would get me into space, then ride I would."

Tick, tick.

The metronome stopped.

CHAPTER 1

J ust sit there . . . don't *touch* anything and don't *do* anything until I tell you."

Twelve-year-old Jerrie Cobb nodded gravely to her father. He gave her seat belt one last tug to make sure it was as tight as it could be, then turned to face the controls in the front seat of the cockpit. The tiny plane roared to life before beginning its bumpy trot down the runway. A 1936 Waco biplane couldn't go very fast. In fact, it maxed out at around 90 miles per hour in the air. But for a kid sitting on a stack of pillows in an open cockpit, the sense of speed was overwhelming. Jerrie might as well have been riding a rocket.

The blonde and freckle-faced girl knew some of the basics of flight, things she'd picked up from her father: *Don't climb too fast or you'll stall. Don't lose sight of the horizon. Keep steady pressure on the stick. Watch your fuel levels.* But there was so much more to learn.

They skipped once, twice, and then lifted off. If Jerrie

made any sounds, surprised gasps or happy shrieks, they were whisked away by the wind. It felt like the sun was warmer up here. Brighter, too. Her tiny backseat was brilliantly lit.

Below them, the little Waco's shadow traced a wobbling path across a dusty brown-green landscape. Clusters of neat, boxy structures proudly dotted the scrubland. They were Army Air Force barracks, mess halls, and airplane hangars. Troops of cadets in crisp green uniforms scurried between drills and lectures. Sheppard Field was cranking out the soldiers and airplane mechanics needed to supply American efforts in World War II. Down there on the ground, all anyone seemed to think about was war, bullets, bombs, and victory. But up in the air, things were different.

Jerrie's eyes grew wide behind a pair of enormous flight goggles. She'd begged her father for weeks for the chance to fly. And now she was overcome with wonder. The Waco's engine buzzed and its wood propeller spun. The fabric-covered wings hummed and sliced cleanly through the air. Jerrie realized just how foreign flight really was. Everything was different in the sky. Her feet, which hung a full twelve inches above the pedals, started to happily bounce.

Then, from her backseat perch, Jerrie saw her father raise both hands into the air to signal her. They were at 1,000 feet. It was her turn to fly. She reached down to take the stick between her legs. Her father tipped his hands forward. Jerrie pressed the stick forward and felt the nose of the Waco dip. Her stomach lurched. The plane growled deeply. She pulled back on the stick gently, careful to avoid a stall, and watched as the horizon dropped out of her line of sight. The growl changed into a whine and then a cheerful hum. Amazing! She was flying.

The next hour was a happy, bright, meandering dance. Jerrie tried out different maneuvers following the hand signals of her father. Together, they climbed, dipped, and banked. When he finally gave her the "hands off" signal, she had reached a level of joy that bordered on delirium.

That afternoon, a pilot friend of Jerrie's father watched the unlikely duo climb out of their little biplane.

"Good flight?" he asked.

"Training flight. Jerrie just had her first lesson," her father answered.

"Better log it," the pilot said, turning to look at Jerrie. "Every student pilot must keep a log."

The pilot then pulled a memo book out of his pocket and drew a few quick columns down the first page. He grinned a little while he worked. This was, after all, a bit silly. She was just a kid!

But none of this was funny to Jerrie. She knew that pilot logbooks were a record of their time in the air. They were like résumés. The very best pilots were the ones with the most hours.

Jerrie watched seriously as the pilot scrawled her first entry in the makeshift log. Below it sat rows and rows of empty spaces. She made a promise to herself: All those spaces *would* be filled. She *would* become a pilot.

PILOT'S NAME	DATE	LOCATION	FLIGHT HOURS
Jerrie Cobb	1943	Wichita Falls, TX	1

In truth, Jerrie's dream was a long shot. Few pilots in the 1940s had even seen a woman in an airplane hangar, unless of course she was a secretary or cleaning lady or somebody's sweetheart. Flying was men's work, plain and simple. It was physical, technical, and dangerous. It was dirty, too. It was everything women had been told they couldn't handle.

Despite this, Jerrie Cobb wasn't the only girl dreaming of a career in the air. While she was logging that first hour of flight, women across the nation were already gazing at the skies, their eyes filled not with wonder but with raw ambition. They stepped out onto their penthouse balconies, their suburban backyards, their tenement back alleys, and they squinted as airplanes buzzed overhead. The Great Depression had come and gone. They'd budgeted and farmed and scraped and saved, and here they were. Still standing. Now a new frontier presented itself in the sky and they dared to ask, *Why not?*

In 1929, two years before Jerrie Cobb was born, a group of pioneering female pilots had gathered in a dusty airplane hangar for a historic meeting. They saw the sky for what it was: a new, brave, uncharted world for both men *and* women. They were a ragtag crew that day; some were dressed in flapper attire, with ankle-length skirts and bell-shaped hats. Others were dressed to fly. They wore trousers, boots, and fur-lined bomber jackets. One woman looked as though she had just stepped off a rough flight. Her oil-stained coveralls fell in crumpled folds around her wrists and ankles, and she hadn't even bothered to take off her flight helmet or goggles. She had work to do. They all did.

These women met that day to lay the foundation for an organization of female pilots that would outlive them all. They called it the Ninety-Nines. The unusual name came from the number of members that first year: ninety-nine. There were ninety-nine women who were bold enough not only to be pilots, but to seek out a community of like-minded adventurers. In later years, the Ninety-Nines would span the globe. Members would fly airliners, fighter planes, and even spacecraft. But during that first meeting in 1929, the women's goals were modest: Organize. Unite. Encourage. Flight was hard for women. The Ninety-Nines hoped to make it a little easier.

At first, many female pilots came from very wealthy backgrounds. Flying was expensive. Ruth Nichols, one of the women who attended that first meeting of the Ninety-Nines, was a New York socialite. She used family money to fund her passion. She shelled out $500 to get her private pilot's license in 1921. This was an almost unthinkably expensive sum at a time when most Americans earned between $1,000 and $3,000 a year. Flight lessons weren't the only expense. Pilots also needed something to fly. They could try to buy a plane, but with price tags that were almost always $500 or more, plane ownership was often out of the question. Women who didn't own their own planes had to rent them, which meant paying for their time in the air. Amelia Earhart, another founder of the Ninety-Nines, worked as a telephone company clerk and photographer in order to pay for her early flight lessons. Her instructor's fee was steep: $1 for each minute in the air.

Over time, as airplanes became more common and airtime more available, the population of female aviators began to grow and change. By the 1930s, the sorority of women pilots was no longer dominated by socialites and the daughters of business tycoons. It was diversifying. Farm girls, schoolteachers, and housewives had begun climbing into the cockpit. Earhart did her best to describe female pilots in her 1932 autobiography, *The Fun of It*: "There are slim ones and plump ones and quiet ones and those who talk all the time. They're large and small, young and old, about half the list are married and many of these have children. In a word, they are simply thoroughly normal girls and women who happen to have taken up flying rather than golf, swimming, or steeplechasing."

Of course, Earhart wasn't referring to just any "thoroughly normal girls." She was talking about *White* girls. Aviation was an activity for a predominantly White population. Only a very small number of minority men—and an even smaller number of minority women—found flight schools willing to admit them, teach them, and certify them safe to fly. Bessie Coleman, the first Black American woman to fly, had to go all the way to France to find someone willing to teach her. Despite this, she earned her international pilot's license in 1921, becoming what American journalists called a Negro Aviatrix. An Asian American woman wouldn't become a pilot for another eleven years. When she got her pilot's license in 1932, newspapers across the nation showed enlarged photos of Katherine Sui Fun Cheung's beaming face, proclaiming "Miss China Goes Aloft."

The early 1940s, the era of Jerrie Cobb's first flight lesson, would see a brief surge in the number of women pilots. In 1941, the Ninety-Nines counted 935 licensed female pilots in the country. That number would more than double when an experimental national flying organization, the Civilian Pilot Training Program (CPTP), allowed a generous female enrollment ratio: one girl for every nine boys. The idea was that women typically controlled their household finances, and would be more likely to allow their husbands to do things like buy airplanes if they themselves had had the chance to enjoy flight. It was a sexist premise, but hopeful female aviators jumped at the opportunity all the same. With the help of the CPTP, the number of licensed American women fliers rose to about 2,000. Compared to male pilots, it was still

Ruth Nichols, decked in fashionable attire, waves from the cockpit of her Lockheed Vega

a measly number. Females made up just over 1% of the American piloting community. But it was progress. Their tiny wedge of the pie was expanding.

Then in mid-1941, a war loomed large on the horizon. The CPTP started to take on a military feel, and women were promptly punted out of the program. It seemed as though nobody wanted to "waste" aviation instruction on women when the country's future war fliers needed it first.

World War II soon bloomed into a deadly global conflict, and the face of America's aviation force changed drastically. Able-bodied male pilots were plucked from their familiar cockpits and transplanted into different, weaponized versions in Europe, or the Pacific, or Africa. Hundreds of thousands more earned their wings through military flight training programs. These aviators flew new, sophisticated aircraft. Giant bombers. Zippy fighters. Seaplanes. Gliders.

As men grew comfortable flying their war planes overseas, the women on the home front settled into the sturdy old planes the men had left empty. They flew commuters to and from meetings, transported goods, and crop-dusted fields. Their time in the cockpit was not glamorous. They earned small but livable wages while learning confidence in the air and a love for flight.

Some women joined the Civilian Air Patrol (CAP). During the war, male CAP pilots were encouraged to fly along American coastlines, searching the inky seas for the telltale shadow of German U-boats. Female CAP pilots weren't allowed to fly the coasts. They were, however, allowed to teach and receive CAP flight training. For women with no other access to a cockpit, the CAP seemed just fine.

At the same time, a short-lived program called the Women Airforce Service Pilots (WASP) gave a select group of women military flight training. Between 1942 and 1944, WASPs flew transport missions and shuttled military personnel between American bases. They also worked as test pilots, trying out newly repaired airplanes before they were handed off to male pilots for use in the war. Training to become a WASP was grueling. It involved months of classroom instruction, physical exercise, and flight lessons. Despite the intense training, graduates of the WASP program didn't enjoy the fruits of their labor for long. In December of 1944, the program was disbanded. The public just wasn't ready to see a woman fly a bomber, even it ship wasn't anywhere near combat.

In 1945, the war ended. Seasoned male pilots flocked back to their old jobs in droves. New pilots, freshly equipped with military flight training, flooded the job market. And employers greedily scooped them up. You're a navy pilot? Hired! Army man? Welcome aboard! Their planes and passengers would be safer than ever before. Airlines, ferrying companies, and flight transport business owners signed their paychecks with pride. Anything to support a war hero.

At the same time, female pilots were quietly pushed to the side. Their novelty had faded. The sense of solidarity and sisterhood that sustained the home front during those

A group of WASPs pose in front of a military aircraft, *Love Field*, in Dallas, Texas, 1943.

long years now felt wilted, embarrassing. Sidelong glances and drawn-out silences sent the clear message: You're not wanted anymore. Go home.

Some women pilots welcomed their sweethearts home from the war with open arms, but others greeted these veterans with a scowl. Each triumphant warrior striding down Main Street represented another cockpit filled. Another job denied.

The conclusion of the war ended many female aviation careers, but not all of them. The women who could afford it maintained their skills by paying for their flight hours. But very few managed to sustain livable wages just from flying planes. Some women stuck it out anyway, finding odd flight jobs here and there. They worked as flight instructors, stewardesses, even airline bookkeepers. Anything to stay close to the airfield.

Among these many amazing women who managed to maintain a healthy flight habit in those postwar years, thirteen of them, spread all over the country, were setting the stage for an incredible future.

There was Myrtle Cagle, who at age fourteen had been the youngest person ever to earn a pilot's license in North Carolina. Jane Briggs Hart and Jerri Sloan Truhill had both started their piloting careers in secret, sneaking out of their respective childhood homes to take flying lessons that their parents had forbidden. There was Bea Steadman, a spark-plug inspector who worked as many hours as she could to afford precious time in the sky. Rhea Hurrle had grown up in Minnesota, staring at planes above her and telling anyone who would listen, "Yeah. I can do that." Sarah Gorelick and Gene Nora Stumbough were both impressive air racers who made a habit of tearing across the skies in high-speed battles. Jan and Marion Dietrich were identical twins living in California. Jan was a flight instructor and corporate pilot. Marion juggled flight with her career as an aviation journalist. Jean Hixson was a WASP turned schoolteacher who never gave up her flight ambitions after the program dissolved. Irene Leverton was a Chicagoan who could fly and fix just about every plane at her local hangar.

Wally Funk was the youngest of the bunch but made up for lost time by earning flight credentials at a breakneck pace. And finally, there was Jerrie Cobb. That first flight in the Waco was a prelude to decades of joy in the air.

These thirteen women didn't know much of one another yet. Some had never even met. Despite this, their lives would soon intersect in one of the most significant events in American aviation.

CHAPTER 2

THE SKY BELONGED TO MEN

C aptain John Glenn strode confidently through a San Francisco airport. It was 1945, World War II was over, and the strawberry-blond, freckle-faced, twenty-three-year-old Marine pilot was homeward bound.

As he made his way from California to his home state of Ohio, dressed in his crisp olive-green uniform, Glenn noticed something unusual: His mere presence had an effect on bystanders. People stared. Some came right up to him to offer their thanks. He was humble and bashful, but also proud. He had done marvelous things over there. He knew it.

Glenn had flown fifty-nine combat missions in the Pacific, firing countless rounds of bullets and dropping hundreds of bombs on enemy targets. He'd had plenty of close calls, too. On five separate occasions, Glenn's aircraft had been socked by enemy fire. Once, the hole in his plane's wing was big enough to fit his head through. But he'd managed to bring his aircraft in safely every time, and that was what counted. His skills didn't go unnoticed. He'd been awarded two Distinguished Flying Crosses and a whopping ten Air Medals for his work in the war.

John Glenn was a real-deal, bona-fide war hero.

But now that the conflict had drawn to a close, it was time to decide what to do with his life. He'd begun college before the war, studying chemistry at Muskingum College, but had dropped out to join the fight. He could go back and finish school. His dad asked him to leave the marines and join the family plumbing business. His old neighbor wanted him to become a dentist. But Glenn? He just wanted to fly.

The male pilots like Glenn who came home after World War II were lucky. Not only had they survived an epic conflict that claimed the lives of more than 400,000 of their countrymen, but they'd also been granted a gift: some of the best flight training available in the world. Unlike female aviators, who often had to fight—and pay—for time in the air, returning military pilots were treated to a wide range of job options. Back in the United States, the skies were theirs to own. They just had to figure out what to do up there.

Glenn decided to stay in the marines. He flew for a while at the Naval Air Station in Patuxent River, helping to service test fighter planes fresh off the assembly lines. These aircraft needed someone to fly them hard and fast, do landings and takeoffs, fire bullets and drop bombs, and do loops and barrel rolls. Essentially, someone had to make sure the planes would hold together in the air.

Service testing was technical, important, and often very fun. During the day, Glenn and his fellow pilots would stage mock aerial battles in the sky, dodging and diving and chasing one another through the clouds. At night, Glenn would prank a friend who lived nearby by flat-hatting his house. He'd shove his stick forward and dive right down toward his pal's roof, then pull back to skim a foot or two over the shingles before climbing back up into the clouds. His engine's roar would shake the walls and roof of his friend's house, surely sending him into a panicked, bewildered frenzy. It was a pretty good stunt.

It wasn't a bad life for a pilot: pranks and stunts and fast, new planes. Glenn was reaping the rewards of his war-tested skills, of course, but also of his gender. While he zigged and zagged through the air in spanking-new fighters, women pilots who managed to fly at all were stuck in slow, old planes, doing the jobs that nobody wanted.

In 1946, Glenn was transferred to the Marine Corps Air Station El Toro, in sunny California, where he and his squadron were often hired to perform at air shows or other outdoor events. They roared over the crowds in sparkling war planes, sometimes flying in formation, other times simply showing their adoring fans just how fast their aircraft could go. For a while, these air shows sustained Glenn. But soon, he grew bored. He wanted to be challenged. Glenn wanted more.

John Glenn wasn't the only military pilot who wondered what to do with himself after the end of World War II. Deke Slayton, a twenty-one-year-old Army Air Corps pilot, was also questioning his future after the war ended. The tall, tanned, dark-haired pilot had flown a total of sixty-three combat missions in Europe and the Pacific. The war had changed him from a wet-behind-the-ears Wisconsin farm boy to a seasoned soldier. He'd flown nervous. He'd flown tired. He'd flown angry, confident, and even—dangerously—rip-roaring drunk. He'd muscled his planes through glowing sheets of flak on countless occasions. Once, he'd ducked for cover under a parked airplane as enemies bombed the base around him to smithereens. How could a guy go from that kind of life into the boring, safe world of civilians?

After the war, Slayton briefly considered taking a job as an airline pilot, but he later said, "It looked like kind of dull flying . . . I didn't have any enthusiasm for that." He spent a year working as an Army flight instructor, which kept him close to the airfield but still left him unsatisfied. In 1946, he left the Army and enrolled in college under the GI Bill to study aeronautical engineering. It was free tuition to learn about his passion. While he studied, he joined the Air National Guard, which paid him $40 a month to do exactly what he really desired: fly.

Slayton spent his hours outside of the classroom strapped into various cockpits. He screamed through the skies in fighters called P-51s, darted around clouds in nimble bombers called A-26s, and thundered across the heavens in hulking transports called C-47s. While women pilots had to scrape by, flying whatever old aircraft they could get their hands on, Deke Slayton was learning exactly what makes aircraft work, and at the same time getting *paid* to fly what he wanted. It was a great gig for a war veteran, and an unthinkable dream for a woman.

When Slayton graduated from college in 1949, he gazed into the horizon and wondered: What next? The skies were limitless. So was his future.

Glenn and Slayton were both fortunate. They were genuine war pilots and, therefore, could shoot for the most coveted flying jobs. There were plenty of other men who had wanted to fly during the war but hadn't quite made it into the air before the Japanese surrendered. Unlike women aviators at the time, who had few options for flight, even these men could still pursue a wide range of careers in the air. They could get their pilot's license and then look for any number of aviation jobs. They could run an aircraft company, something that a woman wouldn't accomplish until 1930. They could become passenger airline pilots, a position denied to women until 1973. Or they could pursue military flight training, something that women wouldn't be allowed to do again until 1973.

Military flight training was a shining, lofty goal for pilots. It was a demanding, rigorous program that churned out row after row of confident, competent aviators. Each man who made it through got the ultimate badge of honor: a gleaming set of wings pinned to his chest. This tiny token was a symbol of discipline, precision, and honor in the air.

Wally Schirra was a brown-haired, dimple-faced navy sailor who longed for a pair of those wings. He had always known he would become a pilot. He was the product of a stick and rudder family. His father had been a World War I ace pilot and his mother had plenty of aviation tricks up her own sleeves. The two lovebirds had spent the early 1920s stunt flying at county fairs across the country. Schirra's father would stay in the cockpit while his wife walked on the top wing to the shock and delight of seas of drop-jawed spectators. Schirra's mother stopped her wing walking only when she realized they had another passenger on board: little Walter. She was pregnant.

Wally Schirra as a young naval midshipman.

Schirra had spent his childhood surrounded by planes. He first took the controls of the family two-seater airplane when he was only thirteen years old. Flight just seemed to be in his blood. It was his destiny.

So it was especially painful for Schirra that he missed his chance to fly during World War II. He had barely made it into the war at all, landing himself on the naval battleship the USS *Alaska* in the final months of the war. At the time, many hopeful naval aviators were required to put in two years at sea before they could get themselves into flight school. This meant that Schirra was out of luck. The closest he came to a fighter plane was when four F8F Bearcats buzzed the deck of the *Alaska* in a staggeringly tight formation. It had been a brain-rattling experience. The small and nimble planes absolutely roared with power. Naval aviators said the Bearcat was essentially just an engine with a saddle on it. Schirra wondered how it would feel to rip through the air in such a magnificent machine.

Schirra finally got himself into flight school at the end of 1946. He earned his wings in 1948 and never looked back.

Another wannabe pilot who was still at sea when the war ended was Alan Shepard. The whip-smart twenty-two-year-old from New Hampshire had served two cruises on the destroyer the USS *Cogswell* during the last years of the war. When the *Cogswell* pulled alongside an American aircraft carrier, Shepard would sometimes abandon his duties just to sprint to his ship's rails to watch. He was fascinated by aviation, and especially by the hotshot pilots capable of these seaborne missions.

Shepard desperately wanted to fly. While he was still on the *Cogswell*, he turned to a shipmate and said dryly, "One of these days . . . One of these days—if I don't get killed—I'm going to learn to fly."

Shepard didn't get killed. He made it home, and then, just as soon as he could, to the airfield. He got his wings in 1947.

Virgil "Gus" Grissom was a high school student when the United States entered World War II. While Glenn, Slayton, Shepard, and Schirra served overseas, dodging bullets and bombs, Grissom was stuck behind a school desk.

The short, broad-shouldered teen yawned through classes and dreamed of joining the fight. He'd first flown in an airplane as a young teen, and while he later confessed that he wasn't a "flying fanatic" as a youth, the idea of becoming a war pilot was certainly an attractive one. He made it through high school with decent grades in math, but not much else. His principal later recalled that Grissom "had studied just about enough to get a diploma." He enlisted in the air force in 1944 but took a brief break to get married in 1945. He returned to service just as the war ended. He'd missed his chance.

Whereas Slayton and Glenn had their pick of impressive piloting jobs, Grissom was nineteen years old and hopelessly lost. He worked a few air force desk jobs but soon lost his enthusiasm. This wasn't what he wanted at all. He left the service and took a job working as a bus mechanic. Then he decided to get an education. He enrolled in some engineering classes at Purdue University during the day and flipped burgers at night. He was a grease-stained, tired husband. This sure wasn't the heroic pilot's life he'd envisioned.

Grissom had had some bad luck. His timing was off and he'd missed his window to fly in combat. But as a White male, he still had plenty of chances to achieve his dream. He'd just have to work at it.

In 1950, Grissom graduated from Purdue with a degree in mechanical engineering. He reenlisted in the air force and got his wings the next year. Finally, he was in the air.

Scott Carpenter was another ambitious, sky-eyed youth who missed the action in World War II. He'd raced to join the navy after high school graduation and was whisked off to training, even managing to snag a few hours of flight lessons. After his first hop in a navy trainer, an open-air biplane, he wrote to his father in breathless excitement: "We did every aerobatic maneuver in the books and then some. I had a lot of fun and I think I'm going to like this flying business a lot." He'd had a taste of freedom and adventure in the air, and he wanted more. But, like Grissom, Carpenter's timing just stank. He was still in training at the end of the war, and he was released from duty with nothing to do and nowhere to go. Without the promise of battlefield glory, twenty-year-old Carpenter was adrift.

But Carpenter couldn't let go of his dreams of flight. Reluctantly, he enrolled in engineering courses at the University of Colorado. He hated them, but at least the classes kept him busy until he could find his way back into a cockpit. Finally, in 1949, Carpenter heard that the navy was looking for engineering students for a program that promised flight training. It was perfect! Carpenter abandoned college, one credit shy of graduation, and jumped at the chance. He rattled off a postcard to his father: "I'm as happy now as any person could possibly be . . . This is what I've wanted all along."

Carpenter had to wait a little and work a lot, but he got his wish. He earned his wings in 1951.

For eighteen-year-old Leroy Gordon "Gordo" Cooper, missing his chance to fly in the war stung. Cooper's dad had fought in both world wars and had made a point of getting his son into formal flight lessons by age fourteen. His family owned a little biplane with so much power that Cooper later bragged that it could "almost do a loop on takeoff." Cooper's dad was a real-deal pilot. He hadn't just flown in battle, he'd brushed shoulders with greatness over friendly skies as well. Young Gordo grew up listening, transfixed, to his dad's stories of flying with celebrities such as Amelia Earhart. What a magical time it had been! He wanted in on that magic.

By the time Cooper graduated from high school, neither the navy nor the army needed any more pilots. He reluctantly enlisted in the marines and went to boot camp, but the war ended before he was able to see any combat. What a bust. He moved to Hawaii and enrolled in college there, but Cooper never stopped dreaming of a career in the air. He just had to fly.

During college, Cooper was commissioned into the U.S. Army ROTC. He transferred to the air force and got his wings in 1950. At last, he soared.

The years after World War II were, for most Americans, a time of growth and security and relief. The war was over. They'd made it through. Couples, drunk off of peace and prosperity, started families. There was a baby boom, and then a rush to the suburbs. America, it seemed, was settling down.

But there was a small community of aviators who weren't interested in settling down. They were looking *up*. Men like Glenn and Slayton, who had tasted airborne battle, wanted more. There was just something about the adrenaline of it that tugged them back to the airfields. Men like Schirra and Shepard, who had missed their chance to fly during the war, felt this same pull. They wanted to fly, too. They *needed* to fly. For new aviators like Grissom, Carpenter, and Cooper, the sky represented a giant, blank canvas. They knew their futures would be scrawled upon it, but when? How?

For these seven men, the sky called. And beyond that, the stars.

CHAPTER 3

LIGHTNING FAST AND ALWAYS LOVELY

Early in the morning of September 14, 1947, as hundreds of thousands of American male pilots began their days, sipping coffee or reading newspapers at their kitchen tables, a pair of petite, raven-haired sisters stepped onto a scale in front of a small crowd. The twins' weight was recorded (a combined 189 pounds), and air race officials began their scribbled calculations. They needed to determine how many sandbags to pack into the sisters' airplane, an Aeronca Chief, to make the day's air race fair for their competition. They soon realized sandbags wouldn't be enough. Air race officials had to load the tiny twins' plane up with lead bars until they were satisfied that it was heavy enough to compete.

Another twenty-seven sets of pilots and planes were then weighed and balanced. Finally, they were ready. It was time to race.

Jan and Marion Dietrich were unlikely competitors. They were young, just twenty-one years old. They didn't have much experience. They had flown less than one hundred

Jan (left) and Marion Dietrich smile in their cockpit, 1961.

hours each. Their plane was slow. Nobody thought their Aeronca could win an air race. Everyone figured another brand of plane, a Cessna, would take the trophy. And of course, the Dietrich twins were women.

The 1947 Chico–San Mateo Air Race pitted a group of mostly male aviators against one another in a mad dash across the California skies. Only four of the planes were piloted by women that year. The prizes weren't anything spectacular—a few hundred bucks and a trophy—but air races offered all of their contestants, and especially their female racers, something far more precious than a trophy: the chance to really cut loose in the air.

Marion slid into the pilot seat of the Aeronca. Her sister Jan strapped herself in as copilot. And then, at their precise starting time, the girls gunned it. Their plane was only certified to travel at speeds up to 88 miles per hour, but as they soared over Mount Diablo, their airspeed exceeded 110 miles per hour. When the twins flashed across the race finish line in San Mateo, a crowd of more than 10,000 spectators burst into applause. What a race! What a show!

In the years after World War II, American airfields had resumed their familiar buzz, with busy runways and boisterous hangars. Male pilots climbed into cockpits big and small and thundered into the air, hauling freight, passengers, or stacks of mail through the great blue expansive sky. This was peacetime flying. It was a safe, if dull, ordeal for most men, but one that could pay extremely well. Airline captains, for example, made between $8,000 and $10,000 a year, more than twice the national average. Male pilots were ushered into the sky in gilded cockpits.

At the same time, female pilots often struggled to find their new place in aviation. They weren't allowed to fly in the military, so those magnificent war planes enjoyed by the likes of John Glenn and Deke Slayton were officially out of their reach. As for civilian air jobs, men scooped up most of the good gigs. Women aviators were left with the scraps. Some were able to find jobs as flight instructors. Others cobbled together careers out of little flying jobs, transporting goods one day and crop dusting fields the next. Many, like Irene Leverton, picked up non-aviation work in their spare time to make ends meet. Leverton juggled her time as a flight instructor with her shifts at a Ford motor plant. It could be a hard life with few rewards. But still, determined female aviators stuck with it.

While men got to fly fast and high and far, women often were stuck with slow and short hops. They puttered along at low altitudes, guiding bumbling students through their first bone-rattling landings, or skimming cotton fields from dawn till dusk, filling their lungs with a mixture of exhaust and chemical fertilizers.

There weren't many opportunities for female pilots to engage in high-stakes flight. So, when they had the time and money to enter into an air race, adventurous female aviators like Jan and Marion leapt at the chance.

Air races had been around for decades. These were popular spectator events in which pilots would do aerial stunts before rapt crowds, or dart from one city to another as fast as their planes could go. They could be very dangerous. Aviators would scream through the air at impossible-to-imagine speeds. This meant that any error in pilot judgment or plane malfunction could have deadly, and fast, consequences. In 1949, air racer Bill Odom pushed his little green plane to nearly 400 miles per hour before losing control and punching right through a suburban home, killing not just himself but also a resident woman and her baby. A year later, a twenty-one-year-old pilot named James Vosyka died in a fatal crash at the Continental Trophy Race in Detroit. A wing on his racing plane collapsed on a hard turn, and his aircraft slammed into the ground in front of 12,000 spectators. Competing in air races was not for the timid.

Like the rest of aviation, most early air races were intended just for men. Air race organizers bristled at the thought of female competitors. What if, they fretted, a woman died? After all, plenty of male pilots had perished during air races. It was only a matter of time before a woman suffered the same fate. In 1929 and 1933, two women air racers had indeed died in competition. Their deaths were tragic losses and also devastating setbacks for other hopeful female air racers. While the public was able to accept the deaths of male pilots, they just couldn't seem to stomach the notion of a woman dying under the same circumstances. Pioneering women air racers had to go to great lengths just to be allowed onto the starting line. When Jackie Cochran, a wealthy socialite and aviator, wanted in on the 1935 Bendix Air Race, for example, she was forced to first get permission from each of her male competitors.

Over time, though, bold female aviators nudged their way into the air racing scene. By the late 1940s, women pilots even had a handful of female-only air races to choose between, and a few mixed-gender events as well, such as the Chico–San Mateo race.

One event that drew talented aviators from all corners of the country was called the All-Women's Transcontinental Air Race (AWTAR). It was a challenging cross-country event that tasked pilots to fly fast and stay alive. AWTAR pilots had to be smart and shrewd. They had to know their planes inside and out, understand how to shave off an extra second or two on takeoff, and what to do in case of engine trouble in an empty and desolate sky. Lots of competitors limited

Planes line up at the AWTAR starting line, 1958.

their liquid intake during the races, since they couldn't afford a bathroom break. They'd suck hard candies in their sauna-like cockpits, growing increasingly dehydrated, but knowing that their sacrifice might just earn them a trophy and the recognition of their peers.

Air races were a chance for women to show the world what they could do. And in the years after World War II, plenty of people still doubted that a woman should do something as complex and dangerous as fly airplanes.

Female air racers were often patronized by the press. Journalists called them aviatrixes or fly girls. They described what the women wore in their airplanes, and how they had styled their hair. Even the AWTAR, a grueling and technical race, earned a dismissive nickname from the press. They called it a Powder Puff Derby. This name recalled the first-ever all-women's air race, a 1929 event in which racers like Amelia Earhart and Louise Thaden raced across America in clunky, unreliable airplanes. That first race was also nicknamed the Powder Puff Derby. It seemed that, if the American public couldn't stop women from racing, they could at least mock them by associating their competitions with cheap, disposable makeup applicators: powder puffs.

In the air, AWTAR pilots could feel genderless. They zipped low through mountain saddlebacks and dodged storm clouds. They searched the skies for the altitude with the best winds. Sometimes the fastest altitude was one that was so high that there wasn't enough oxygen for the pilots to breathe. Staying at this height could be incredibly dangerous. Pilots could get confused, dizzy, or pass out from lack of vital gas. So the women improvised. They carried oxygen in tanks with portable masks. If a race had them tearing through the thin air for too long, they'd strap on the thick plastic masks and breathe their bottled oxygen.

But on the ground, the AWTAR teams were still expected to act and look feminine. Many racers wore skirts and high heels, despite the fact that climbing in and out of their airplanes was an occasionally gymnastic feat. After spending hours sweating in hot, sunbaked cockpits, they often paused to reapply makeup before exiting their planes. Women pilots knew that their audiences expected beauty as well as heroics.

Jackie Cochran sponsored some air races. She owned her own cosmetics empire and believed strongly that all women—even women pilots—should appear feminine, delicate, and flawless. Once, after surviving a brutal plane crash, Cochran refused to allow rescuers to pull her from her crumpled cockpit until she had shimmied out of her flying suit and touched up her makeup.

Cochran thought other women aviators should follow her lead. One year, she even supplied each of the participants in an air race with a box of makeup. This was a not-so-subtle reminder for the competitors. They should be fast, of course. But also, they must always be lovely.

As years passed, air race rosters bulged with female pilots who craved speed, competition, and something more: friendship. Many events encouraged two-person teams. This meant hours and days spent in cramped cockpits, laughing and sweating and most of all, racing. Long-distance events involved several overnight stops. Racers who overnighted in the same town could spend long evenings bonding over airplanes, men, families, and anything else. Participating in these races gave women pilots the precious knowledge that they weren't alone in this challenging world of aviation. They might be the only woman in their local airplane hangar, but during competitions, they were part of a community.

Out of this community, thirteen pilots would soon emerge as women to watch. They were a motley crew, with wildly different backgrounds, and flying different types of planes. But they all had something in common: a desire to push limits, fly high, and fly fast.

In addition to the Dietrich twins, there was Bea Steadman, who had been flying since she was seventeen years old. She'd spent her childhood days watching planes take off at her hometown airport and making countless model airplanes. She knew she would become a pilot. Her first years in the air were rambunctious and wild. Steadman and her friends roared through the skies, playing a risky version of airborne follow-the-leader. She said "the first pilot would lead us through loops, climbs and dives" and the rest would do their best to follow along. It was dangerous, reckless, and incredibly fun. It wasn't long before Steadman became one of the best female pilots in Michigan.

Steadman often raced with Janey Hart, a wealthy Michigan politician's wife and mother to eight. Hart had grown up in a giant stone mansion in Detroit, riding horses, playing tennis, and studying with her governess. But Hart wanted more than that quiet, privileged life. After briefly considering becoming a spy, she decided to become a pilot instead. She spent her teen years sneaking out of her family estate to take flight lessons in secret. By the time she was twenty, she had her pilot's license.

Jerrie Cobb, who had first flown with her father as a pig-tailed twelve-year-old, often raced as an adult. She took fourth prize in the Skylady Derby as a twenty-two-year-old and later went on to race in competitions such as the International Women's Air Race and the AWTAR. Cobb only managed to win one race, the 1958 Sky Lady Derby. But even in the races that she didn't win, Cobb showed both her competition and the spectators what she was made of.

Four female aviators pose for a photo in front of their airplane. Bea Steadman is second from left. Janey Hart is third from left.

She was a capable, driven aviator. She knew what she was doing in the air.

The spirit of female air racing, while competitive, was also deeply supportive. These women were painfully aware of how hard and lonely aviation could be. They nurtured relationships, which often stretched across the country, and cherished their brief airfield encounters. They wanted to win these races, of course, but they also wanted to have a good time.

One air racer who was perhaps more determined than most to have a good time was Wally Funk. The young, adventurous New Mexico aviator had spent her whole life pursuing thrills. When she was four years old, Funk climbed to the top of her family's barn and leapt into the air, hoping to take flight. She tumbled to the ground, brushed herself off, and decided to try something else. At age nine, she took her first airplane ride and beamed. Ah! *This* was what she wanted to do! Funk enrolled in aviation classes in college and all but surrendered to the call. She later admitted, "The bug bit and that was it." Wally just had to fly. And after she learned to fly, she learned to race.

Jerri Sloan was another regular in the air race circuit. She had first sat in a cockpit as a four-year-old on a flight her father had chartered for business. The experience sparked something in the young girl, and she bubbled with joy as she told her father that she wanted to fly more. He responded with a condescending nod, telling her, "Work hard, do well in school, and you can grow up to be an air hostess and fly all the time."

Well, that just wasn't enough for Sloan. As a fifteen-year-old, she snuck out of the house to take flying lessons. Her mother learned about the lessons and became enraged. She sent her daughter off to a Catholic school in an attempt to break her passion for aviation. It didn't work. Young Sloan came home just as flight crazed as ever. Her father once again tried to talk her out of her interest. He told her gently, "Honey, girls just don't fly airplanes. That's men's work." As an adult, Sloan went on to win the Dallas Air Championship three years in a row.

Another air racer, Gene Nora (pronounced "Janora") Stumbough, often flew with a coed college flight team called the Air Knockers. Stumbough was pretty. So pretty, in fact, that her male teammates once nominated her for a beauty pageant against her will. They thought Stumbough, with her lovely smile and rich chocolate-colored hair, would make the perfect "Sky Queen." Gene Nora disagreed. She wanted to race, not prance around in evening wear. Stumbough would later get hooked on the AWTAR. A perk of flying in the women-only competition was that she didn't have to worry about sexist practical jokes.

But getting to an air race wasn't always easy. Many working women had to use their precious vacation time to participate. Sarah Gorelick, an electrical engineer from Kansas, raced in six AWTARs and a handful of others. The blonde, bubbly pilot accomplished this feat by carefully collecting her vacation time at work and using it not for relaxing beach trips but for cutthroat, ragged, heart-pounding races across the American skies. Gorelick wasn't satisfied with her demanding technical job. She wanted more. And in the skies, she got what she wanted.

Despite their sacrifices, some female pilots' early air races weren't quite as heroic as they might have wished. In 1949, former WASP Jean Hixson was ushered into the National Air Races in Akron, Ohio, not as a competitor but as the race's "air caravan queen." Rather than speeding across the course, Hixson floated slowly past the crowds on board a bloated Goodyear blimp. She was a spectacle to behold, not an air racer, that year. Hixson wasn't content to be somebody's mascot. She would later participate, and actually race, in other competitions, such as the AWTAR.

Irene Leverton also stumbled a bit in some of her early aviation events. She founded the Illinois Women's Air Meet in 1948 but didn't manage to win it until 1954. Leverton cited her empty pockets as the reason for her poor performances. Fast planes were expensive, and Leverton was often strapped for cash. "The rich women were the ones who won those races," she later recalled. Over time, both Leverton's skills and ability to borrow fast planes improved. She inched her way through the ranks of female pilots, eventually placing third in an AWTAR.

The last of the thirteen women pilots to watch, Rhea Hurrle and Myrtle Cagle, felt the pull of air racing as their unique, precious chance to really push their limits in the air. However, both had late starts to their air racing careers. Each woman was hard at work establishing herself as an aviation professional in her hometown, a task that could be difficult for women. Cagle juggled a varied career. After working as a military nurse, she spent the years following World War II working as an aviation writer, pilot, flight instructor, plane mechanic, and owner of her own North Carolina airport. Though she didn't race much in her early years, she still supported the air racing community by hosting overnight stops at her airport and cheering from the sidelines as her sisters in flight screamed across the skies. Hurrle was equally busy, flying seven days a week in Texas, first as a private pilot, then as a commercial pilot, and later as a flight instructor. When both Hurrle and Cagle finally rumbled across the starting lines of races such as the International Air Race and the Dallas Doll Derby, they were ready. They wanted to soar.

This group of thirteen pilots would participate in a wide

variety of air races that crossed state lines and international borders. Some would take home armloads of trophies. Others would cherish a precious few ribbons. But they would soon become bonded in a new type of race. It had higher stakes than any competition they'd yet seen and was far more dangerous. But they would be drawn into it, all the same, by that magical temptation to fly high and fast and hard. In the end, this new, unfamiliar race would change everything. It was the race to space.

CHAPTER 4

THE JET AGE

On March 23, 1952, Gus Grissom's short, broad frame was squeezed into the narrow cockpit of a shining new swept wing jet called a Sabre (F-86). Below him, Korean hillsides shot by in a green-gray blur. He was flying wingman, a role he took seriously. It was his job to fly to one side of a group of American planes and keep an eye out for the enemy. If he saw anything, he'd been ordered to do whatever it took to keep his countrymen safe. As one of his superiors would later command, "nothing but kills."

Grissom squinted into the sunlight, searching the horizon for a telltale silver flicker or a chalk-white contrail. He was a hunter, sniffing for prey. And then he caught a glimpse of something in the distance. It was a Soviet MiG! And not just that—this MiG was in a dive! An attack! Grissom spotted its target: an American reconnaissance plane below him. *Oh no.* Grissom knew that plane was essentially defenseless. The men inside were dead meat. Grissom peeled away from his squadron and thundered toward the MiG, pulsing his jet's powerful guns at the same time. The MiG tore away in a flash, disappearing into the deep blue sky.

Grissom had spent years hoping to get into air combat, and now that he'd finally gotten his chance, he was thriving. His actions saved the men in the recon plane that day and eventually earned him an Air Medal and Distinguished Flying Cross. The awards praised him for what he was already growing to understand: He was good at this flying business. Very good.

Grissom was a member of the elite 334th Fighter Interceptor Squad during the Korean War, a conflict that stretched between 1950 and 1953. It was a time of heroism and fear and sacrifice, but also a time of innovation. The skies were no longer cluttered with only propeller planes. A new breed of aircraft was punching through the clouds: jets. These powerful machines were changing everything for pilots like Grissom.

For one thing, jets could travel far faster than propeller planes. They were more powerful, too. Jets offered a completely different style of flying, and pilots just loved it. The introduction of jets also separated aviators into two groups: those who flew them and those who didn't. The military had jets. Civilians, for the most part, did not. Since women could no longer fly in the military, this created a clear gender barrier. Jets were for men.

While women like the Dietrich twins raced across domestic skies in propeller planes that topped out at 90 or

100 miles per hour, men flying in Korea were streaking through the air six or even seven times as fast. It was as though these men, who were already granted more opportunities and planes and jobs, were suddenly transplanted into a fantastic future, filled with superpowered aircraft. Their jets were gray-silver-blue blurs in the sky, propelling them light-years ahead of women.

The American armed forces had several types of jets in its arsenal: the Thunderjet (F-84), the Shooting Star (P-80), and the Sabre (F-86), among others. They were all fast and deadly, with the Sabre holding the title of fastest and deadliest. It could rip through the skies at 650 miles per hour and had a ceiling of 45,000 feet. But there were other reasons to love the Sabre, too. It was, at least among trained pilots, a pretty easy plane to fly. In fact, in 1956, an air force mechanic took a Sabre for an unauthorized joyride all on his own. Despite the fact that he'd had only two hours of flight instruction in a prop plane, the mechanic was just fine flying the Sabre. A couple of experienced jet pilots talked him through a remarkably smooth landing, after which he exclaimed, "This bird really can fly itself." This suggested that it didn't take a genius to fly a jet like a Sabre. Pilots just needed the chance.

Of course, even if flying a Sabre was fairly easy, getting through the Korean War wasn't. American military pilots had a fearsome enemy to contend with: the Soviet MiG. Like Sabres, MiGs had a sleek, swept wing design. These Soviet-made jets were lightning fast and murderous.

In 1951, the kill ratios between MiGs and Sabres were very nearly even. For every one Sabre shot down, 1.4 MiGs were lost. This matchup meant that combat outcomes were almost entirely dependent upon the skills and instincts of the pilots.

Korean War jet pilots had to be good. They had to be brave, too.

Flying in combat could be downright terrifying. Few pilots discussed their fears out loud, but they were there, the silent companions of those who flew and faced death. The thing was, in those last moments before a combat mission, nobody knew who would live and who wouldn't. Dying in combat could be fast and merciful, or slow and agonizing. A pilot could slam into a hillside and be done with it, or he could crash and slowly die of his injuries. If he was shot down over the ocean, he might drown, trapped in his cockpit, his blood staining the seawater crimson. He might even be eaten by sharks! The horror! The possibilities were limitless, and plenty of material for years of nightmares. As each pilot roared off to

Gus Grissom in his air force uniform.

fight, he had to understand, deep down in his gut, that he might be chasing his demise. Knowing this and still punching the throttle, still thundering off into the clouds, required heroic bravery.

Gus Grissom was incredibly brave. Sure, he got spooked here and there, but he just did his best to stay focused and keep flying. He grew to love the thrill of it all, and flew in one hundred combat missions in Korea. In fact, before his tour there ended in 1952, Grissom applied for an extension. *Just twenty-five more missions. Please!* The air force denied his request and sent him packing. The rejection was a sucker punch for Grissom. Couldn't they see? He wasn't done! He had more to do up there.

Grissom wasn't the only pilot who flourished in the Korean skies. Wally Schirra also grew into a star aviator during the conflict. Schirra was on a naval aircraft carrier when the Korean War started in the summer of 1950. He volunteered for an air force exchange program and got in, one of only twenty naval aviators who made the cut. Before long, he was training to fly combat in a rugged, tank-like jet called the Thunderjet (F-84).

Schirra flew ninety combat missions in Korea between 1951 and 1952. One day, he was flying in a protective formation around a group of giant bombers called B-29s. Suddenly, Schirra looked down and bam—right there under him was a MiG. Out of sheer luck, Schirra was in the perfect position. He later recalled, "He was slow, and I was above him—in the right place at the right time." Schirra zeroed in and "nailed him."

As he flew back to base that day, Schirra was hardly able to contain himself. A MiG! He'd shot down a MiG! He was a twenty-nine-year-old "hotshot Navy kid" and holy smokes did it feel good. Schirra figured he might as well announce his presence to his new air force buddies with a good old-fashioned airport flyby. He jammed his stick forward and dove toward the low building, pulling up just in time to avoid a disaster. But he wasn't quite done yet. He yanked back on the stick to do a couple of half loops, right there where everyone could see it.

Showboating was officially against the rules, but Schirra just didn't care. Later that day, an air force colonel let the cocky pilot have it. It was a doozy of a lecture. The colonel warned Schirra that if he pulled another stupid stunt like that, he'd be grounded. Schirra wasn't worried. In fact, he smirked through the whole encounter.

Schirra went on to shoot down another MiG in Korea. As it turned out, his showboating didn't get him grounded after all. By the end of the conflict, Schirra would return home with two Air Medals and a Distinguished Flying Cross. He was an amazing pilot.

John Glenn, that freckle-faced World War II pilot, didn't get to Korea until 1953, but the thirty-two-year-old made up for lost time by flying aggressively, skillfully, and precisely. He flew sixty-three missions with the marines and an additional twenty-seven combat missions in an air force exchange program. In his last nine days at war, Glenn shot down three MiGs. He was just as good in a jet as he'd been in a propeller plane. He went home with an additional

John Glenn returned from the Korean War a highly decorated military aviator.

eight Air Medals and another two Distinguished Flying Crosses.

Like Grissom, Schirra, and Glenn, Scott Carpenter made it to Korea. But unlike them, he chose to opt out of flying jets. The twenty-six-year-old pilot volunteered instead to fly the navy's slow and lumbering multi-engine propeller planes. His choice was unexpected but not irrational. Carpenter had a lovely wife and two little kids. Flying fighter jets was very dangerous, and he had a deep fear of leaving his children without a father.

Of course, flying multi-engine planes in the Korean War wasn't the safest career choice in the world. His big, hefty aircraft had to be wrestled down to extremely low altitudes over the Yellow Sea for crucial surveillance missions. His goal was often to find submarines or spot enemy ships. Flying "low and slow" made a pilot's job incredibly difficult. Planes flying at low altitudes and slow speeds can stall easily. Or they can lose control. Flying low means there isn't much room for error. A pilot at 20,000 feet has a minute or two to recover from an issue. A pilot at 200 feet has mere seconds.

Much of Carpenter's training focused on these low and slow flights. On one practice run over a Pensacola, Florida, air field, Carpenter remembered flying so low and so slow that he looked down and spotted a kid riding a bicycle. The kid looked up and waved. Carpenter returned the gesture. The two seemed to be going almost the same speed.

Carpenter's time in Korea was not glamorous. He did not return home a celebrated war hero. But he had done an important duty, and he had become an excellent pilot.

Just as it was during World War II, there were plenty of pilots who wanted to get into the conflict but just couldn't seem to make it happen. Members of the military can't simply pick a battle to participate in. They go where they're sent.

Deke Slayton spent most of the Korean War outside of the conflict but intensely hoping to get in. In 1952, he wound up in Germany working as an air force maintenance inspector. The job was okay, but it wasn't combat. And it forced him to fly a plane he'd first flown with the Air National Guard and now had come to loathe: the giant, hulkish, propeller-powered C-47. Slayton called it the Gooney Bird and said he'd developed an allergy to it. It was just so slow. And big. And clumsy.

Finally, in 1954, thirty-year-old Slayton got his break. He was transferred to a fighter unit in Germany. They flew Sabres. These were fast, sensitive, and powerful, and Deke loved everything about them. It wasn't long before

Slayton was telling people he could fly a jet using just his fingertips.

Like Slayton, Gordo Cooper flew in Germany during the Korean War. His slow, twangy Oklahoma drawl and aw-shucks grin often seemed at odds with his deadly precision in the air. He was a natural pilot, quick and gifted in the cockpit. Cooper spent four years mastering two jets, the Thunderjet and the Sabre. His excellence in the air was recognized by just about anyone who saw it, and he was soon promoted to flight commander of the 525th Fighter Bomber Squadron stationed in Munich.

By the time Cooper came back to the States in 1954, the twenty-seven-year-old pilot was as comfortable in the air as he was on the ground. He would later reminisce on his early years in the sky with starry-eyed fondness: "Flying was my whole life . . ."

After earning his wings in 1947, Alan Shepard worked hard to become one of the navy's best fliers. Shepard had a gift for it. He was bold yet precise. It was just the right combination for a successful pilot. As the Korean War erupted, Shepard was pulled, not into combat, but into the navy's most elite aviation program: test pilot school. There, Shepard would fine-tune his flying ability even further, learning to be the very best and the very fastest and the very brightest.

By the time he left the program in 1953, Shepard had developed an unusual morning routine. He'd face his bathroom mirror each day, leaning in close, and search his reflection for any signs of weakness. He'd "look for signals" that something was off, a sluggish reflex or a twitch in his eye. Alan Shepard couldn't afford a single slipup. He wanted to be better than his peers. He needed to be the *best*.

For a male aviator in the 1950s, being the best usually meant flying in combat. But Shepard never saw air combat. He spent the last months of the war doing a different kind of high-tension, dangerous flight. He worked as an operations officer on board the aircraft carrier the *Oriskany*. This wasn't easy flying. Aviators had to bring their powerful, heavy planes down for landings onto the flat ship decks, hoping desperately to snag a cable with a hook on their plane's belly, bringing them into skidding, neck-snapping, squealing stops. But that wasn't the hardest part of carrier landings. What made landing on an aircraft carrier suicidally difficult was the fact that the runway *moved*. The carrier decks bobbed and swayed and lurched on the waves, rising and lowering five or ten or even fifteen feet at a time. A pilot whose timing was even slightly off could slam right into the side of the ship, killing not just himself but whoever happened to be nearby at the moment. Shepard would later say that it was the kind of flight that "separates the men from the boys."

High-stakes military aviation often did, in fact, separate aviators into two groups. But they weren't the groups Shepard was thinking of. Rather than separating men from boys, military flight separated men from women. It cordoned off whole categories of aviation—combat flight, jet flight, carrier-based flight—and marked them as suitable for men only.

For a select group of female pilots who craved speed and adventure, and who weren't afraid of risk, that just was deeply unfair. These women wanted their chance to soar.

CHAPTER 5

"A MAN'S WORK"

I n the mid-1950s, while scores of military men tore through the air at 600 miles per hour or more, Bea Steadman found herself at a standstill.

The tall brunette had an airplane to start. It was an old Fairchild, a bird that, once airborne, chugged along at up to 130 miles per hour. Starting a Fairchild was an almost comedic task. Someone, usually the pilot, had to perch outside of the cockpit and hand crank a mechanism near the plane's nose until the engine could start. Pilots tended to do it by throwing their weight onto a crank over and over in a heaving, bobbing motion. It wasn't easy work under the best of circumstances. Steadman had recently undergone appendix surgery. Her abdomen was still swollen and tender. Starting that plane would be pure agony.

Just then, Steadman spotted a man in the hangar. Thank goodness! She asked him for a hand with the Fairchild.

"No, if you're going to do a man's work, then you're going to do a man's work," he gruffly responded.

So, the twenty-one-year-old flight instructor went ahead and "did a man's work." She started the plane herself, bobbing and heaving and cranking away, despite the fresh pink scar stretching across her belly.

The years after the Korean War hadn't been easy for Steadman, though she knew she'd fared better than most female pilots. In an environment where women aviators were often distrusted and disliked, she'd managed to build a thriving career as a flight instructor in Flint, Michigan. She'd even developed a niche: war veterans who knew how to fly in battle but had no idea what to do on a civilian runway.

By 1956, Steadman was the only female flight operations instructor for the Air Force Reserves. The Korean War was over. However, air force reservists still needed to stay up-to-date and familiar with aviation in case they were called back into duty. Steadman taught advanced aviation topics, such as high-tech navigation, meteorology, and even new types of radar flight. Her students were all officers. The lowest rank in her class was a colonel. Later, one of her students would tell a local reporter, "She's one of the best instructors I've ever had . . . as good as any man."

Steadman didn't fall into her successful career. She worked hard for it. Fearing that she'd be pushed aside after the war, she'd devoted herself to learning everything about flight. She wanted to be the most qualified instructor out there. She spent her days poring over flight textbooks. She studied aerodynamics and engine functions. She brushed up on airframe technology and made sure she knew how to use

Bea Steadman poses with one of her aircraft, 1957.

the latest aviation tools. She also wrangled a couple of test flight gigs for herself. One involved ironing out the bugs in an aircraft tail wheel. The other had her flying endless loops in front of an unarmed gun sight, helping developers improve the accuracy of a future weapon component. On top of all that, during her few free hours, she paid a neighbor girl to come to her house and read technical manuals aloud. She listened intently as the girl read, visualizing "every detail in every system." Steadman already had plenty of flight ratings. But after the war, she made sure she got "every rating there was."

Steadman's actions showed how tricky it could be for women who wanted to work in aviation. They were up against a vast sea of male competitors. Even after getting a job, women knew that their employment wasn't necessarily secure. They could be replaced in an instant by a man with a pair of gleaming military flight wings. So some women approached their jobs the way Steadman did. They set their sights on becoming experts. Better than that, they decided to become the *best*.

Even those women who were the best still suffered abuse from their male peers. Female pilots regularly experienced unwanted comments and rude jokes from men in the hangar. Some endured outright sabotage.

Jean Hixson was one of only about 1,100 women who flew with the elite WASPs during World War II. The WASP program was designed, in part, to relieve male pilots from some of the easy domestic tasks that took up their precious time. It sounded so convenient: The men could shrug off the boring stuff—the maintenance flights and the transport flights and the training flights—and hand them off to the ladies. Then these brave and masculine warriors could zip on overseas and win the war.

In reality, WASP work could be very dangerous. They flight-tested planes that had just been repaired to make sure they were safe enough for combat. This meant that women were often flying planes with serious issues that could only be discovered in the air. WASPs also flew gunnery practice missions. They'd fly over a military base while dragging a giant white target on a cable behind their planes. Male cadets squinted into the sky and did their best to shoot the target full of holes. This put the female pilots uncomfortably close to streams of red-hot bullets shot by jittery amateurs.

Hixson used her time as a WASP to become an expert pilot of the B-25, a twin-engine military bomber. She'd take the giant beast up in the dead of night and test out its navigational tools. She had to do this to make sure the B-25 was up to snuff for combat. If there were any quirks or problems in the plane, it was Hixson's duty to find them and have them fixed.

Once, when she was on a test flight 1,000 miles from her base, Hixson's B-25 lost its radio, lights, and navigational tools. The twenty-one-year-old pilot was suddenly on her own and in the dark. Relying on her pilot's instinct and muscle memory, she fumbled in the inky black to find her controls. Her left hand gripped one side of the cold metal control yoke and her right hand rested tensely on the throttle. Her eyes grew impossibly wide, searching for something, anything to see. She had to get back to her base. She just had to.

Hixson tugged the yoke to swing the enormous plane in what she thought was the right direction. She searched the horizon until she saw them: tiny pinpricks of light. Civilization! Salvation! She nudged her nose toward the lights. As she got closer to them she started to recognize familiar landmarks. She used these to navigate her way to her base. But she still wasn't out of trouble. Hixson didn't have a radio. This meant she had to land her plane without alerting anyone that she was coming in. She had no way of knowing whether the runways would be cleared or if anyone else was coming in for a landing at the same time. Hixson did the only thing she could. She scanned the skies, gripped the control yoke, and brought the B-25 down safely.

The WASPs represented the best of American female aviation. In fact, some statistics show that they represented the best of all military aviators, regardless of gender. WASPs made fewer mistakes than men flying the same types of missions. They died less frequently from domestic, noncombat air accidents as well. WASPs had a fatal accident rate of 0.060 per 1,000 hours. This meant that roughly one female pilot would die for every 16,667 hours flown. The male rate was just slightly higher, at 0.062 per 1,000. This wasn't a big margin, but it was significant. In an age when many people thought women were too incompetent to fly, it was mind-blowing to learn that they could outperform their male peers.

Some male pilots didn't like the WASPs. They might have been threatened by them. Or maybe they just didn't like seeing women sitting in cockpits. *Their* cockpits. They quietly set about sabotaging WASP flights.

Many WASPs were forced into emergency landings on routine flights only to discover that someone had put rags in their engines. Or grass in their gas tanks. Some women's airplane tires were slashed. Others discovered that their parachutes had been splashed with acid. One WASP even found her flight controls coming loose after she'd taken off from the runway. These incidents were never officially attributed to any men, though of course that was the idea around WASP bases. There must have been some men, angry men, who didn't want women flying for the military.

And if they couldn't prevent women from becoming military aviators, they could certainly knock them out of the skies.

Jackie Cochran, the cosmetics entrepreneur and air racer, was in charge of the WASPs. She could have flagged these incidents. They were clearly foul play. Once, this meddling even had fatal consequences. On a fall day in 1943, WASP Betty Taylor Wood's airplane slammed into the ground near a runway, killing both Wood and her passenger. Cochran personally investigated the incident. What she found was chilling: Someone had dumped sugar into the plane's gas tank. This was an outrage! It was murder! But Cochran didn't protest. She and the rest of WASP leadership actually made an effort to downplay the sabotage. They worried that the program would be canceled if there was any hint of trouble. No, it was best to stay quiet and keep flying. And fly they did.

Girls across the country saw the WASPs and dreamed of joining them, regardless of the dangers this might entail. Just like so many male combat pilots who faced their fears overseas, they were ready to show their bravery over domestic skies.

Irene Leverton was one of the young women who had fantasized about becoming a WASP. Despite being too young and inexperienced for the program, Leverton had still applied using a borrowed birth certificate and a forged flight log. The recruiters saw right through the ruse and sent Leverton packing. But the young aviator wasn't derailed by this. She just set to work finding other ways to fly.

Leverton spent the late 1940s working as the only woman on a Chicago airport line crew. The job turned her into an aviation expert. A wide variety of planes pulled into her hangar, and it was her job to gas and clean them. However, Leverton wasn't content to do only that. She used her paychecks to pay for flight time in just about every plane she could, and then she'd poke around in their engines for good measure. Before long, Leverton knew exactly what made each plane tick.

By 1956, Leverton was a twenty-nine-year-old aviator with a commercial pilot's license and plenty of experience under her belt. She took a job flying giant cargo planes called DC-3s around the country. The job mostly had her ferrying military personnel from base to base. On one flight, an ex-military pilot slid into the captain seat beside Leverton. She watched as he gunned the engine and sent the big bird rumbling down the runway without remembering to lift the flaps on the wings. The DC-3 was heavy. Leverton knew that it could never get the lift it needed to take off with its flaps down. She reached across the cockpit to correct the issue herself, and the male pilot became enraged. The two fought, right there in the cockpit, as Leverton struggled to lift the flaps before the plane crashed into the hill at the end of the runway. She succeeded. The hefty DC-3 heaved off the runway just in time.

Then the man in the captain's seat had her fired.

This incident haunted Leverton. The man spread the story of the crazy female aviator throughout his community of military pilot friends, and suddenly Leverton couldn't find a job. She spent the next few years bouncing from gig to gig, barely scraping by.

Women pilots often struggled to show people that they knew what they were doing in a cockpit. A female aviator could have years of experience, and it still wouldn't be enough to prove that she could be trusted in the air. That she belonged. This attitude toward female aviators

Irene Leverton in the cockpit of her plane.

wasn't unique to male pilots and flight crews. People who had nothing to do with flight also bristled at the notion of a woman in the cockpit.

Once Janey Hart had her pilot's license, she flew all sorts of planes for all sorts of reasons. She competed in air races alongside Bea Steadman. She flew to family events. She flew her eight kids to and from summer camps. She owned a twin-engine Bonanza with enough room for her family plus their baggage. She said she'd load it up "and thunder off in whatever direction I wanted." The freedom of it was thrilling. Hart became quite famous for flying her senator husband to and from his political campaign stops. Phil Hart didn't mind his wife's flying one bit. She was great for publicity. When she later earned her helicopter pilot's license, becoming the fifty-eighth woman in the world to do so, it guaranteed headlines for the eager politician. Waving to a crowd of admirers beneath the giant, chopping blades of a helicopter struck quite the image in voters' minds. Phil fully supported his wife's interest in aviation. Many of his peers, however, found it nauseating.

On more than one occasion, politicians and well-meaning bystanders approached Phil to tell him to control his wife. Sometimes it was a whispered warning. Other times it was a crude joke told over drinks. Quite often, it came in a tersely worded letter. But the message remained the same: *Get that woman under control. Flight is a man's job. Put your wife in her place.* The Harts weren't swayed by these comments. However, every time an angry letter landed in their mailbox or a drunk senator slurred his sexist judgments, it was a reminder that plenty of people just didn't think women were up to the task of flying airplanes.

Many female pilots spent their entire careers bumping up against this men-only message. In 1953, when twenty-two-year-old Jerrie Cobb applied for an unpaid job flying passengers in powerful twin-engine DC-3s, the same type of plane that would cause Leverton so much grief three years later, her interviewer promptly turned her away. "We can't expect our passengers to fly with a girl copilot," the hiring manager told her. "They're already scared of flying, and a girl in the cockpit will frighten them even more." He went on to assert that "no airline passenger will ever fly with a woman in the cockpit." Then, as if to soften the blow of rejection, he suggested that Jerrie look into the stewardess training program just down the hall.

Gender discrimination was a real issue for women pilots. Some women responded to this by trying to blend in. They didn't call attention to themselves, spoke politely and softly, and stayed out of the way, happy to get whatever flying jobs they could scrounge. Others, like Bea Steadman, Jean Hixson, and Jerrie Cobb, tried to prove everyone wrong by being skilled, educated, and competent aviators.

Male pilots didn't have to overcome this type of discrimination. This meant that they could devote their energy to their flights, their planes, and their dreams. Many of the very best male pilots shared a dream that was utterly unattainable for women: military test flight.

CHAPTER 6

THE TEST PILOT YEARS

Alan Shepard barked out a surprised laugh. The engine in his Tiger (F11F) had just flamed out 60,000 feet above Earth, and he'd lost all power. He'd tried restarting his engine, but no luck. The Tiger's cockpit frosted over, and the jet began to fall out of the clouds in a looping, lazy corkscrew. Shepard tried to stay calm. He knew he had plenty of sky to use up before he was in real trouble. At 40,000 feet, he tried starting the engine again. Still nothing. He fell. And fell. And fell. In total, Shepard plummeted more than nine miles before, finally, at 12,000 feet, he got the engine running and the Tiger growled back to life.

Shepard brought the Tiger down onto the runway, climbed out, and began walking away. Then he turned and flipped the jet the middle finger. It was 1956, and thirty-three-year-old Alan Shepard was one of the best military test pilots on the planet. He wasn't about to let a Tiger take him out. No way.

Only the most skilled military fliers could become test pilots. Shepard had attended the navy's prestigious test pilot school at Patuxent River, Maryland, back in 1950. He stayed for two years before being called to serve on the *Oriskany*. Then, in 1956, he'd returned to test flight. The job was dangerous, grueling, and hard. But it was also an incredible adventure. Shepard was thrilled at the chance to do more.

Test pilots were the tip-top of the military pile, the bravest and fastest and best. They spent their days crawling into brand-new planes and testing their limits—pushing them high and fast and far. Shepard said he spent his test flights trying to get his planes to their "critical area." This was that risky spot where an aircraft was just on the cusp of stalling or spinning or burning right up.

Test pilots ironed out each new plane's issues—and they all had issues—so that they could be certified for general use. When Shepard took the Tiger up, he knew he'd have problems. But he also knew he could handle whatever happened up there. Test pilots were specially trained to do this kind of work. On top of their flight training, test pilots had additional lessons in engineering, aerodynamics, mechanics, and advanced mathematics. Their skills and education made them more likely than just about anyone to be able to take a new plane up into the air and survive if something went awry. Of course, test flight could still be deadly. Test flight programs across the country occasionally noted death tolls as high as one or two pilots per week.

Test flight attracted an elite, highly talented crowd of men. The ones who made it through training and out onto the runway were pilots with the right instincts. It wasn't enough for them to be by-the-book aviators. They had to have something more. They needed the ambition to fly where others wouldn't or couldn't.

Shepard fit the bill. His peers described him as a genius, the best pilot they'd ever seen. But Shepard wasn't a model aviator all the time. He was also prone to goofing off and pulling stunts. In 1952, he'd gotten busted for using the half-completed Chesapeake Bay Bridge in Maryland as an acrobatic prop. He'd taken a jet called a Banshee (F2H-2) in a full loop under, over, and back under the bridge again. Later that same year, he pushed a Banshee into a shallow flyby just above a crowded Ocean City beach. Shepard flew so low that he'd sent the sunbathers into hysterics, reportedly even blowing some women's bikini tops right off. His boldest stunt that year happened when he buzzed a full formation of men who were standing outside a naval base. His low pass sent hundreds of uniformed men diving for cover, sure that they were about to be obliterated by some maniac's reckless moves. But of course, it was just Shepard, pulling a fast one on his friends.

Shepard's superiors were annoyed by his stunts. They doled out minor scoldings and punishments, grounding him for ten days after he buzzed the navy men and then letting him back into the air again. They were never too hard on him. After all, he was one of their best pilots. He had a knack for this stuff. A little rule breaking here and there could certainly be forgiven.

The American armed forces had bigger problems to worry about than a frisky test pilot's unauthorized maneuvers.

Alan Shepard sits in the cockpit of a F-106, 1961.

While Shepard was busy terrorizing Maryland sunbathers, the United States was in a frantic race to churn out newer, faster, and better planes than their shadowy communist enemies. The Soviets were updating and improving that Korean War murder machine, the MiG, and cranking out other fighters, interceptors, and helicopters as well. Americans wanted to be more advanced than the Soviets in case the building tensions between the two nations turned violent. This meant that test pilots were up to their ears in shiny new aircraft with little time to study their quirks before they took to the air.

Test pilots had another reason for their lack of preparation: They didn't want it. They delighted in what they called the grip and rip approach. They'd glance at a plane's handbook to get the gist of what to expect. Then they'd just grip the throttle and let it rip. They figured out the details in the air.

In the 1950s, military test flight was a profession that dripped masculinity. Despite the fact that WASPs like Jean Hixson had flight-tested countless planes in the 1940s, the new world of test flight that embraced men like Shepard oozed testosterone. It was rough and rowdy, technical and ruthless. Definitely not a woman's work.

Test flight was also a racially exclusive field. Only a small number of minority aviators were able to nudge their way into the program. This is likely because American test flight mirrored many of the nationwide stereotypes of the time, which held firmly the idea that the best and brightest were, and would always be, white men.

Scott Carpenter snagged himself a coveted spot at Pax River in 1954, two years before Shepard would return postwar. Carpenter flew a wide range of planes there. While his peers racked up a thousand hours or more in jets, Carpenter was mostly assigned other types of aircraft for tests. While at Pax, Carpenter only logged about 300 jet hours. This was okay with Carpenter. He learned to savor his precious time in the jets and came to enjoy one jet in particular: the F11F-1. It was a version of the Tiger that would later send Alan Shepard into his nine-mile plummet.

The F11F-1 was a lightweight fighter with a great call sign: "Foxtrot One One Foxtrot One." Carpenter liked rattling it off into his headset radio. He appreciated its speed, too. This plane had the unique distinction of being able to

Scott Carpenter climbs into a jet during his time as a test pilot at Patuxent River.

shoot *itself* down. It could fly so fast that it could overtake its own bullets, which would easily turn its wings into Swiss cheese.

Like Shepard, Carpenter got into some trouble for showboating here and there. Once he took a hefty twin-jet bomber called the A3D on a test flight and decided to roll the bird to see what happened. Big planes don't usually do well in a roll. They lose thousands of feet of altitude and can fail under the increased gravitational forces on their heavy parts. Carpenter got lucky. The A3D held together beautifully. Minutes after Carpenter landed, a red-faced superior officer yanked him into his office and ripped into him. Carpenter flinched through the lecture. Then he got right back out there, testing and flying.

After he left Korea, Wally Schirra felt disappointed when his superiors didn't send him to Pax River to work alongside his fellow hotshots. In 1952, he was instead ordered to report to the Naval Ordnance Test Station at China Lake, in California. His job there would be testing out a new air-to-air missile called the Sidewinder. As soon as he laid eyes on the Sidewinder, his disappointment disappeared. The missile had a clear glass dome on its nose. As Schirra moved, he could see a little device inside the dome following him. It was a heat seeker, and it had zeroed in on Schirra's cigarette.

Schirra worked as an engineering pilot at China Lake. He helped smooth out the bugs in the Sidewinder and the planes that carried it. Once, after launching a Sidewinder from his plane out over the California desert, he watched in horror as the deadly missile doubled back in hungry pursuit of its prey: him. *Yikes.* If that heat seeker closed in on his red-hot tailpipe, he'd be in trouble.

Wally's piloting instincts snapped into action. He pulled back hard on his stick to bring his Skyknight (F3D) into a tight loop through the hot, dry air. It was a lightning-fast, roller-coaster escape. It was smart, too. Schirra's quick thinking brought him behind the Sidewinder and into a position of safety. He breathed a sigh of relief. *Phew.* The engineer who had been riding along to monitor the missile was less relaxed about it. Schirra would later notice that the poor guy ended up with a case of the "clanks," which, he explained, was "pilot talk for the shakes."

After China Lake, Schirra bounced around different air bases in California, flying jets and teaching airborne combat to new aviators. It was chal-

lenging, technical, and fun. In 1955, Schirra became one of the few naval aviators with a flight log that boasted 1,000 hours of jet time. In 1958, he got his invitation to Pax River. He had made it. Finally.

While elite naval aviators went to Pax River, for the air force, there was Edwards. This dusty, desolate base in the middle of the California desert had

A man shows off the Sidewinder's heat seeker, located inside its nose cone.

grown from a ramshackle outpost into a famous aviation hub. The place had a mythical, almost storybook appeal. Men went to Edwards to become legends.

Pilots from all over the country fantasized about getting a gig at Edwards. They knew about guys like Chuck Yeager, who'd been the first man to break the sound barrier back in 1947 when he flew a plane at a then–mind-boggling speed of 700 miles per hour. This was an event so significant that it had its own name: Mach 1. When his plane made it to Mach 1, something amazing happened. Shock waves, formed by air that couldn't get out of the way fast enough, created enormous pressure waves around his jet. This caused a deafening, thunderous double crack. People on the ground were slapped with the explosive noise: *ba-BOOM*. It was the first time anyone had heard a sonic boom.

Yeager was an Edwards man. Scott Crossfield was an Edwards pilot, too. He became the first man to fly at twice the speed of sound, Mach 2, in 1953.

Deke Slayton got himself to Edwards in 1955, after returning from time serving overseas. He sailed through test flight school in six months and then tumbled out onto the runway, flying five or even six days a week. Slayton flew all sorts of planes, including the F-105. The plane's official name is the Thunderchief, but everyone who flew it called it the *Thud*.

The *Thud* got Slayton into one of his trickiest situations ever when, out of the blue, it snapped him into a series of rolls. One minute, he was flying in a swift, banking path, and the next he was tumbling wildly while fighting to regain control. Then, somehow, the plane chucked him into an inverted spin at 37,000 feet. That meant his plane was belly up and whirling around and around like some devious, vomit-inducing carnival ride. Except this wasn't a ride. It was a very real emergency. Poor old Deke fell a full 10,000 feet in that spin.

Slayton did everything he could think of to right his plane, even attempting to reach his ejection handle. Pilots loathe ejecting from their jets and only attempt it as a last resort. Ejecting from a jet is awfully dangerous. Powerful explosives blast pilots clear of their aircraft. But they also often seriously injure them in the process. Human bodies just aren't built to withstand the force of ejection. Even the most battle-hardened military men turn soft and fragile when blasted out of their seats. Sometimes their shoulders or knees or wrists, made floppy by the sudden detonation just below their tailbone, slam into the edge of their cockpits on their way up and out of the plane. At the very best, this can result in impressive bruising. At worst, it can rip a limb right off. Once they manage to shoot free of their planes, ejected pilots are still in mortal danger. Their incredible airspeeds mean they can be knocked unconscious when their doll-like bodies hit the air. Their shoulders can dislocate. Their necks can break. Their parachutes can be yanked away, leaving them to fall freely to their deaths. Ejection is a last resort.

Slayton couldn't even eject from the *Thud*. He was spinning too fast. The force of the spin pulled him out of his seat and made it impossible for him to reach down for the ejection lever. He stayed calm and tried a few more things. He opened a set of flaps on his tail. This slowed him a bit but not enough. He tried it again and realized he was still spinning, but with his nose pointing down. Now he had something to work with! Test pilots are trained to recover from nose-down spins. Slayton nudged the stick and wham! Just like that, he snapped out of the spin. Alive. And he'd even saved the government a $15 million plane. Slayton estimated that the "whole business took forty seconds." He hadn't been afraid because there just wasn't any time for it.

A lot of pilots died at Edwards. In 1956, Edwards pilot Mel Apt became the fastest man alive when he brought a rocket-powered plane to Mach 3. He seared across the desert sky at 2,178 miles per hour before his plane began to violently roll. Apt ejected but died when he and his parachute slammed into the hard desert sand.

Slayton knew he was lucky to escape that fate. In fact, he only sustained a few minor injuries as a test pilot. He'd once gotten a hernia while falling out of a burning plane on an Edwards runway. It was unpleasant, sure, but it was a lot better than what would have happened if he had been stuck in the cockpit.

Gus Grissom and Gordon Cooper found themselves at Edwards test pilot school together in 1957. The two pilots had met a few years earlier at the Air Force Institute of Technology in Ohio, where they both studied aeronautical engineering. It was the perfect topic for a couple of sky-crazed hotshots. They learned about the nuts and bolts of aviation—how to design aircraft, how they work, and how to make them better. Grissom and Cooper were close friends and became closer still as they weathered the dangers and thrills of life at Edwards. They flew experimental interceptors and fighters, such as the Delta Dagger (F-102). These planes flew higher than 50,000 feet, which could be a toxic altitude without the right safety precautions.

At high altitudes, the air pressure outside is low enough to be extremely harmful to a human body. When exposed to very low air pressure, humans tend to puff up like gas-filled marshmallows. The low air pressure outside pulls a pilot's chest outward, yanking their lungs open in a perpetual inhale. Exhaling is a feat of incredible strength, a great huffing effort. Pilots breathe bottled oxygen at this height, but it doesn't do them any good if they can't actually get the stuff in and out of their lungs.

Pilots flying at high altitudes have to be in pressurized cockpits. These are sealed microhabitats that mimic the denser air pressure that human bodies are used to. But cockpits can lose pressure. This means pilots also need a backup plan. That's where partial pressure suits come in. In the 1950s, these emergency "get-me-down" suits were a lifesaver for high-altitude pilots. At Edwards in the 1950s, they were often long johns–style garments with air-filled tubes running along the arms, legs, and torso. If a plane lost pressure at a great height, the tubes inflated to apply the crucial pressure a pilot needed to keep breathing and stay conscious. They gave pilots a full-body squeeze—a lifesaving hug.

Grissom and Cooper knew about the dangers of high altitude. They understood that the suits were designed to help them, but boy were they uncomfortable. Cooper later grumbled about what happened: "As you went higher, the [tubes] would inflate, grabbing and pinching chunks of skin and hair as they did."

Two years after Grissom and Cooper reunited at Edwards, a marine pilot named William Rankin got a brutal lesson on the hazards of high-altitude flight. Rankin's jet engine stalled while he was flying at about 47,000 feet and he was forced to eject. This was, Rankin knew, a life-or-death moment. He wasn't wearing a partial pressure suit. An unprotected human body might not survive ejection at such a high altitude. He was about to find out why.

Immediately after exploding through the glass canopy of his cockpit, Rankin was overwhelmed by the searing, stabbing cold. He guessed that it was about -70 degrees Fahrenheit up there. His exposed skin froze almost instantly before going blissfully numb. And then the real pain started. The low air pressure attacked his vulnerable body like an enormous, hungry vacuum. His abdomen swelled. His skin stretched. Blood sprayed from his eyes, ears, nose, and mouth. Rankin made it to the ground alive but barely.

Rankin's brush with death reminded military pilots of an undeniable truth: Flying high and fast was exciting, but it was also exceptionally hazardous. Anyone willing to push an aircraft to its limits had to be comfortable facing danger.

Despite the terrible stories, the close calls, and the near misses, test pilots in the 1950s were aglow. They basked in a marvelous, unmentionable sense of greatness. They felt it in the pits of their bellies, this knowledge that they were making history. A man could wake up a nobody and become a national celebrity after a single flight.

And unlike women pilots at the time, these men weren't up against the same pressure to be picture perfect all the time. They could make little errors, moan about problems, even come close to crashing a $15 million plane, and nobody was rushing to say that their gender couldn't hack it in the air. Male test pilots were allowed to be human.

John Glenn was a Pax River guy, just like Carpenter and Shepard. He'd graduated from test pilot school in 1954 and spent the following two years there flight-testing a variety of aircraft. In 1956, he went to Washington, D.C., to help design a jet called the Crusader (F-8). It was an excellent plane, but Glenn's pals at Pax thought it needed more test time in the air. That gave Glenn an idea. He decided to fly the Crusader across the country. It would set a record for transcontinental speed and give the plane a respectable distance flight test. It would also draw attention to the hot new Navy plane.

As an additional bonus, this cross-country flight test would keep Glenn, a World War II and Korean War hero, in the spotlight. Glenn knew that the Crusader could fly faster than 586 miles per hour, the same speed as a bullet shot from a .45-caliber pistol. Glenn named his transatlantic flight Project Bullet.

On July 16, 1957, Glenn climbed into his Crusader and set a new record by crossing the United States in just three hours and twenty-three minutes. His lightning-fast trip averaged 723 miles per hour and required three mid-flight

John Glenn smiles from the cockpit of his Crusader (F-8), the aircraft he flew for Project Bullet, 1957.

refuelings. These difficult maneuvers forced Glenn to slow down so that giant air force tanker jets, heavy with the flammable fuel, could pipe the liquid right into his plane. It was tricky flying, but Glenn was one of the best. An Associated Press story that ran across the country the following day heralded his flight as a "New Aviation Miracle Written into History."

Glenn's aviation miracle helped earn him a place among some of the country's greatest pilots: Chuck Yeager, Scott Crossfield, Mel Apt, and now John Glenn. The list was all male, naturally. Only men were allowed to be military test pilots.

But men weren't the only ones breaking records.

CHAPTER 7

SETTING RECORDS, SPUTNIK, AND THE START OF THE SPACE RACE

Sunlight streaked across the curved glass of the cockpit. In the distance, Oklahoma City sprawled lazily over the flat landscape. Jerrie Cobb knew it was now or never. The twenty-six-year-old pilot hoisted her hips away from the leather seat and shimmied out of her watim flight suit. Cobb then began the familiar squirm required to ease into stockings while flying a twin-engine airplane at 10,000 feet. It was a one-leg-at-a-time, don't-smack-your-nose-on-the-throttle kind of dance. Cobb had done it plenty of times, though, and so she made quick work of it. Lastly, Cobb reached for a neatly folded polka-dot dress she'd tucked into the corner of her cockpit. She slipped it over her head and threaded her arms through the sleeves.

It had been four years since a hiring manager had told Jerrie that the mere sight of a woman in the cockpit was enough to send potential passengers into fits of terror. In those intervening years, she'd taken a job ferrying old military planes from the United States down to South America and over to Europe. She'd done test flight work, taking rebuilt DC-3s up and into the air to work out their bugs. She'd even set a record for speed in 1955, when she shaved twelve hours off the fastest airplane delivery time from Toronto, Canada, to Bogotá, Colombia. She'd seen the world, flown a lengthy list of airplanes, and become a very skilled pilot.

Those skills had come in handy today. The flight hadn't been easy. Cobb had steered her airplane, the *Boomtown 1*, around clusters of bruise-colored storm clouds, hail, torrential sheets of rain, and even tornadoes. The press plane that was supposed to follow along on her historic flight had bailed long ago. Its pilot didn't want to risk being struck by lightning or knocked out of the skies by powerful winds. Cobb had been all alone up there.

Now her solitude was coming to an end.

A crowd of reporters stood in the blistering heat awaiting her. The moment her wheels bounced down onto the runway, the mob surged forward. From a distance, it would have looked choreographed, this mass of fedora-wearing, notepad-clutching men on the move. Cobb taxied slowly toward them. The coarse growl of her plane's engines gave her one last moment to collect herself. She couldn't hear anything over it, and neither could the reporters. Finally, she cut the engines. Her ears filled with a familiar ringing brought on by the sudden absence of the noise. She slipped on a pair of low heels and then climbed out of the cockpit. A forced smile stretched across her face.

It was May 25, 1957, and Cobb had just set the world record for a nonstop long-distance flight in a light propeller plane. Her 1,504-mile trip from Guatemala City to Oklahoma City had lasted just over eight hours. The previous record had been set by a male Russian pilot flying a Soviet plane. Any victory over the Soviets was welcome, but a victory in aviation was especially sweet.

In the years since World War II, Americans and the Soviets had fallen into a tense and hostile state. This period of almost-war was called the Cold War and would ultimately last more than forty years, with both sides scrambling to show superiority in technology, weapons, and of course, aviation.

As cameras flashed, journalists pestered Cobb with questions. They wanted to know how it felt to beat the Soviet record. Her fast flight had given the U.S. a leg up in the Cold War.

Cobb did her best to politely answer as many questions as she could. A speech impediment made these occasions nearly unbearable, but she knew they were part of the gig. She planned on setting many more world records, so she figured she might as well get used to talking to the press now.

The news stories that followed Cobb's impressive flight praised her for her skills, but also focused on her appearance. One reported that she "looked as fresh as if she had just dressed for a date." Another noted that her dress, jewelry, and stockings looked more appropriate for "a luncheon than a grueling world record endurance flight."

Cobb didn't dwell on the press. She had bigger things to think about—namely, her next world record. She wanted to push a light twin-engine plane as high as it could go.

Jerrie Cobb stands near her twin-engine airplane, five days before attempting her world-record long-distance flight in 1957.

Three weeks after setting her long-distance record, Cobb climbed into another Aero Commander, this one named the *Boomtown II*, and flew it to 30,330 feet. It was another world record! But something went wrong with her instruments, and the altitude hadn't been properly recorded. Cobb didn't despair. She just tried again. On July 5, 1957, she pushed *Boomtown II* even farther. This time, she climbed nearly six miles into the sky. As her altimeter rose, finally settling at yet another new world record of 30,560 feet, Cobb stared in wonder out of her cockpit. The sky was achingly blue. She could see no horizon, no limits, no boundaries. This was the closest she'd ever been to space. She was entranced.

Cobb wasn't the only female pilot pushing aviation boundaries in 1957. Earlier in the year, Jean Hixson had become the second woman in history to break the sound barrier. She flew at over 840 miles per hour in a jet called a Starfire (F-94 C) over Lake Erie. Hixson had been a WASP, which made her an experienced and elite aviator. When she climbed into the Starfire, she had nineteen years of flight under her belt. Hixson's extensive background made it more than a little frustrating that she wasn't allowed to actually *fly* the jet that broke the sound barrier. Oh, no. A male air force pilot took care of that for her.

Hixson had actually found her way onto the flight through a little luck and a solid argument. At the last minute, the reporter scheduled to ride along on the flight developed an inner ear infection. Not wanting to experience a simultaneous sonic boom and ruptured eardrum, he had bowed out of the mission. Hixson saw her opportunity and pounced.

Hixson was a schoolteacher and a member of the Air Force Reserves. She argued that as an educator and pilot, she was the perfect person to fill the seat on the bullet-shaped jet. She could even incorporate something about the sound barrier into her curriculum! The air force agreed, with one important stipulation: Hixson had to keep her hands off the controls. She would be a passenger on this flight. Not a pilot.

As the Starfire zipped over the lake, the force of the jet's incredible speed shoved Hixson back into her seat with building pressure. "Gravity assured me it was there," she said, "and I squashed real hard into the seat." Then it happened: A deafening crack shattered the air. A sonic boom! Hixson didn't hear it. She was traveling so fast that the sound occurred behind her plane. She watched out the cockpit as the lake disappeared below in a blue-gray blur.

The thirty-five-year-old math, science, and astronomy teacher reveled in the experience. She was fascinated by all things aviation and knew that even riding as a passenger on this flight was the chance of a lifetime. When she gingerly climbed down from the Starfire's cockpit after the newsworthy flight, she beamed at a swarm of reporters. Her delight soon turned to irritation when the press ran the story. The reporters didn't refer to her as a pilot. They called her "Akron's flying school teacher."

While male test pilots were climbing in and out of all

Jean Hixson shakes hands with Army General Henry "Hap" Arnold, 1944.

sorts of jets at Edwards and Pax, it remained an incredibly rare opportunity for a woman aviator to fly in one. The military occasionally doled out jet flights to women as prizes for winning an air race, or for publicity. Even then, these jet flights were often short and micromanaged.

The year after Hixson's flight in the Starfire, the air force agreed to let her take control of another jet called the Delta Dagger. This was the same jet that Gus Grissom and Gordon Cooper had tested out over the California desert in those pinching, squeezing pressure suits. Hixson wasn't allowed to take off from the runway, but the second she was in the air she said she "put [the jet] through every manoeuvre they would allow." The *Akron Beacon Journal* breathlessly reported on her flight the next day. It noted that Hixson's mother remained calm during her daughter's flight, even when Hixson did a loop at an altitude of nine miles.

Flying jets was a thrilling activity, and for talented aviators like Hixson, it wasn't too hard, either. Her freewheeling flight showed that. It also suggested that other women pilots might take to jets just as easily, if only they could have the chance.

Despite the fact that women pilots still faced resistance and discrimination, 1957 was a thrilling year in American aviation. In January of that year, three giant Boeing planes called Stratofortresses completed a nonstop around-the-world mission. During their monumental 45-hour flight, the wide-winged planes had to be refueled mid-flight four different times. This meant even bigger planes called

Stratotankers had to fly just above the Stratofortresses, lower fuel pipes, and fill the planes as they roared through the skies. A few months later, a U.S. Navy blimp set a record for an unrefueled, continuous flight by soaring an astonishing 9,448 miles in 264.2 hours. John Glenn's Project Bullet made headlines across the nation as he crossed the country at 723 miles per hour. In September, President Dwight D. Eisenhower became the first president to fly in a helicopter.

American aviation seemed to be an industry of immeasurable growth. But on October 4, 1957, the Soviets dealt a swift blow to American confidence with the successful flight of something far more impressive than a jet or a helicopter. The Soviets had launched a *satellite*. A spacecraft! The twenty-three-inch metal orb was the first artificial object ever sent into Earth's orbit and represented a huge leap in technology. Americans reeled at the news and shaped their mouths around its unfamiliar Russian name: *Sputnik*. Within hours of its launch, horrified shortwave radio operators could pick up *Sputnik*'s tinny robotic beeps as it passed 560 miles overhead.

Many Americans responded to *Sputnik*'s launch with hand-wringing terror. If the Soviets could lob a satellite up there, what else would they do? Would they use this advance for peaceful scientific exploration, or would they weaponize their next satellite? Senate Majority Leader Lyndon B. Johnson warned that the Soviets could use their space technology to drop bombs on American soil "like kids dropping rocks onto cars from freeway overpasses."

In December, the U.S. Navy trotted a satellite of its own out alongside a tricky little rocket called the Vanguard. The satellite was about the size and weight of a cantaloupe. Engineers balanced the pint-sized device atop the Vanguard, stood back, and lit the ignition. The rocket lurched about four feet off the launchpad and hovered there for an excruciating moment. Then it exploded in a giant fireball. In the midst of the blast, the satellite fell from the top of the rocket and rolled across the launchpad, chirping its chipper signal along the way. Navy engineers were mortified. The press was elated. Journalists delighted in making up nicknames for the disastrous event, such as "kaputnik," "stayputnik," and "dudnik."

The Space Race had only just begun, and Americans were already losing. This battle to show superiority in space would occupy the minds of both Americans and Soviets for nearly twenty years as each side toiled in labs and on launchpads. Following the *Sputnik-Kaputnik* debacle, President Eisenhower knew it was time for the United States to prioritize space exploration. He signed the National Aeronautics and Space Act in 1958, which turned the National Advisory Committee for Aeronautics (NACA) into the National Aeronautics and Space Administration (NASA). This move showed that the United States was taking this space business seriously.

Soon, it would be time to select the first group of astronauts.

The Vanguard missile explodes shortly after launch, enveloping the pad in flames, 1957.

CHAPTER 8

ASTRONAUT TESTING AND SELECTION

Scott Carpenter struck quite the figure. He stood at just over 5' 10" and was powerfully built. His face was tanned and worn and scarred, a little like a movie star cowboy. His eyes were a brilliant green. They even twinkled when he smiled. He was casually handsome. In 1959, he was a veteran of the Korean War and a Pax River test pilot. Dressed in his navy blues, Carpenter looked like the ultimate American hero.

That chilly winter morning, however, Carpenter wasn't in uniform. The dashing test pilot walked down the gleaming halls of the Pentagon wearing a stiff and unfamiliar civilian suit. He'd recently received a set of painfully brief top-secret orders: "You

Scott Carpenter smirks for a photograph.

are hereby ordered to report to the Pentagon at 0700 on 2 February 1959 . . ." They didn't explain what he'd be doing, or why he'd been invited. They just specified to be here, now, dressed like a civilian.

Carpenter took a deep breath and walked into the Pentagon assembly hall. Inside, thirty or so men milled about awkwardly. They looked to be around his age, height, and build. The number of crew cuts in the room made it fairly clear that they were all military. He recognized a few fellow test pilots. John Glenn was there. So was Wally Schirra. Carpenter knew them both from Pax.

The room hummed with nervous tension and low, murmured conversations. What were they all doing here? Any ideas? A few hotshots guessed that the Department of Defense was working on a new plane. Maybe a rocket plane. They must need pilots.

Three older men entered the room and took their seats on a stage at one end of the hall.

"Gentlemen," one began, "we've asked you here to discuss Project Mercury."

He went on to explain that he represented the country's new space agency, NASA. They wanted to send a man into Earth's orbit within the next three years. The details were still a little shaky, but they had a basic plan. The agency would use a ballistic missile called the Atlas booster to propel a tiny metal capsule into space. The capsule would be called the Mercury. NASA needed men to fill it. These brave passengers would be called astronauts.

An electric current of excitement shot through the room. *Astronauts?* Space pilots? It sounded like something straight out of science fiction!

The speaker went on to explain that, at least during the early missions, the astronauts wouldn't actually do much flying. Their capsule's flights would be automated. Engineers on the ground would program it all ahead of time using something called an electronic computer. These room-sized devices were capable of staggering workloads. They had enough memory to hold more than a thousand words at a time. All this computer power meant that the engineers could monitor and control the missions from their desks.

So, the astronauts wouldn't exactly *fly* their capsule. They wouldn't *land* it either, at least not in the traditional sense of the word. There wouldn't be any runway landings for the Mercury capsule. It would plunk down into the ocean instead, slowed by a set of parachutes.

At this, flickers of doubt and disgust rippled through the crowd. The astronauts wouldn't do any flying? No thank you. These were test pilots, the best and the brightest and the fastest. They weren't *passengers.* And this landing business? These men were used to bringing all manner of aircraft down onto runways or water or even hard-packed desert sand. A parachute? How embarrassing.

Sensing the mounting hostility, another figure on the stage stood up. It was Warren J. North, a well-known test pilot. North assured the men in the room that whoever wound up in the capsule would still be a pilot. He'd make important observations and monitor his instruments. In the event of an emergency, he *could* take over the controls. A few sets of shoulders in the room relaxed at this. Still, many remained tense, defensive.

The presentation went on. Carpenter and the others learned that Project Mercury would be risky. Perhaps the riskiest thing they'd ever done. The Atlas was still a little unreliable. The giant rocket booster had a tendency to blow up here and there. But, the speaker assured the group, the engineers at NASA were working on correcting that problem. They had already ironed out quite a few of the bugs.

NASA needed the best astronauts it could find for this pioneering program. That was where the men in this room came in. The agency had considered a wide variety of possible candidate pools. They'd seriously debated whether acrobats, deep-sea divers, mountain climbers, or meteorologists might make the best astronauts. However, in the interest of time, NASA had settled on choosing its astronauts from the pool of active military test pilots.

This move made sense for a few key reasons: test pilots were talented aviators who had experience in dangerous situations, and they were generally in good health. Also, they had already been granted security clearance for their military employment. This last point might have clinched the deal for the test pilots. The pressure to beat the Soviets into space weighed heavy on their shoulders. NASA was in a frantic rush to get this project underway. Any paperwork shortcuts were enthusiastically welcomed.

In December 1958, two months before Carpenter was called to the Pentagon, NASA's astronaut selection committee had begun sorting through the military's 540 active-duty test pilots. The engineers had given them a list of requirements for potential astronauts: They wanted pilots who had logged at least 1,500 hours of flight time, experience flying jets, military test flight experience, and a bachelor's degree in science, engineering, "or the equivalent." In addition, the pilots had to be younger than forty years old, weigh less than 180 pounds, and be under 5' 11".

The last specification was perhaps the most practical of all. The Mercury capsule was tiny. NASA engineers didn't want to design a new version to accommodate a taller astronaut. Filtered through these requirements, NASA came up with a list of 110 possible pilots. They started inviting them right there, to the Pentagon. In fact, Carpenter was among the first group of pilots to hear about the project.

At the end of the meeting, a NASA official gave a few final remarks to the assembled pilots. He told them that this decision was theirs to make. No one would judge them for their choices here. He advised them to take the night to think this over. If any of them decided to volunteer, his team would follow up with a series of medical, physical, and psychological tests. The room remained silent as the test pilots gathered their things and left. They had a lot to think about. Project Mercury could be their most important, and dangerous, test flight yet.

Carpenter didn't wait. He volunteered that afternoon.

He wasn't alone. Thirty-one other test pilots volunteered as well. This group included some of the very best military pilots alive: John Glenn, Wally Schirra, Gordo Cooper, Deke Slayton, Alan Shepard, and Gus Grissom.

The thirty-two men were soon directed to report to Lovelace Clinic in Albuquerque, New Mexico, for Phase I of their astronaut testing, their physical screening. This didn't seem like it would be a big deal. Military pilots were used to routine physical exams. What awaited them at the quiet desert clinic, however, was like nothing they'd ever experienced.

They arrived at the Lovelace Clinic in groups, again dressed like civilians and under strict orders to keep the whole thing a secret. Instead of using their names, physicians referred to them by their patient numbers. They were Unit 28 and Unit 3 and Unit 19. For seven long days, each candidate's body was tested, measured, weighed, analyzed, poked, and prodded. Deke Slayton later said, "If you didn't like doctors, it was your worst nightmare."

The pilots spent a full week hobbling between exam rooms and suffering every kind of test their doctors could think up. They stripped naked and floated in giant vats of water to determine their exact body densities. They displayed the health of their hearts and lungs by blowing little balls into the air and trying to keep them aloft for as long as possible. They ran on a treadmill until their fatigued muscles gave out. Doctors used new technology to map the pilots' hearts. Then they mapped their colons for good measure. The pilots grimaced while doctors scraped the inside of their throats. Then they withered in embarrassment while doctors inserted a device they called the steel eel into their rectums.

The fact was that the medical establishment just didn't know what spaceflight might do to a human body. Therefore, the doctors tried to ensure that any astronaut NASA sent up there was as healthy as possible. If something went wrong in space, it wouldn't be because their guy was a lemon.

John Glenn blows into a tube during medical testing at the Lovelace Clinic, Albuquerque, New Mexico, 1959.

The next two phases of testing took place at the Wright-Patterson Air Force Base in Ohio. Phase II and III of astronaut testing determined how they might respond to the stresses of outer space. Again, the test administrators weren't exactly sure what those stresses might be. So, they improvised.

The pilots were strapped to seats and vibrated violently while clusters of scientists stood nearby, scribbling observations into their notepads. They were blasted with loud noises and forced to sit in baking-hot rooms. They sat in pressure chambers that simulated flight at staggeringly high altitudes. Medics studied their reactions as the pilots' feet were plunged into icy water. Isolation tests challenged the men to sit in a dark room for three hours, armed only with a pen and pad of paper for entertainment.

The men spent their days at Wright-Pat alternating between bizarre physical tests and invasive psychological exams. They stared at inkblots, doing their best to come up with astronaut-worthy responses. They described themselves in one word, then twenty words, then one word again. They ranked themselves against their peers and described their dreams. Days of extensive psychiatric interviews, tests, and activities left one pilot feeling as though "nothing is sacred anymore."

These tests served more than one purpose. Sure, they showed which candidates were healthy and sane, but they also showed doctors something else as well. They made it crystal clear which men really, truly wanted this opportunity. The tests were embarrassing and long. Many were tedious. Some were very painful. They required composure and patience and a sense of humor. One of the doctors admitted that he was pushing the astronaut candidates on purpose. He confessed, "We were trying to drive them crazy."

NASA planned to spend about $1 million in 1960s currency to train each astronaut. Today, that number would equal around $9 million. The people at NASA wanted to be sure they weren't about to waste all that money on a candidate who wasn't passionate about this project or able to handle the stresses of the experience.

Eighteen men, 56% of the test pilot volunteers, performed well enough to be recommended "without medical reservations." They hadn't all scored perfectly, and some hadn't actually met the agency's exact requirements. Glenn and Carpenter didn't have engineering degrees. In fact, the two hadn't even graduated from college. Glenn had another strike against him: He and Schirra were at the very top of the weight limit. They'd have to diet if they made the cut.

NASA engineers figured they would send up a half dozen or so astronauts on Project Mercury. This meant they needed to narrow down the group of eighteen test pilots further. While the test pilots waited anxiously to hear if they'd been deemed worthy, the selection committee began ranking the candidates. They placed the best at the top, and the worst at the bottom.

No one knows exactly how the selection committee judged the men. Its official ranking of the eighteen pilots remains a secret even today. However, it is clear that in addition to considering each pilot's performance, NASA also considered his personality, ability to charm a crowd, and willingness to work in a team. Officially, NASA's selection committee wanted pilots "who were not only in top physical condition but had demonstrated that they had the capability to stay alive under tough and dangerous assignments." Unofficially, a NASA employee admitted that the agency "looked for real men."

Finally, after agonizing review, seven men were chosen to become the nation's first class of astronauts. Each pilot received a phone call from the committee in which he was asked one final time to confirm his willingness to volunteer. Every one of them enthusiastically complied.

On April 9, 1959, the seven pilots met in Washington, D.C., for their debut press conference as the Mercury 7, America's first astronauts.

The men sat at a long banquet table at the head of a conference room. Lined up like this, it was easy to see their similarities. They were all white men of medium build and stature. Their haircuts were trim and neat. They were all between the ages of thirty-two and thirty-seven. Though some wore bow ties and others wore neckties, each of them had the sharp, buttoned-up look of military men.

The Mercury 7 smile at a crowd during their first press conference, April 9, 1959. From left, Brigadier General Donald Flickinger, Deke Slayton, Alan Shepard, Wally Schirra, Gus Grissom, John Glenn, Gordon Cooper, Scott Carpenter.

A NASA official stood behind a podium in one corner of the room and introduced the pilots to the already adoring press. "Malcolm S. Carpenter, Leroy G. Cooper, John H. Glenn, Virgil I. Grissom, Walter M. Schirra, Alan B. Shepard, Donald K. Slayton." The men rose to their feet as the speaker continued, "These, ladies and gentlemen, are the nation's Mercury astronauts." Reporters ogled. Cameramen peered around their enormous lenses to gape. The room was awash with admiration. After all, these were the seven men who would represent the nation and perhaps all of mankind in its first forays into the cosmos.

In his brief remarks to the crowd that day, Captain Norman Barr, the director of NASA's Astronautical Division, said, ' All ul uo ᴨᵗᴴ vᵢᵢᵣʸ ouₑᵣₑ that the correct men have been selected for this program." A cluster of unilormᵘᵢ ₙᵢçₙ in the room listened with confident, satisfied expressions. Yes, these men were good candidates. They had the right background, flight experience, and temperament. They were the right physical build and age. Yes, these men would surely help the United States beat the Soviets in the Space Race.

Barr's comment also acknowledged an important assumption: the astronauts would be men. The question of whether women should be considered probably had not crossed his mind. That was likely true of almost everyone in the room that day, with two important exceptions: Brigadier General Donald D. Flickinger and Dr. William Randolph "Randy" Lovelace II. Flickinger was NASA's director of human factors. Dr. Lovelace was chairman of NASA's Committee on Life Sciences. He had helped design and host the Mercury 7's medical testing program at his clinic in New Mexico. This pair of men, who sat to one side of the astronauts that day, had been quietly cooking up a little theory that women might make better astronauts than men. And in fact, they were just about ready to start testing it.

CHAPTER 9

FEMALE, UNIT 1: TESTING BEGINS

T hings at NASA were moving fast in 1959. The Space Race was in full swing, with the United States enjoying a momentary lead. Americans had managed to lob eleven satellites into space. This put them way ahead of the Soviets, who had only three satellites looping around the planet. And now, everyone's attention turned to the next big step: putting a human up there.

NASA prepared frantically for this monumental task. Engineers worked hard to design a capsule that just might keep its passenger alive through a rocket launch. They wondered: *How many g's would the astronaut need to survive? Six? Eight?* That would mean six or eight times the force of gravity. Standing on Earth subjected a human to one g. Whipping around a corner in a race car might exert two g's on a passenger. But six or eight? That kind of thing could easily knock a pilot into g-LOC, or g-induced loss of consciousness. An unconscious astronaut might as well be a sack of potatoes. The engineers needed to keep their pilot awake. They ended up deciding on a cone-shaped capsule that would launch with its inhabitant lying on his back. This position, they figured, gave a pilot a fighting chance at staying conscious during launch.

And then there was the issue of reentry. How could they stop the whole capsule from burning up as it cut through Earth's atmosphere? A capsule tearing through the thick layer of gases surrounding the planet would get hot. Very hot. NASA's engineers experimented with different types of materials for the capsule's heat shield, the flat edge that would take the brunt of the scorching temperatures. Should they use metal? Polymer? They ended up coating it in a type

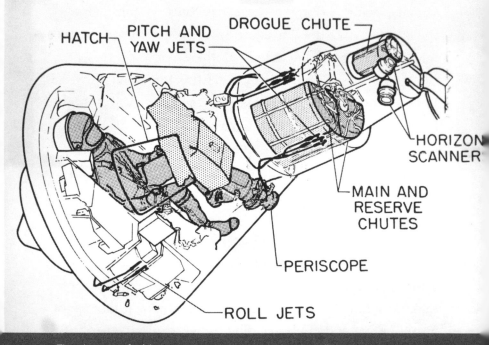

This diagram of a Mercury capsule shows just how small it was.

of modified resin. It melted in goopy globs when it got hot, but it would keep the capsule from turning into a flying lump of charcoal.

And their questions didn't simply focus on the details of the flight. They also had to worry about what would happen during landing. What kind of impact would they be dealing with when the capsule splashed down into the water? What if it hit land instead? Engineers began strapping live pigs into the Mercury capsule and dropping it from great heights onto concrete. They needed to see how much of a walloping someone could take in there and still manage to walk away with a heartbeat.

Four pigs endured these tests, which subjected them to up to fifty-eight g's, and often attracted crowds of eager viewers. Engineers and audiences alike were relieved each time to see their pigs trot away with only slight injuries. The pigs had made it. Maybe the men could, too.

Of course, everyone knew that all of this work could be for nothing if it turned out that spaceflight was toxic. Some people had guessed that the very act of floating around in outer space caused a heart to stop beating or eyeballs to explode. Others thought spaceflight might feel so good, so intoxicating, that the astronauts would refuse to come home. They called it the breakaway phenomenon. The fear was that pilots suffering from breakaway phenomenon might just try to steer their capsules away from Earth and disappear into the inky depths of space. The fact was that scientists at NASA just didn't know what would happen out there. No one did.

Air Force Brigadier General Don Flickinger worried about the pace at NASA. He said the United States was "trying to do too much" at a "horribly fast" speed. Flick, as he was called by his friends, was a hard worker, but not a fast worker. He favored slow, deliberate research. Flick thought that the best discoveries were the ones made while a man was fishing or gazing off into a sunset, deep in meditative thought. No one was making time for that now. The Soviets were breathing down their necks. NASA was a freight train, chugging forward with all the strength and speed it could muster. Flick worried that all this urgency might just send NASA off its tracks.

He thought the agency was likely to miss something in its frenzy to beat the Soviets into space. First of all, he questioned, had they even chosen the right astronauts? The Mercury 7 were all men. What about women astronauts? Months before they were seated behind the astronauts at their debut press conference, Flick had teamed up with his friend Dr. Randy Lovelace to explore this topic. Would women make good astronauts? Was it possible that they might be *better* space travelers than men?

In the fall of 1959, Flick proposed an air force research program he called Project WISE (Women in Space Earliest). He hoped to work with Lovelace to investigate just how, or if, women could contribute to the nation's space program. This project would have sounded radical to a male-dominated society, but it was built upon solid science. Previous studies had shown that women fared better in isolation and small spaces than men. They also had fewer heart attacks than men. This suggested that they might make hardier, more resilient astronauts.

On a practical level, investigating women astronauts seemed like it could help NASA solve a serious problem: cutting weight in the space capsule. Most women weighed less than men. They also breathed less oxygen. They ate and drank less,

Brigadier General Donald D. "Flick" Flickinger.

too. NASA engineers were hard at work making their space capsule as light as possible to ease the load on their rockets. Flick wondered why NASA wasn't considering female astronauts who might weigh forty, fifty, even sixty pounds less than males. After all, every pound an astronaut weighed required approximately 1,000 pounds of fuel to launch. A lighter passenger who required less oxygen and fewer rations would certainly be a welcome relief for the frazzled engineers. As it was, they were tearing their hair out trying to strip weight from the capsule anywhere they could.

Flick knew his project would be unpopular within the air force, and probably within NASA, too. Most people in aviation circles believed that women wouldn't be able to hack it in space. They didn't have the right constitution. Plus, what would they do about menstruation? First, it would pose a practical problem—all that blood! How could the engineers deal with liquid in space? Second, this brought up a familiar stereotype about women pilots: that their periods changed their brains so drastically that a menstruating woman might not be able to make rational decisions. The idea of training an astronaut who could lose her mind once a month was just nonsense.

Another reason that Project WISE was bound to get pushback was that it didn't make much sense given NASA's current astronaut requirements. The agency wanted its astronauts to be military pilots with test flight and jet flight experience. Women had not been allowed to fly in the military since the dissolution of the WASPs back in 1944. This meant they couldn't check either of those boxes. So, why fuss with Project WISE when the outcome didn't really matter anyway?

Flick didn't care much about pushback. He was curious. Lovelace was, too. And the two friends had a hunch that they were onto something. They decided to do some research on women astronauts first, then come up with some hard data. If they were able to show that women could score well on the same astronaut tests that the men had taken, then maybe NASA would consider the idea of sending females into space.

The two men soon found the perfect test subject on a

Miami beach. Jerrie Cobb was in town for the September 1959 Air Force Association meeting. It was a gathering of some of the top minds in American aviation, and Flick and Lovelace were attending it as well.

Their first interaction was a little awkward. Lovelace and Flick were in their bathing suits, still dripping from an early morning swim. Cobb was starstruck. Both men were well known for their work with NASA. Cobb, a flight and space enthusiast, might as well have just bumped into John Wayne. These men were heroes.

A mutual friend introduced the three, and their talk soon turned to planes. Cobb mentioned something about aviation and noticed the two men snap to attention.

One blurted, "Are you a pilot?"

Cobb smiled and replied, "Oh, yes. I've been flying for sixteen years."

The men's eyes grew wide as they learned that twenty-eight-year-old Cobb had more than 7,000 hours in her flight log. She held three speed and altitude records. Cobb was the 1959 Woman of the Year in Aviation and the National Pilots Association Pilot of the Year. They had very clearly found their girl.

Flickinger and Lovelace were fresh from a trip to Moscow. While there, they'd heard quiet, buzzing rumors that the Soviets might be training women for spaceflight. If this were true, if the Soviets were ready to launch a woman, then the United States didn't have a moment to waste.

"What can I do?" Cobb asked eagerly. "How can I help?"

The answer was more than she could have hoped for: "Would you be willing to be a test subject for the first research on women as astronauts?"

A wave of excitement hit her. She remembered all of her first flights—her first hop in the Waco, her first taste of airborne freedom, and her altitude record that had taken her so close to the stars. Now, she was stepping closer to another first. *Space.*

"I would," Cobb answered. Happy tears stung her eyes.

The three began to hatch their plan. Flickinger and Lovelace would put a group of women through the same testing that the Mercury 7 had undergone. All the men who went through the testing were elite pilots, so the women should be elite pilots as well. Cobb promised to help come up with a list of talented female aviators for the tests. She had participated in enough air races and worked in aviation long enough to know which women were the best.

One month after meeting Lovelace and Flick, Cobb got an incredible opportunity for any female aviator, but an especially golden chance for someone about to undergo astronaut testing: She got to fly a jet! And not just any jet. It was a gorgeous, powerful, glimmering Delta Dagger and she was at the controls for forty glorious minutes. Of course, the air force assigned a man to fly alongside Cobb. He handled the other twenty minutes of the hour-long flight. But Cobb was delighted nonetheless. She pushed the jet to Mach 1.3 and experienced the delicious satisfaction of breaking the sound barrier. After landing, she echoed the sentiments of many other pilots: Flying a jet was a cinch. "It's really effortless flying," she said.

On the eve of her astronaut tests, this short hop on a jet was important to Cobb. Astronauts were jet pilots. And now she had flown a jet, too. The differences between her and the Mercury 7 were beginning to dissolve. She was inching toward them, flight by flight, and soon, test by test.

Cobb wouldn't actually be the first woman to undergo astronaut testing. Around the same time that Cobb was breaking the sound barrier, a pilot named Ruth Nichols was quietly invited to Wright-Patterson Air Force Base to take some of the tests herself. She rode on training devices and endured hours of solitude in the isolation test. Nichols excitedly wrote about her experience in the press, saying that women were "naturals" for spaceflight. When air force leadership caught wind of her public report, they became furious. Nichols was making it seem like these guys were on board with the idea of lady astronauts. This couldn't have been further from the truth.

In November 1959, the air force canceled Project WISE. That meant that Flick, an air force man, had to bow out of the project. He handed the research entirely over to Lovelace to continue on his own.

The official reasoning behind the cancellation was that there was "too little to learn of value to Air Force Medical interests and too big a chance of adverse publicity." In other words, the data didn't matter enough, and the risk of a negative news story just wasn't worth it. It is likely that the air force also canceled Project WISE for a financial reason. Women would need pressure suits in order to complete their astronaut tests, and, thus far, the air force didn't have any that would fit women. If Project WISE were to move forward, someone would have to pay for a suit redesign. The air force didn't want to foot the bill.

Ruth Nichols was devastated by the fallout. Nine months later, she died by suicide. Those close to her suspect that her death was related to her deep disappointment at not becoming an astronaut.

Another pilot named Betty Skelton managed to take some astronaut tests before Jerrie Cobb as well, though hers were essentially a publicity stunt staged by NASA. Skelton earned her fame as an acrobatic pilot. Her signature move involved flying a prop plane upside down over ribbon-cutting ceremonies. She'd fly so low that her propeller would slice right through the ribbon. Crowds adored the red-haired beauty.

On February 2, 1960, *Look* magazine hit newsstands with Skelton on the cover. The acrobatic pilot was pictured wearing a silver space suit and holding her helmet—the better to see her curled red hair and flawless makeup. On one side of Skelton sat the Mercury capsule. On the other side was a question: "Should a girl be first in space?" The photo essay inside showed Skelton giggling with the Mercury 7 during various tests and training exercises. The story cutely noted that the men nicknamed Skelton number 7½. Just one half. Not quite a whole.

NASA had no real intentions to invite Skelton to become

an astronaut. The story simply gave the agency a chance to drum up positive attention about how its astronauts trained for space. The article made sure to caution its readers that there was "at this writing, no announced program to put women into space."

Despite the experiences of Nichols and Skelton, Cobb held on to hope for her own testing. Perhaps it might lead to an American woman in space, she told herself. Maybe she could be that woman. On February 15, 1960, Cobb walked into the Lovelace Clinic in Albuquerque, New Mexico, to begin her Phase I astronaut tests. She reported to the front desk, where she received her new secret identity: Female, Unit 1. Cobb had heard about the tests the Mercury 7 had endured at Lovelace. It had been all over the news. At the astronauts' very first press conference, John Glenn hinted at how invasive it had all been. When asked which test he'd liked least, Glenn replied that it was tough to answer. "If you figure how many openings there are on a human body and how far you can go into any one of 'em . . . now, you answer which would be the toughest for you!" The crowd of reporters had dissolved into laughter.

On that brisk February morning, Cobb didn't feel like laughing. She steeled herself for the trial of a lifetime. After all, if she did well on these tests, she would open the door to the idea of women in space. If she performed poorly, she could blow it for her whole gender.

A friendly charge nurse handed Cobb a schedule. She smiled and said, "Good luck, and I mean it." Cobb reviewed the list of tests awaiting her and gulped. With the exception

Betty Skelton poses by an airplane, 1948.

of an added gynecological exam, she would face exactly what the men had.

Cobb promptly began. Before long she found herself lying on her back on a table in the middle of a large exam room. Wires were taped to her chest and a blood pressure cuff hugged her upper arm. Abruptly, the table lurched and her whole body tilted. The blood pressure cuff squeezed. Someone asked if she felt dizzy. She shook her head no. Then the table pitched again, and she tilted at a new angle. It lurched again. And again. Cobb did her best not to fall off while remaining calm and answering the doctor's questions. She later discovered that this was a tilt table, a test that had "been the nemesis for a good many healthy, hearty, ox-strong pilots." It determined whether a pilot had any problems with circulation. If a pilot passed out on the tilt table, he or she would make a lousy space traveler. Scientists figured that astronauts would be spending as much time in outer space upside down as right side up. If they couldn't hack it on the tilt table, they definitely couldn't hack it in space. Luckily, Cobb did just fine.

Later, Cobb sat through a fairly routine ear exam. A doctor peered into her ear and tested her hearing. Just when she thought it had ended, he directed her to stare up at the ceiling. She did. Suddenly, she felt the jarring and painful sensation of 10-degree supercooled liquid spraying against her tender inner ear. The liquid froze the bones inside her ear. The effect hit her instantly. The ceiling swirled, her eyes darted from side to side, and her arm fell off the table. Cobb knew this was vertigo, but she was powerless to stop it. She

Jerrie Cobb endures the tilt table test at the Lovelace Clinic, February 1960.

was completely, helplessly disoriented. She couldn't see. She couldn't move.

The doctor explained that a pilot who was especially vulnerable to vertigo wouldn't be a good choice for an astronaut. Outer space would surely present enough challenges with balance as it was. As soon as Cobb regained her composure from the first ear, she saw the doctor preparing to do the whole test again on the other side.

"Ugh," she groaned quietly.

Cobb knew she had to behave politely at the Lovelace Clinic. This was especially difficult during one exam. Scientists stuck a hefty needle into the muscles in her hand and then pulsed electricity through it. The test had something to do with measuring the speed of her muscular and nervous reactions, but that was hard to focus on while staring at a needle that looked as thick as a nail. Cobb managed to remain composed through the test, noting later that "it is a strange feeling to wait for an electric shock, and to see your hand twitch uncontrollably."

Another exam brought Cobb into a room where a stationary bike was perched among a tangle of medical equipment. The head of the Lovelace physiology department, an older man named Dr. Ulrich Luft, told her, "Miss Cobb, this test is to see how your body reacts to hard physical work. It is part of our special dynamic examinations here to measure body efficiency."

"Just what do I do, Dr. Luft?" Cobb asked. "Pedal as fast as possible, as if I were racing?"

The gray-haired physician smiled kindly. Cobb realized he wasn't going to tell her how to beat this test. It would be up to her to figure it out. Ulrich gave her simple instructions: Pedal along to the beat of a metronome.

Cobb began, huffing and pedaling, but doing well. Then someone slid a sandbag against the rear wheel of the bike. Her pedals dragged. Her legs burned. Cobb kept pedaling. The test would measure how well her lungs worked, but it was also a test of resolve. A tech increased the resistance on the back wheel. Cobb kept pedaling. Ulrich gave her a quiet nod of encouragement. Cobb began silently praying for strength. She just had to pass this test. She just *had to*.

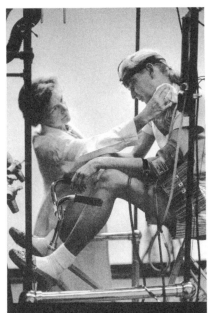

Jerrie Cobb slumps in exhaustion at the conclusion of her bicycle test, Lovelace Clinic, 1960.

Finally, when her heart rate hit 180 beats per minute, the test stopped. Scientists believed that a heart beating that fast was at its total exhaustion point. They had pushed Cobb to the brink, and there she was, still breathing. Still determined.

The male pilots who tested at Lovelace did so in groups. They chatted in waiting rooms and competed to perform the best on this test or that. Cobb took her tests alone.

When she swallowed three feet of rubber hose as part of a test on her stomach acids, she gagged and coughed and sputtered by herself. When she ran on the treadmill, endlessly sweating and panting and plodding ahead as scientists watched and scribbled their judgments, she was alone. She was alone at breakfast and at dinner. But she was used to the solitude. After all, she was a woman pilot. She'd spent years alone in her cockpit, with just the clouds for company. As one of her doctors would later observe, Cobb "excel[led] in loneliness."

At the end of seven days at the Lovelace Clinic, Cobb appeared for her very last appointment. It was a meeting with one of the physicians, to sum up her performance. Her heart pounded in her chest as she took her seat opposite the doctor.

Then he spoke. "You've passed the Mercury astronaut tests, Miss Cobb."

CHAPTER 10

G ordo Cooper was struggling to stay conscious inside his space capsule. His vision narrowed into a shrinking gray disc, and he feebly reached for his instrument panel. An incredible weight pressed against his body. He felt the familiar, sluggish tug of his brain turning off.

And then, just before Cooper passed out, the pressure pinning him into his seat began to lift.

Cooper wasn't in space. He was in Pennsylvania, strapped into a model space capsule that was currently whipping around a giant circular room on the end of a fifty-foot centrifuge arm. As the machine slowed, the g-forces lessened and Cooper's field of vision began to grow. The pressure lifted. Finally, the huge spinning arm came to a complete stop, and Cooper felt the bizarre relief that followed such a brutal training exercise. How simple it felt to lift a hand! To breathe!

Cooper's run in the centrifuge had subjected him to eighteen g's. On the ground, Cooper weighed about

150 pounds. Under eighteen g's, Cooper felt like he weighed 2,700 pounds. He'd managed to push a few buttons and answer a question during the centrifuge run, but nothing more. As the Mercury 7 were learning, humans couldn't do much under that kind of pressure.

A couple of the aides helped Cooper out of his mock space capsule. He was a bit wobbly, but the techs expected that.

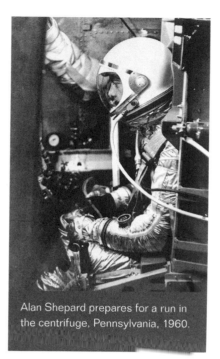

Alan Shepard prepares for a run in the centrifuge, Pennsylvania, 1960.

Everyone wobbled after a hard run, and eighteen g's wasn't just hard. It was vicious. Then Gordo soon noticed something odd. The backs of his legs, arms, and torso were wet.

Good grief, he was soaked with his own blood! The centrifuge had forced blood to pool at the back of his body. At a certain point, it must have burst through his skin. Gordo's bruises from the run would last him a couple of weeks. They also taught his peers a key lesson about g-forces: Anything higher than 15 g's was too tough on a human body.

The truth was, no one knew quite how to prepare for spaceflight. The Mercury 7 couldn't exactly hop on a rocket and take it for a quick ride to get a feel for things.

Instead, they had to work with engineers who did their best to simulate different parts of a space mission right here on Earth. That was where the centrifuge came in. They used it to mimic the g-forces an astronaut might face on launch and reentry. This wasn't just so that the astronauts could get familiar with the sensation, though that didn't hurt. The engineers needed the astronauts to be functional under high g-loads. If things went screwy during a launch, an astronaut needed to be able to hit an abort switch that would knock his spaceship to safety—well away from his explosive and fuel-filled rocket. Even something as simple as pushing a button was quite tricky under high g-loads. So, the astronauts trained.

Their centrifuge training started out gradually. The early runs simulated just five or six g's. These had the astronauts feeling clumsy and sluggish, but still capable. At eight g's, they struggled to lift their arms away from their chairs to reach their instruments. Blood drained away from their heads and pooled in their bellies. As the g's increased, the astronauts learned to tense their muscles and breathe in great, grunting puffs. This, along with their pressure suits, helped keep a little blood going to their brains, a little oxygen in their systems. But it was still a dicey exercise. If they relaxed for even a second, it was lights out.

NASA engineers had by now figured that the force of launch would be about eight g's. But there were scenarios that would hit their guys with much, much more. An aborted launch, for example, where a capsule had to be blasted away from an ascending rocket. If that happened, an astronaut could get slammed with twenty-one g's. Twenty-one! Can you imagine? The most any American had survived was twenty g's, and that was for a measly six seconds. Even still, the poor guy had stumbled away vomiting like crazy and covered in bruises.

And these mission simulations were just part of the Mercury 7's workload. Shortly after their first press conference in April 1959, they had been whisked off to their new astronaut headquarters at Langley Aeronautical Laboratory in Hampton, Virginia. There, they sat behind seven identical desks and listened to lectures on space, astrophysics, and engineering. The program needed to transform these men from pilots into space experts. NASA was counting on them. America was, too.

Most of the Mercury 7 had engineering degrees. This was one of the requirements set out at the beginning of the astronaut selection process. An engineering degree would ensure that the astronauts could help with the design of the capsule and then give valuable feedback after their missions. Of course, this degree wasn't strictly necessary, as proven by the presence of Glenn and Carpenter.

The Mercury 7 soon got to work alongside NASA's engineers. They divvied up their responsibilities according to their own individual expertise. Scott Carpenter helped out with the communications and navigational tools. John Glenn helped design the instrument panel. Wally Schirra got to work on the astronauts' space suits. Gus Grissom worked on the control systems for the capsule—the spaceship version of a steering wheel and gas pedal. Gordon Cooper and Deke

The Mercury 7 listen to a lecture in their office at NASA's Langley Aeronautical Laboratory in Hampton, Virginia, 1959.

Slayton worked on the boosters and rockets. They punctuated their flurry of work with trips to various factories or labs across the country to check in on different components of their spacecraft and rockets.

On May 18, 1959, the Mercury 7 were summoned to Cape Canaveral, Florida, to watch their first rocket launch. It was an Atlas, the very rocket they planned to ride into space. The seven men gathered about half a mile from the launchpad and watched in awe as it ignited and lurched off the ground. The burst of flames against the pad was blinding. Magnificent. As the men started to crane their necks to watch the Atlas soar, the whole thing blew up. Huge, flaming chunks rained from the sky. They all ducked for cover.

Alan Shepard broke the silence that followed with a dry joke: "Well, I'm glad they got that out of the way."

Several months later, at the end of 1959, the astronauts went to St. Louis, Missouri, to check in on their space capsule. What they saw troubled them. The tiny, cone-shaped contraption stood roughly ten feet high by six feet wide. The astronauts would be absolutely jammed into the thing. Shepard later said that once he had squeezed into it, he could "move his eyeballs and not much more." Glenn joked, "You don't climb into the Mercury spacecraft, you put it on."

The size wasn't the problem. The capsule lacked something crucial. The engineers had designed the thing without a window! Sure, it had a little porthole, but someone had tucked it way back behind the astronaut's left shoulder. The only real way for the man inside to see anything was to peer through a periscope located between his knees. It was a funny little fish-eyed gizmo, and it definitely wasn't the same as a window. The astronauts gawked, dumbfounded. How could they navigate if they couldn't *see*? What if an emergency occurred and an astronaut needed to find his way back to Earth? Did the engineers really think he should pause amid the chaos and slowly crank out a periscope? Or twist completely around and squint through the little porthole? It had to be a joke!

The Mercury 7 were angry and baffled. They all remembered that first meeting at the Pentagon, where they'd learned that engineers on the ground would control much of their missions. Maybe NASA's reassurances had been wrong. They wouldn't be space pilots after all. Gus Grissom grumbled that a man in that capsule would be "almost as useful as a baby in an incubator."

The astronauts complained, and the engineers reluctantly agreed to a redesign. They'd see what they could do about a window. It might take a while, they cautioned, but they'd look into it. The Mercury 7 breathed a sigh of relief. It was a step in the right direction.

Between capsule design and classroom instruction, the early days of Project Mercury were packed. There was just so much to learn and do and try. The astronauts trained for the weightlessness they would experience in space on a plane they called the Vomit Comet. It was an F-100 that took its passengers on a series of dips and dives to give them short bursts of zero gravity. Glenn said the sensation felt a bit like "that brief moment when your car goes over a rise in the road and you're lifted out of your seat." In the Vomit Comet, the feeling of weightlessness lasted a bit longer than that. The astronauts would float for forty-five seconds or a minute while trying to quickly practice a task they'd need to do during a mission—take a bite of food or press a few buttons—before falling back into their seats.

Then engineers started to worry about what would happen to the astronauts if they lost control of the capsule during reentry. What if it started to tumble end over end? They'd be slammed backward into their seats and then thrown forward against their restraints. Could a human survive that kind of ride? Should they redesign the seat belts? Back to the centrifuge, boys!

The Mercury 7 were soon grimacing through a run they

Gordo Cooper poses in front of a prototype of a Mercury capsule, 1960.

nicknamed "eyeballs in, eyeballs out." The centrifuge would start them up, spinning and facing forward, with the force of the acceleration smashing their eyeballs into their skulls. Then, mid-ride, they'd flip 180 degrees and keep spinning, now enduring the very odd sensation of their eyeballs being pulled out of their heads.

Then the engineers realized that reentry wasn't the only time that the astronauts could lose control of their ship. It could happen at any moment! What would they do if, while tearing through space at 17,500 miles per hour, they caught themselves in a relentless spin? Without gravity or air particles to slow it down, the capsule might just spin and spin and spin out into what might as well be eternity. It was a ludicrously frightening thought. Could a man even recover from something like that? In February 1960, the astronauts started to train for this terrifying scenario on a machine called the Multi-Axis Space Training Inertial Facility, or MASTIF.

Glenn called the MASTIF "diabolically perfect." It was a set of three giant rigs, one set inside the other, with a cockpit at the very center. It could spin a pilot on three axes—pitch, roll, and yaw. This meant they could be somersaulting, rolling, and twisting, all at once. The men did not enjoy the ride. As Schirra said, "The seven of us rode the stupid thing, and we all lost our cookies or nearly did."

Once inside, the pilot's job was to manipulate the controls in the cockpit to bring the MASTIF to a standstill. It wasn't easy. It was a stomach-churning torture device. MASTIF came with an abort button, but everyone called it the Chicken Switch. After all, only a chicken would quit, right?

Alan Shepard hit the Chicken Switch on his very first ride. Aides scurried to the queasy pilot and helped him out of the cockpit. Then they gingerly laid him down on a nearby cot. Someone gave him a bucket, just in case.

Nevertheless, the astronauts gamely returned to the MASTIF day after day, riding and puking and riding again. Eventually, the Mercury 7 mastered the MASTIF at speeds of up to 30 revolutions per minute in each direction.

The astronauts didn't just train for flight, either. They trained for what might happen after they landed, too. NASA planned to station rescue ships and planes all along the space capsule's route, but engineers fretted about what would happen if the capsule landed somewhere unexpected. What if they crashed down in the jungle? Or the desert? NASA engineers figured they could find the astronauts just about anywhere they landed, but they still had to deliver rescue crews to them. That could take as long as two or even three days. A man could freeze to death in that time. Or suffer from dehydration.

The Mercury 7 were taught basic survival skills and then, as a test, dropped into the wilderness and left to fend for themselves. They sweated through 120-degree days in a Nevada desert, assembling makeshift hats and robes from their billowing orange-and-white parachutes, and doing their best to avoid deadly snakes. After three long and hot days, they emerged, sunburned and dehydrated, but eager to keep working.

Next, and more important, came water survival training. People at NASA knew it was far more likely that their guys would plunk down into an ocean than thwack into land—it was a matter of probability. Earth has more water than land. So, NASA needed its astronauts to know how to float. The agency sent the Mercury 7 to a water survival training course off the coast of Pensacola, Florida. Crews brought the astronauts out into the choppy seas and dropped them overboard with only their capsule survival kits. Then the crews sailed away, leaving the men alone in the salty waves. The astronauts treaded water while inflating their life rafts, then carefully climbed aboard, applied zinc oxide,

The Mercury 7 transform parachutes into clothing during their desert survival training, Nevada, 1960.

and activated their location beacons to help rescue crews find them.

It wasn't easy work, but it was important. The hopes of the nation rested on the Mercury 7's broad shoulders. They had to be ready for anything.

By the fall of 1960, NASA had introduced a specific tool for the astronauts called a procedures trainer. It included a mockup of the capsule cockpit, complete with a functional instrument board and a little video screen mimicking the view through the periscope. The astronauts could climb into this fake capsule and practice, really train, for spaceflight. Engineers presented them with different scenarios: Your oxygen's low! Your parachute won't deploy! You're out of fuel! Then each pilot tried to figure out the best way to respond to each crisis. This was as close as they were going to get to spaceflight before liftoff, and so they relied heavily on it. But it wasn't enjoyable work. Shepard absolutely despised it.

The trainer was arranged exactly like the actual space capsule, which meant that the astronauts were positioned as though they were sitting in a chair that had tipped back. Their knees were directly over their hips and they had to reach up to touch their instruments. They could handle an hour in the trainer, sure. But six hours? Eight? It felt like torture. Plus, taking a bathroom break was so inconvenient. They had to be unstrapped and unhooked from restraints and wires, and it all took such a terribly long time. Soon, astronauts in the procedures trainer just started to urinate right there in their flight suits. Glenn said it wasn't so bad. A little liquid never hurt anyone.

The Cold War and the race against the Soviets had created a sense of urgency around NASA. They wanted to get a man up into space, of course, but they also wanted to be *first*.

Shepard told anyone who would listen that they needed to launch as soon as possible. "We're ready to go," he'd urge. "Let's go now." One day, he even cornered NASA's leading rocket scientist, Wernher von Braun, and nearly begged him: "For God's sake, let's fly now." Shepard knew the clock was ticking. This was a race. The United States needed to win, and he wanted to be the man to get the trophy.

What Shepard didn't know was that another source of competition was creeping up just behind him. And it wasn't a Soviet cosmonaut. It was a female pilot named Jerrie Cobb.

CHAPTER 11

GOING PUBLIC

The MASTIF towered over Jerrie Cobb. She had to crane her neck to take it all in. It was giant, a tangle of brightly colored metal beams. And at the heart of it all sat an electric yellow cockpit with a stiff-looking chair. Restraint straps dangled from the seat like leathery tentacles. It was the spring of 1960, but Cobb might as well have stepped into the future. This was as cutting-edge as it got.

A crew of technicians helped Cobb hoist herself into the rig. She looked absolutely tiny, and not only because she was settling into a training device the size of a two-story house. The air force had given her a standard-issue orange flight suit. These coveralls were loose-fitting, comfortable flying gear for most male pilots, with lots of pockets for pens and sunglasses and flight plans. But loose-fitting for a man equaled tentlike for Cobb. She'd rolled the sleeves and ankles to get a better fit, but there was no mistaking the fact that it was meant for a male aviator. No one at the air force had thought to design a flight suit for a woman.

A technician quickly taught Cobb how MASTIF worked.

Jerrie Cobb grasps the controls of MASTIF, 1960.

The cockpit sat inside three separate rigs that could spin in different directions, all at once. He showed Cobb how to control each of the rigs with a handheld stick. She could nudge it this way or that to release little puffs of a gas. This action would propel the rig in one direction or another. It worked exactly how the Mercury controls would work in outer space. It was sensitive. Too much pressure on the stick wouldn't bring MASTIF under control; it would send it careening in another direction. The technician buckled Cobb into her seat with a chest harness and straps across her waist and legs. Another strap pinned her helmet firmly against the headrest.

Finally, he asked, "Are you ready?"

"Yes," Cobb replied.

MASTIF growled into action, and within moments Cobb was flipping and twisting and rolling all at once. Her vision blurred. Her body bucked against the straps. Her stomach heaved. Cobb squinted at the blurry instruments directly in front of her and slowly, slowly, things began to take focus.

Witnesses couldn't tell what Cobb was up to in the cockpit. She was hidden at the center of a huge, mechanical blur. But the young pilot was already working out a meticulous plan. She would tackle MASTIF methodically. First, she focused on the pitch. She nudged the stick ever so slightly until she was finally free of the relentless somersaulting loops. Then she got to work on the roll, bumping the stick from side to side to gently slow and then stop the wicked cartwheeling. Finally, she tackled the yaw. A few light twists on the stick eased her out of the top like spin. And just like that, Cobb was motionless. She felt dazed. Her head spun.

"You want some more?" crackled a voice over her headset radio.

"Why not?" Cobb responded. The cockpit whirled back into action.

Cobb stayed on MASTIF for a full forty-five minutes. When she finally climbed off, the technicians on hand were stunned. Alan Shepard had to be peeled off the thing, and some woman had just mastered MASTIF on her first try!

"You did very well," said one of the techs. "Your response was exceptionally quick."

The MASTIF ride was the next step in Jerrie Cobb's work for Dr. Lovelace. After her remarkable performance on the medical tests, Dr. Lovelace pushed Cobb further. He wanted her to follow in the male astronauts' footsteps, taking the same psychological tests and training on the same simulators. Up until this point, Cobb's testing had been kept quiet. She wasn't promised a spot on a space mission. She was simply helping Lovelace collect data so that he could learn more about whether women might make good astronauts. But something in the air made Cobb feel like she had a chance at becoming an astronaut.

The MASTIF handlers seemed to think so, too. As she stepped off the rig that day, one of them told her, "Don't worry—the space capsule won't be nearly as bad as the ride you just took."

Then, in August 1960, Lovelace went public. He announced his findings at a conference in Stockholm, Sweden. He stated that a female test subject had undergone Phase I astronaut testing and done very well. And not just that. Lovelace also suggested that "certain qualities of the female space pilot are preferable to those of her male colleague."

Reports from the conference soared over the Atlantic Ocean and splashed across American front pages. They referred to some yet unknown "Lady Astronaut," and the public went wild. Who was she? Where was she? When would she launch? *LIFE* magazine found Cobb and ran a story featuring her. The headline proclaimed, "A Lady Proves She's Fit for Space Flight." Overnight, the shy female pilot was transformed into an international celebrity.

It wasn't long before Cobb faced a throng of reporters in her first major press conference.

"Miss Cobb," the questions began, "aren't you afraid of space flight as an unknown, unexplored quantity?"

"No, not really," she answered.

"Are you afraid of anything?" the reporter asked.

"Yes, of course," Cobb said.

"Specifically, what?"

"Grasshoppers," Cobb said, seemingly offhand.

The crowd of journalists laughed and the mood in the room lightened. It seemed friendly and warm, a welcome relief for the quiet pilot with a speech impediment.

The reporters wanted to know why Cobb thought women should become astronauts. She repeated the reasoning she'd learned from Lovelace and Flickinger. Women were lighter, they ate and drank less, and they breathed less oxygen than men. Then she went on: "Women are psychologically better suited for space flight. Under stress, they are on record as being able to withstand pain, heat, cold, monotony, and loneliness for longer periods and with less ill effects than men."

Satisfied with the brief scientific discussion, the press moved on. "Can you cook, Miss Cobb?" asked one journalist. Other reporters' hands shot up with questions of their own about recipes and ingredients. Cobb was annoyed. She was a pilot, not a chef.

The questions continued. One reporter asked, "Why do you want to beat a man into space?" Another asked how she would feel about a coed flight.

Snickers and winks rippled through the pool of reporters. Now this was the story they were after.

Cobb answered clearly and eloquently. She said that she didn't want to "'beat' a man into space" but that she hoped to go "for the same reasons men want to." She thought she could do a good job up there. Then she reminded the press, "We aren't in a contest to beat men in anything."

The articles that followed this first press conference were varied. Some praised Cobb as a talented pilot, a woman who would make a fantastic space traveler. Others downplayed her credentials and focused instead on her appearance. More than one paper printed her bust size. The *Washington Star* reported that "Miss Cobb, who has a 36-26-34 figure . . . stands 5 feet 7 inches and weighs 121 pounds." Several articles noted her blonde hair, her ponytail, and her bachelorette status.

Cobb did her best to stay focused on her goal: spaceflight. In September 1960, she moved on to Phase II of astronaut testing. This phase would test her psychological fitness for space travel.

Like the men, Cobb spent this phase taking inkblot tests, intelligence tests, and personality tests. Her experiences during Phase II were very similar to the men's, with a few exceptions. First, the location was different. The male pilots had taken their Phase II tests at Wright-Patterson Air Force Base, and Wright-Pat wasn't interested in letting women use their testing equipment. Second, Cobb still had to work. She was a company pilot at Aero Commander, one of the only women in the nation to hold such a title. She didn't want to lose it. She needed to somehow juggle a day job with the demands of astronaut testing. She did this by completing her Phase II tests at the Oklahoma City Veterans Affairs hospital, a facility a short drive from the Aero Commander office. It meant long, hard days, but Cobb was motivated. She wanted to prove herself. The third, and most significant, difference between what the men and Cobb experienced in Phase II had to do with their isolation tests. Lovelace had stumbled upon a new type of isolation test that was far more rigorous than what the men had endured. Even though this would make Cobb's testing a little different from the men's, he decided to go for it.

The male pilots' isolation test challenged them to sit alone in a dim room for three hours. John Glenn wrote poetry. Scott Carpenter toyed around with a physics problem. Cobb wouldn't have access to a pen and paper during her test. She wouldn't have access to anything. Her test would subject her to something her doctors called "profound sensory isolation."

These isolation tests were important. The air force used them to identify "subjects who cannot tolerate enforced inactivity, enclosures in small spaces, or absence of external stimuli." In other words, the tests weeded out pilots who might freak out if they were alone in a small aircraft for very long.

An astronaut could easily be alone in a space capsule for hours. Days, even! Some people worried that the extreme solitude of space could cause a person to act irrationally. What if they panicked? Picture this: A frazzled, jittery astronaut wedged inside a cramped capsule jam-packed with sensitive buttons and levers. It wouldn't take much for the astronaut to fire their rockets too soon or make some other flustered, frenzied mistake.

Cobb's test was called the isolation tank. Instead of sitting in a dim room with pencil and paper, she would float in a giant pool of water in a pitch-black and completely soundless room for as long as she could stand it. The lack of sensation was jarring. People who had been in the tank said they couldn't tell whether they were awake or asleep. They wondered if the sounds they heard were real or simply inside their own heads. Previous test subjects had experienced a wide range of responses to the utter lack of stimulation. Some hallucinated. Others talked to people who weren't there, sobbed, screamed, or heard the ghostly bark of non-existent dogs. In short, the test made some people go a little mad.

Cobb knew of all this when she stepped into the tank. A psychologist had briefed her extensively on what to expect during the test. She felt a little nervous but mostly just ready to see what would happen. The water was the exact temperature of her body. This made it almost impossible to feel. A few assistants helped arrange flotation cushions under her neck and torso to allow her to float without effort. They turned the lights down so that the only illumination came from the open door at one side of the room.

And then everyone left. The door softly closed and the room filled with dense black silence.

Cobb waited for the panic, but it never came. She floated quietly for nine hours and forty minutes before softly announcing that she was ready to get out.

"I don't think my feelings are going to change by staying in here any longer," she said.

When she finally stepped out of the tank, an astonished crew greeted her. No previous test subjects, male or female, had lasted longer than six and a half hours.

Cobb hadn't had any outbursts. She hadn't sobbed or screamed or anything else. Rather, she'd remained focused. Relaxed, even. It was an astounding performance.

At the end of her Phase II testing, Cobb's physicians summarized her performance in glowing terms. "It is our opinion that Miss Jerrie Cobb not only possesses no significant liabilities, but also possesses several exceptional, if not

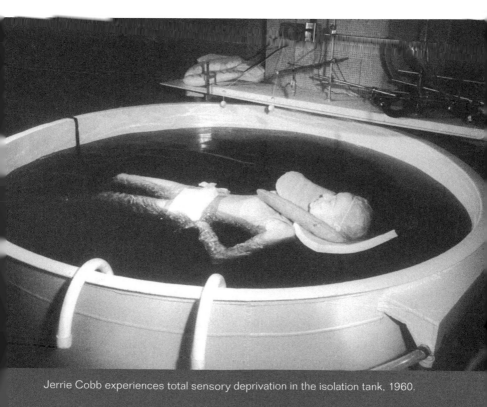

Jerrie Cobb experiences total sensory deprivation in the isolation tank, 1960.

unique, qualities and capabilities for serving on special missions in astronautics . . ." The report ended with a heartfelt endorsement: "she has very much to recommend her for selection as an astronaut candidate."

The press continued to report excitedly about Cobb and her testing. Her successful completion of Phase II testing only increased the public's curiosity about this unusual, high-flying woman.

NASA, on the other hand, went out of its way to clarify that it wasn't interested in women astronauts. Though Lovelace played a critical role in NASA's medical team, and Cobb's tests closely mimicked the male astronaut tests, NASA made it very clear that they were *not* sponsoring these tests. In late September 1960, the agency released a statement that it "never had a plan to put a woman in space, it doesn't have one today and it doesn't expect to have one in the foreseeable future." It seemed that, so far, Lovelace's testing hadn't quite persuaded the agency to take the idea seriously.

That was okay with him. Lovelace hadn't shown NASA any data yet. He was still doing his research. In fact, he was ready to start expanding that research. He had to know: Was Jerrie Cobb some kind of superhuman oddball? Or were there more women like her? He began reviewing the list of aviators Cobb had helped him compile earlier in the year. They certainly were an impressive group of women.

While Lovelace combed through the profiles of other female pilots, Cobb prepared to set yet another world record. An American man had recently taken a light prop airplane to 34,862 feet, besting her earlier record of 30,560 feet. Cobb thought she had the stuff to fly a little higher still. Aero Commander agreed. They gave Cobb a powerful new twin-engine plane called a Commander 680F to fly for a new record.

Climbing that high in a propeller aircraft isn't easy. It takes exceptional skill and bravery. It also requires top-of-the-line safety equipment. There isn't enough air to breathe at that height. An aviation company loaned Cobb one of their new, high-tech oxygen systems for the flight. Everyone hoped that this might increase Cobb's chances of surviving the perilous climb.

On the morning of September 20, 1960, Cobb sat in the pilot's ready room in a Santa Monica airplane hangar, preparing for the flight. Several friends, colleagues, engineers, and test pilots shuffled around the room nervously. This flight would be risky. The air at 34,000 feet can be 50 degrees below zero, or colder. Nobody knew how the Commander would handle those temperatures. Its fuel lines could freeze. If an engine quit, Cobb wasn't sure if she'd be able to get it running again. The plane's builder himself stopped by to warn Cobb that if the airplane started acting up, she shouldn't try for the record. Cobb wasn't going to chicken out now. "I'll go for broke," she told him.

The minutes ticked by. Cobb ate a little food, then stared at her new oxygen system. Idly, she wondered aloud, "What happens if you get sick when you're wearing a helmet and oxygen mask?" Everyone fell silent. Cobb's mother looked horrified.

Vomiting inside a fitted oxygen mask and helmet could be deadly. A pilot could choke on it. If she made any real effort to take off her mask and clean it out, she could pass out from oxygen deprivation. If Cobb puked up there, it might actually kill her.

"You unhook your mask real fast and dump it," an equipment expert quickly answered, shutting the conversation down.

Cobb shrugged and thought to herself, *Bad timing for a question like that.*

Finally, it was time. Cobb dressed in layers of warm

Jerrie Cobb prepares for her high-altitude flight in the Commander 680F, September 20, 1960.

flight gear and climbed into the Commander. At 11:56 a.m., she roared down the runway and started climbing, fast. She yanked back on the yoke to drive the Commander up at a rate of 2,000 feet per minute. A chase plane flew alongside Cobb to monitor the early stages of her flight, but she was too fast. It soon lost sight of her.

Cobb climbed. She flew through blinding sunshine and dense white clouds. Grainy ice crystals began to creep along the cockpit's windows, then interior. Her engines labored and grew sluggish. Cobb checked her fuel. It was low.

But Jerrie wanted this record. She leaned forward against her seat restraints as if to urge the plane higher. She climbed and climbed and climbed. Alarms began to sound inside her cockpit. Her plane was about to stall. But she was so close! Jerrie urged the Commander on: "Come on now, you can do it, just a few more feet, and we'll have it made." The plane began shaking violently. She couldn't hold on much longer. And then she looked at her altimeter: The gauge read 37,010 feet. This was 2,148 feet higher than anyone had ever managed to wrestle this type of aircraft. She did it!

Just then, the screaming alarms ceased. The sudden silence hit her like a slap. *Uh-oh.* Cobb had stalled.

The frosty cockpit was ghostly quiet as the plane nosed over and began to drop. Cobb stayed calm and began systematically working to revive her aircraft. She knew the fundamentals for recovery. Keep the wings level. Build airspeed. Point that nose down and no matter what, keep the plane out of a spin. A Commander wasn't built to withstand a spin. If a wing dipped and forced the aircraft into a rotation, it might start going around and around and around up there. And with a frozen instrument panel, there wouldn't be much Cobb could do to recover. Her plane would break up as it corkscrewed down to Earth, first one wing snapping off, then the other. Witnesses on the ground would watch as Cobb, trapped helplessly in her cockpit, slammed right into the ground.

Engine trouble wasn't a death sentence. But a high-altitude spin? Maybe.

Cobb wrestled with the controls to keep her wings level as her plane fell out of the clouds. She plummeted 1,500 feet before managing to get her propellers churning again, but she did it. Once again, it was an astounding performance.

The newspaper stories that followed Cobb's record-breaking flight didn't mention her masterful recovery of the frozen aircraft. They mostly focused on how she looked, as usual. Headlines, such as "Pretty Blonde Sets World Altitude Record," were followed by careful descriptions of what Cobb wore to stay warm on the flight: "three arctic survival suits, fur-lined boots and three pairs of gloves . . ."

Nearly all of the press stories noted that Cobb was hoping to get into space one day soon. Some even called her an "astronautess" or "lady astronaut." Cobb made sure to caution journalists that she hadn't been accepted into NASA just yet. She even acknowledged that "men are more qualified for space flight at this time" than women. To the casual reader, it might have seemed as though Cobb was simply stating the obvious: Male pilots had a better chance at getting into space than female pilots. But for Jerrie, these words had a different message. They were a challenge. A call to action.

Jerrie Cobb had just broken an astounding altitude record. Why couldn't she push for space next?

CHAPTER 12

MONEY, MONKEYS, AND MEN

While Jerrie Cobb looked to the stars, the rest of the nation fixed its gaze on its first class of astronauts. And oh, what astronauts they were! The nation was nearly bursting with love for these seven men. The press called them the Magnificent 7. The name itself glittered with celebrity. They were handsome, healthy, strong, and brave, each one a variation on good, clean American heroism.

When the Mercury 7 weren't training, fans followed them everywhere. They staked out the astronauts' favorite lunch restaurants, eager for a glimpse of a real-life space pilot. They showered the men with gifts and free drinks, hoping for a good story or maybe even an autograph. Journalists started attending John Glenn's church, not for the sermons, but for a chance to brush shoulders with the astronaut as he walked to his car after the service.

At first, the attention had been intoxicating. The astronauts stumbled from base to base in a drunken haze of celebrity. They were like gods! But soon, the novelty faded and it was all too much. The astronauts just couldn't do their jobs without tripping over some fedora with a notepad, busily scribbling down their muttered comments. Gus Grissom even experimented with dressing in disguise to avoid the attention. Once, before trying to sneak through an airport, he put on a straw hat and a pair of dark sunglasses. He turned to Deke Slayton with a sly smile and asked, "How do I look?"

Slayton eyed the unmistakable test pilot. Grissom was easy to spot. He was short, broad-shouldered, tan, and fit. His face had been in countless magazines and newspapers.

"You look just like Gus Grissom in dark glasses and a hat," Slayton told him.

NASA leadership recognized early on that the astronauts couldn't deal with a tidal wave of fans and press all the time. "Sounds like you're being nibbled to death by ducks," the director of the Office of Public Information, Walt Bonney, told Glenn. The agency needed to do something to protect the astronauts from the public.

At the end of 1959, NASA allowed the Mercury 7 to sign an exclusive deal with *LIFE* magazine. This meant that the astronauts had to deal with only one publication, *LIFE*, instead of a growing gaggle of reporters, and that they could get on with their work. It didn't hurt at all that the magazine agreed to pay each of the astronauts $24,000 a year (about $216,000 in today's currency) for three years for their access. For a group of military pilots whose base pay usually came out to between $5,500 and $8,000 a year (about $49,000–$72,000 in today's currency), this was a delightful perk.

The Mercury 7 pose for a group portrait, 1959.

The astronauts were stars even within NASA, a place that absolutely buzzed with some of the best brains in the country. The Mercury 7 could suggest changes to the rockets or space capsule, and the engineers, experts who had been working, really slaving over this stuff, would listen! This was partly because of their backgrounds as test pilots. They knew what made aircraft fly. But it also had to do with their status. The astronauts stood on a glorious, fame-built pedestal above the scientists and engineers. They weren't actually in charge. NASA's administrator was. But the astronauts occupied an unusual role within the agency. They were pilots, yes, but they were also leaders.

The Mercury 7 sauntered through the agency, peering over shoulders to read blueprints or double-check someone's math. They traveled to visit the various factories where their space craft parts were being built. There, they'd cross their arms over their muscular chests and stare knowingly at a circuit board or rocket booster, inspiring both fear and admiration in the hard-working laborers.

Occasionally, the astronauts could be cruel rulers. They were critical and sometimes impatient. Deke Slayton admitted to timing technicians as they worked. Surely, the presence of an astronaut with a stopwatch added stress to their workdays.

Mostly, though, the astronauts were beloved leaders. They cracked jokes and patted the workers on the back for jobs well done. On a visit to the Atlas rocket plant, Gordon Cooper grabbed a marker and scrawled a note on the side of the giant rocket: "Launch this way!" with an arrow pointing up. The work crews loved it. Photographers gleefully snapped photos of Cooper's act of graffiti, knowing the American public would eat it up.

The other astronauts checked on the Atlas, too. Once, on a visit, Gus Grissom found himself standing in front of a crowd of 18,000 eager plant workers, hoping to hear the short astronaut say a few words. Grissom wasn't one for public speeches. Actually, he wasn't really one for private speeches, either. The astronauts joked that he was such a quiet copilot he could fly "East Coast to West Coast in ten words or less."

Grissom stared blankly out at the crowd, paused for a beat, and then blurted: "Well . . . do good work!"

The crowd burst into rowdy applause. *Did you hear that? Do good work!* Grissom shifted uncomfortably as they shrieked and hooted. Not long after, the work crews had his sage advice emblazoned across a giant banner that they then hung inside their work bay: "DO GOOD WORK." Grissom's celebrity had transformed his gruff words into something profound. To the starstruck crews, they weren't the awkward grunts of a stage-shy pilot. No, they were sheer poetry.

But the Mercury 7 weren't celebrities everywhere. One small cluster of Americans didn't idolize the astronauts. Ironically, it was the very community that trained them, tested them, and spit them out onto the runway. Test pilots. These aviators saw the astronauts as failures. Washouts. Jokes. Rumors buzzed around military airports that the astronauts weren't even flying over at NASA. They were too busy sitting through lectures and working on simulators.

Test pilots were used to flying five or six days a week,

morning till night. Aviation flowed through their veins. To the pilots, the astronauts had swapped real flight for practice, and that seemed downright shameful.

Chuck Yeager, that brave Edwards test pilot who'd been the first to break the sound barrier, thought the astronauts were making fools of themselves. And he made it known. They sure weren't going to be pilots in space! Not even close. Engineers on the ground would do all the flying for them. He and his fellow test pilot hotshots agreed: The astronauts would be "Spam in a can." The joke spread like wildfire through the aviation community. Pilots dissolved in fits of laughter at the thought of it. Tears streamed down their sun-worn cheeks as they pictured them: seven ex-pilots, jammed into tin cans and lobbed skyward like 180 pounds or less of deli meat.

The Mercury 7 knew about the Spam-in-a-can joke. They still bumped into test pilots here and there, and they couldn't ignore the snickers. Shepard thought Yeager had it all wrong. He saw Project Mercury as a thrilling frontier, something "new and important." Slayton figured Yeager was just jealous. These guys had gotten the chance to ride a rocket, and old Yeager was just smarting from a lost opportunity.

The astronauts did their best to hold their heads high and hope, really pray that this gig might turn into something great. The ugly truth was that the joke was painfully accurate. The astronauts weren't flying. Their hands, so used to gripping throttles, now held pencils and calculators. Notepads and blueprints. It was all so important, but it sure wasn't flight.

NASA wasn't exactly helping the astronauts feel any

better about trading test flight for spaceflight. The agency was hard at work testing one rocket after another, and things weren't going well. They kept exploding. In July 1960, a Mercury capsule launched atop an Atlas rocket and both were blown to bits. In September and October, more Atlas rockets launched and failed. A few blew up. In November, NASA tried a Mercury launch with a rocket called a Redstone. This effort proved to be the most embarrassing yet.

After the countdown reached zero and the rocket belched flames all over the launchpad, everyone craned their necks to watch the big bird fly. They squinted into the sun, confused. Where did it go?

As soon as the smoke cleared, everyone realized that the darned thing had launched less than a foot before plopping back down onto the pad. The Mercury capsule still sat right there, perched on top of the rocket like a dumb hat. And then, as if to add insult to injury, the capsule sensed that something had gone wrong.

Thwoop! A bright orange parachute shot out the top and flapped in the wind.

Squirt! A spray of vivid green ink dribbled down the side of the capsule.

This neon liquid was meant to stain ocean water to help rescue crews find the floating capsule after a mission. Nobody had anticipated how dreadfully humiliating it would look puddling on the launchpad. The press called it the Four-Inch Flight. People at NASA called it a fiasco.

All of these rocket failures were embarrassing for NASA. But they also emphasized the dangers of spaceflight.

They weren't all blowing up, but the odds weren't good. NASA's Atlas rocket failure rate hovered around 45%. It was terrible! Abysmal! Nobody wanted to give their beloved astronauts a 55% chance at surviving launch. And there were still so many lingering fears about what would happen once somebody actually made it into space. Would their eyeballs pop? Would their hearts collapse? Clearly, NASA had more work to do before their guys could fly.

The agency decided to determine the safety of spaceflight by sending animals up first. This wasn't anything revolutionary. The Soviets had been doing it for years. Less than one month after launching *Sputnik* back in 1957, they'd sent a dog named Laika up in a craft called *Sputnik II*. Laika survived the launch, but the poor thing died after only a few hours in space. It was just as well. The Soviets hadn't planned to bring her back anyway.

The American press gave Laika a nasty nickname: Muttnick. It was a mean joke. It mocked a dead dog that was trapped in a cold and ghostly silent coffin all the way out there in space. It also showed just how painfully raw this time was. Americans didn't like losing.

NASA had already sent several monkeys up on shorter test flights. In 1959, two monkeys named Able and Baker launched atop a Jupiter rocket. These two tiny passengers made it 360 miles up and experienced nine minutes of weightlessness before splashing down into the water. Their handlers were relieved to see that they were both healthy after the mission, though they admitted that the monkeys were "a little mad about the whole thing."

After Able and Baker, NASA sent more monkeys up on test flights. These tiny astronauts soared across the sky in a series of what were surely terrifying missions. But their terror was unknowable, and besides, it wasn't the point. NASA needed these monkeys to show whether they could *live* through spaceflight. They had. Now NASA engineers questioned whether anyone could *think* through it as well.

Out marched Ham, a chimpanzee who would answer that question.

Ham had spent a month doing his own little version of astronaut training. Like the Mercury 7, he worked in the centrifuge and practiced in a simulator. His trainers taught him to do a series of simple tests inside his capsule. He'd pull a lever or push a button, and if he

The monkey known as Baker being readied for launch, 1959.

did it right, he got a banana-flavored pellet. If he made a mistake, he received an electric shock on the soles of his leathery feet. The point of all of this was to get Ham ready to do these little tests while he flew in space. His performance would show scientists whether or not spaceflight made it hard to think. If Ham did well, then everyone figured a human would probably be okay up there, too.

On January 31, 1961, Ham settled into his Mercury space capsule and launched. After about one minute of flight, things went a little haywire. His rocket fired too hot and too fast. The capsule vibrated so powerfully that an air inlet valve shook itself open. The air pressure inside the capsule dropped, giving medics on the ground visions of their chimp puffing, and puffing, and puffing up until he popped with a splatter of blood, fur, and medical wires. Thankfully, they'd thought to seal Ham inside a tiny pressurized capsule-within-a-capsule. This little lozenge-shaped contraption kept America's first space chimp from exploding, but he still wasn't out of the woods.

Ham's mission had to be aborted. Then, even the abort didn't go well. The chimp plunged toward Earth at 5,587 miles per hour, slamming the tiny astronaut with a gut-busting fifteen g's.

Ham splashed down in the Atlantic 115 miles off target. It took rescuers two hours to find him, and by that point his capsule had flooded with 800 pounds of water. They pried open the hatch to find Ham alive, annoyed, and hungry. His arms were crossed over his chest as if to say, *It took you long enough.*

Nobody at NASA was going to say that Ham's flight had been perfect, but there was some good news to celebrate. He'd lived! And his brain had worked the whole time. It was great news for the American space program.

Not everyone was happy about Ham's flight. The astronauts, who were still salty from the whole Spam-in-a-can joke, knew the test pilots were going to tear them up over this. How could they argue that they were going to fly the Mercury capsule after a chimp completed a mission? A chimp!

Indeed, military pilots came up with a catchy little song to mock the astronauts. The lyrics were as brutal as they were hilarious: "Shepard, Grissom, and Glenn, the link between monkeys and men." NASA was turning even the most seasoned, serious pilots into comedians. A reporter asked Yeager if he wanted in on Project Mercury. He responded: "No. It doesn't really require a pilot, and besides, you'd have to sweep the monkey [poop] off the seat before you could sit down."

For astronaut hopefuls like Jerrie Cobb, this space-chimp business must have been confusing. At the time, NASA was beginning a rigorous primate training program, nicknamed "chimp college," where whole troops of primates were learning to fly in space. Many of these space chimps, like Ham's backup, Minnie, were female. Cobb must have wondered: *If NASA will launch a chimp, and even a female chimp, why not me?*

In addition to the insult, the animal flights posed a practical problem: They took so much time! While Ham's brain had performed perfectly, his capsule experienced several

Ham the chimpanzee looks irritated after his flight, 1961.

glitches. The engineers at NASA wanted another test flight before they launched a human.

This delay highlighted the real issue. Every engineer, researcher, and astronaut felt a constant, lurking threat that the Soviets would send a human into space before the Americans. If that happened, the embarrassment would be excruciating. They'd already beaten Americans to the punch with the first satellite. It couldn't happen again with the first crewed mission.

NASA had secretly chosen the man it would send up first: Alan Shepard. That talented, prank-loving navy pilot was perfect for the job. Naturally, everyone kept this decision under wraps. The *LIFE* magazine deal wouldn't protect Shepard from the flood of attention that was guaranteed to follow the announcement, and Shepard didn't have time for distraction. He had too much work to do.

Shepard practiced on the procedures trainer relentlessly. But as he got better at flicking this switch or that, Americans started to grow restless. When would one of their guys launch? First comedians, and then everyday Joes, started to poke a little fun at the astronauts. The tide began turning on these all-American heroes. The nation was impatient. And with their impatience came some good-natured teasing.

By the spring of 1961, the monkey jokes were everywhere. The press ran cartoons of chimps teaching the astronauts to fly, or warning the astronauts that they might crave bananas in space. A popular comedian coined the phrase, "First the chimp, then the chump." These wisecracks even made it into NASA's training facilities. Some of the astronauts took them in stride. *Very funny*, they'd laugh. *Har-har*. Others didn't find it amusing in the least.

During one simulator run, Shepard felt frustrated and crabby. He moaned about some delay, and an engineer joked about his bad attitude: "Maybe we should get somebody who works for bananas." Shepard picked up an ashtray and whipped it at the engineer's face. He missed his target by a hair. He was a test pilot. A grip-and-rip guy. Enough with the practice runs and the chimp missions. He wanted to launch. He couldn't stand it if the Soviets got up there first.

On April 12, 1961, at 9:07 a.m. Moscow time, a Soviet cosmonaut named Yuri Gagarin became the first human to fly in space. And he didn't simply fly. The man orbited Earth! Gagarin's mission lasted 108 minutes, more than seven times what NASA was prepared to do with its first space missions.

It was about 3:00 a.m. in Florida when Gagarin made it back to Earth safely, and the American press were in a mad dash for details. Had a Soviet really done it? Was it true? If so, the accomplishment was staggering. NASA was scrambling just to figure out how to lob a man up in a simple rainbow-shaped arc, a quick stab at space. The Soviets were way ahead.

A reporter called a NASA spokesperson, Shorty Powers, to get his reaction. Powers was dead asleep and blissfully unaware of Gagarin's mission. He awoke to the shrill ringing of his telephone and growled into the receiver: "If you want anything from us, you jerk, the answer is we're all asleep!"

It was a mortifying mistake.

A few hours later, newspapers hit the stands with the

headline: "Soviets Send Man into Space; Spokesman Says U.S. Asleep."

Shepard was furious. He saw the news early the next morning and hit a table so hard that he nearly broke his hand. Glenn had a more graceful response. He met with the press that afternoon and answered their questions honestly.

"They just beat the pants off us, that's all. There's no use in kidding ourselves about that," he said.

Jerrie Cobb wasn't questioned about Gagarin's flight for several days, and even then, her reaction didn't make headlines. Instead, newspaper reporters focused on another of

Yuri Gagarin in his space suit. The letters on his helmet, CCCP, are an abbreviation for the Russian name for the Union of Soviet Socialist Republics.

her aviation achievements: piloting a Goodyear blimp. Two days before the Soviets successfully flung Gagarin into the sky, Cobb had kicked off her high heels and worked the pedals of the massive blimp in her stockings.

The Mercury 7 were hardly flying. Jerrie Cobb was flying anything she could.

Thirteen days after Gagarin's flight, NASA held another test launch. Gus Grissom had a special mission during this exercise. He was to fly a jet right up alongside the rocket as it launched, spiraling around it to get a close look at the early stages of flight. It would be dangerous, but it would also give him some rare and precious time in the cockpit.

The rocket launched and Grissom zoomed in, watching the massive thing heave off the ground. "And then . . ." he remembered, "*kablooie!* The biggest fireball I ever want to see!" The rocket had begun to veer off course, and a safety officer on the ground decided to destroy it before it crashed somewhere dangerous. Grissom didn't know any of this in the moment. All he knew was that he was now circling an inferno.

He reacted instantly by zipping away from the explosion. His skillful flying was so fast and seamless that people on the ground couldn't keep him in their sights. One friend who had been watching Grissom turned to his wife and said, "Well, now there are only six astronauts."

It turned out that Grissom was fine. The Mercury 7 were all still alive and well. But while Americans waited impatiently for their seven handsome space pilots to launch, a group of thirteen women would soon assemble in the shadows, hoping to join the Mercury 7, or perhaps even overtake them.

CHAPTER 13

TESTING MORE WOMEN

In November 1960, just five months before the Soviets would launch a man into space, Dr. Lovelace prepared to start testing more female astronaut candidates. But he had a problem. This process cost a lot of money. It required a huge staff of medical professionals, expensive machinery, and access to elite training facilities. Lovelace couldn't pay for it all himself. He needed someone with deep pockets who had a real interest in women astronauts, somebody who believed in the power of female aviators. He reached out to his old friend Jackie Cochran.

Cochran was the perfect backer for Lovelace's project. First, she was rich. Her booming cosmetics company kept her flush with cash. She was also wife to one of the country's wealthiest men, Floyd Odlum. But second, and perhaps more important, Cochran had friends in high places. She used these friendships to get whatever she wanted. When jets made headlines during the Korean War, Cochran talked her way into learning to fly one. In 1953, Cochran became

Jackie Cochran poses in front of a T-38, a military training jet, 1962.

the first woman to break the sound barrier in a borrowed Canadian Royal Air Force Sabre. She was unstoppable.

When Lovelace came calling, Cochran immediately agreed to fund his woman astronaut program.

With Cochran's financial support and endorsement, Lovelace could move forward with his research. He'd discovered that Jerrie Cobb could pass the first two phases of the Mercury astronaut tests. Now he needed to see if more women could do the same. Lovelace reviewed the file of female aviators that he, Cobb, and Flickinger had assembled earlier in the year. He also sorted through the various letters from female volunteers that had poured in after Jerrie Cobb's *LIFE* magazine debut. He narrowed his pool of pilots down until they fit a set of rigid standards: Each had to have at least 1,000 flight hours, be in perfect health, and be under thirty-five years old.

Lovelace did not require candidates to have jet flight or test flight experience, as these were essentially impossible for women to acquire. However, he did require candidates to have an instrument rating. This certification allows pilots to fly in the dark, or in poor visibility, using just their cockpit instruments for guidance. Landing an airplane using only its instruments, in clouds or storms or the dead of night, can be a sweaty, frightening ordeal. This requirement narrowed the pool to only those aviators who had real guts. The toughest ones.

From the fall of 1960 until the spring of 1961, when the nation fixated on Yuri Gagarin's mind-boggling spaceflight, Lovelace sent letters inviting women to participate in Phase I astronaut testing. A select group of female aviators across the country opened their mail with astonishment. The Lovelace Clinic letterhead looked so official. And right there on the signature line: W. Randolph Lovelace II, M.D. *The* Dr. Lovelace! He worked with NASA. Everyone knew that. Did that mean . . . could it possibly mean . . . they could become astronauts?

The language in Lovelace's letter certainly made it seem possible: "Will you volunteer for the initial examinations for woman astronaut candidates? The examinations will take one week and are done on a purely voluntary basis. They do not commit you to any further part in the Women in Space Program unless you so desire."

Lovelace's letter included a brief survey and asked the women to reply if they were interested. He reviewed their responses carefully. This next step was crucial. He had to choose the very best pilots out there. If these women did well in their testing, the data he collected might finally persuade NASA to consider female astronauts.

In the end, Lovelace welcomed nineteen female aviators to his New Mexico clinic for their Phase I astronaut tests. They were an exceedingly talented and experienced bunch. Irene Leverton had logged 9,000 hours of flight time. Jan Dietrich had 8,000 hours. In comparison, John Glenn, the most experienced of the Mercury 7, had only 5,100 hours in his log when he underwent testing.

Twenty-two-year-old Wally Funk arrived at Lovelace with some unexpected baggage: her parents. Funk didn't have a car to make the trip to Albuquerque, and so she asked her parents to drive her there. Once they arrived, the Funks went so far as to sign their daughter into the clinic for her medical testing. It was a loving gesture, but also one that was at odds with the scenario. After all, their daughter was by now a highly capable flight instructor. Just a few months earlier she'd become one of the rare women in the country to fly a jet. Funk had experience flying gliders, prop planes, and now jets. She was more than capable of handling the tests set out before her.

Funk was also the only woman to show up at the Lovelace Clinic with company. Unlike the men, who had reported to the Lovelace Clinic together, the women would do their tests alone or in pairs. Lovelace staggered their testing over the course of several months. He had to do this to fit them into his schedule here and there, between his regular patients and meetings. This was his pet project, not a government-sponsored clinic takeover. He couldn't stop everything to make room for the women test subjects.

Despite this, the women's astronaut testing was still just as demanding as what the men had endured. Lovelace wanted to keep things consistent for his male and female test subjects. These women were about to go through the ringer. He needed to know what they could handle.

Lovelace soon learned that the women could handle a lot. They plodded through their tests bravely, rarely complaining or moaning or even wincing. Jan Dietrich remembered that the bicycle endurance test, which challenged subjects to ride and ride and ride until their hearts were ready to give out, had turned her legs into "ribbons of extreme pain." She didn't let anyone know this. In fact, she told the doctors, "I could have gone another minute," and acted as though she was "not the slightest out of breath."

Though they weren't shown the men's test results, the women felt a sense of competition in the air. They wanted to do well, sure. But what if they could do even better than the men?

Several women walked away from their tests believing that they had in fact outperformed the men. A doctor told Bea Steadman that she beat all the men on the bike test. Wally Funk says medical staff informed her that she beat John Glenn and Wally Schirra on several tests, including the bicycle, vertigo, and stress tests.

Maybe the medical staff was telling the truth. Maybe the women really were blowing the men out of the water. It is also possible that they were just trying to encourage the women to do their best on a series of exceptionally uncomfortable exams. Whatever their motivation, their comments had an important impact. They made some of the women believe they were being seriously considered for spaceflight.

Several of the medical staff commented on how tough the women were. One told Jerri Sloan that the men had been "a bunch of gripers." Sloan felt empowered by these comments. After all, the tests were rough. She said, "We didn't even say ouch and, boy, they hurt us."

Bea Steadman endured one especially painful test. It was the same one that had caused Jerrie Cobb to wince a year earlier. Doctors stuck an enormous needle into the meaty part of Steadman's right thumb, and then pulsed it with electricity to test her muscular and nervous response. It was excruciating. The shocks forced her muscles to twitch and contract, dragging her delicate tissue against the thick metal needle.

A technician stood nearby to photograph Steadman as she weathered the agony. About halfway through the test, he ran out of film and couldn't figure out how to load another roll into his camera. Someone briefly suggested starting the whole test over again so that he could get the photographs he needed. No way! Steadman grabbed the camera and reloaded it herself with her left hand, the whole while being careful not to bump the gigantic needle sticking out of her right.

The testing at the Lovelace Clinic also included extensive

interviews. The researchers wanted to know about each pilot's area of expertise. For Sarah Gorelick, this meant an involved discussion about her technical skills. She had a bachelor's degree in mathematics with a minor in physics. She spent her days working as an engineer for AT&T and her evenings and weekends in the air. This made her an especially attractive astronaut test subject. After all, NASA wanted its male astronauts to have an engineering degree or equivalent experience. Researchers questioned Gorelick at length about her skills and education. She left New Mexico wondering if she might have just earned herself a place in space.

Other women were questioned about their private lives instead. Thirty-six-year-old Myrtle Cagle had a brand-new husband when she showed up at the Lovelace Clinic. She loved him deeply and agreed to come to the testing only after he granted her permission. Cagle's credentials were staggering. She had worked as a pilot, airplane mechanic, aviation journalist, *and* as the operator of her own airport. She had 4,300 hours of flight time and a towering stack of flight ratings. That wasn't all. Cagle was also a licensed nurse.

She had flight experience, technical skills, and a scientific background as well. And Cagle was also very pretty. She had been named Miss North Carolina Air Power in 1955, which suggested that she was sociable and looked good on camera. Just as NASA had considered the male test pilot's likability during the selection of the Mercury 7, it seemed as though test administrators were also noting each woman's crowd appeal.

Lovelace warned Cagle that this process might require sacrifices. He told her that she might even need to delay having children. Cagle nodded. "Fine." This was the opportunity of a lifetime. Kids could wait.

Janey Hart was thirty-nine years old when she endured her astronaut tests. That was four years over Lovelace's age limit. Hart was an exceptional pilot who not only had extensive experience racing planes and flying helicopters but also giving birth. Hart had *eight* living children, and one who had died as a toddler. It might have been Hart's status as a mother of so many that earned her the spot at Lovelace. Or it might have been her marriage to the powerful politician Senator Phil Hart. Whatever the reason for her invitation, it must have been a compelling one. In the end, her age didn't hurt her performance. Hart did great on her tests.

For Jerri Sloan, marriage became an issue during her tests at the Lovelace Clinic. Her husband also worked as a pilot, and in the years after World War II he'd been drinking too much. By the time she made it to New Mexico, he was an alcoholic.

Sloan was a born aviator, one of the bravest and the fastest and the best. She'd never set out to compete with her husband. She simply knew her stuff, and everyone around her could see it. But her husband could see it, too. He hated it. It hurt his ego to be married to such a talented woman. Her invitation to Phase I astronaut testing managed to make things even worse between them.

Sloan's husband called her hotel room each night after her tests. He was drunk, angry, and cruel. Sloan did her best to ignore his boozy rants, but this soon became impossible. About halfway through her tests, Lovelace called her into his office. "Are you having problems at home?" he asked.

Sloan responded, "Yes, sir, I am. But it's just not—" she stammered. "My husband is an alcoholic."

"I know that," Lovelace responded. "I've talked to him several times."

Sloan's heart sank. Had Dr. Lovelace heard her husband's slurring, hateful speech? Surely he would send her home. Nobody would keep her around if it meant dealing with her horrible husband.

Luckily, Lovelace didn't kick her out of the program. He simply told her to "get home and take care of that."

As the women candidates trudged ahead with their testing, Jackie Cochran became more involved in the program. She wanted to be sure that people knew she had a hand in all this. In April 1961, she published an article in *Parade* magazine about the Dietrich sisters. The article called them the "First Astronaut Twins." The cover image showed the two beautiful pilots dressed in bright orange flight suits and holding air force helmets. The air force still hadn't come up with a women's flight suit. Both sisters had rolled their sleeves several times.

The article focused on the Dietrich sisters, but not entirely. Cochran made sure to highlight her own role in the project as well. A photo of Jan Dietrich on the treadmill test shows Cochran lurking behind the testing equipment.

Jan and Marion Dietrich smile from the cover of *Parade* magazine, 1961.

She's clutching a pad of paper and watching Jan. It looks as though she's next in line to hop on the treadmill. And Cochran *was* ready to start testing. "I myself, while not an active participant in the present program, still expect to fly into space before I hang up my flying gear," she wrote.

WOMEN in SPACE

Famed aviatrix predicts women astronauts within six years

by JACQUELINE COCHRAN, *first woman ever to break the sound barrier. Miss Cochran has established more international flying speed records than any other man or woman. For her work as head of the WASP (Women's Air Force Service Pilots) in World War II, she won the Distinguished Service Medal. She is an officer in the Air Force Reserve.*

ALBUQUERQUE, N.M.

WOMEN WILL FLY INTO SPACE just as certainly as men will—only not so soon. I would like to predict that a woman will go into space by December 17, 1963—which is 60 years to the day after the Wright brothers first flew—but probably within six or seven years would be more realistic.

In my opinion, women can be just as good "astronauts" as men. A medical research project for possible women astronauts now under way at the Lovelace Foundation for Medical Education and Research here has indicated this in its checks of women volunteers.

Economically, this country can't afford right now to have women pilots flying as a part of the Armed Services. It's considered too expensive when there is no emergency or shortage of this kind of talent. It costs the government several hundred thousand dollars to qualify a jet pilot. Such a government-trained pilot cannot be a sporadic flyer; he must fly regularly. And with women, marriage and children are likely to interrupt their flying careers.

The Lovelace Foundation, out of private donations, is bearing the expense of the women volunteers. The ones who pass will become a group and may later receive specialized training to participate in space flight as astronauts or as engineers or skilled technicians. I am special consultant to the Foundation connected with this program.

So far, this medical research program for women is unofficial and is just a gleam in the eyes of doctors interested in aero-space medicine. I know they'll put at least several men in space over a considerable period of time before they try it with women. But the private research program could eventuate into a government-sponsored program.

Qualified Pilots

Our women are civilian volunteers who:
• are under 35 years of age, in good health and less than 5 feet 11 inches tall;
• are qualified pilots with substantial experience in the air, measured by hours flown;
• hold a Federal Aviation Agency instrument rating and medical certificate.

Approximately 20 women believed to have these qualifications were initially invited to participate by the Lovelace Foundation. Others have since been invited. At least 12 have already agreed to take the test. Five have already passed: Jerrie Cobb, Janet "Jan" Dietrich, Marion Dietrich, Mary Funk and Rhea Hurrle. They are all good pilots.

The medical check of the women is exactly the same as given to the men astronauts. Of special medical interest is the fact that Jan and Marion Dietrich, who live in California, are identical twins (see cover) — of the "mirror" type, in that one is left handed and the other right handed. Both have cow-licks, but on opposite sides of the scalp. They both passed the tests pretty much as if one person were taking the tests twice.

In addition to a thorough medical checkup, special tests are given dealing with resistance to stresses of various kinds. One is the tilt-table test, in which the candidate is tilted on a table that is held up at about a 60 degree angle and pulse, respiration and blood pressure are taken at frequent intervals. The efficiency of the vascular (blood supply) system is checked in this way, and abnormalities in the functioning of the blood vessels are almost surely disclosed.

Physical Strength

Then there is an endurance test, which is roughly the equivalent of pedaling a bicycle uphill for as many minutes as the candidate can reasonably take, during which changes such as pulse and respiration rate are noted.

While women are not as physically strong as men, such strength is not essential for space flight. That women are lighter is not a disadvantage.

The tests are under the direction of Dr. Randolph Lovelace II (who developed the first workable pilot's oxygen mask and who was in charge of the Aero-Medical Laboratory at Wright Field during World War II) and Dr. A. H. Schwichtenberg, head of the Aero-Space Medical Section of the Lovelace Foundation. Only about 60 per cent have passed of those who have taken the tests, either men or women, so it can be assumed that if about 20 women volunteers are checked, approximately a dozen will qualify for any future phase of the program.

No woman volunteer in the present medical phase has any obligation to carry on in any future program. But all of them, so far, want to fly into space and some may get the chance. I myself, while not an active participant in the present program, expect to fly into space before I hang up my flying gear. I think the day of women in space will come sooner than most people believe.

But this program is the first "launching pad" for women in space. If you are a qualified and healthy woman pilot and you want to take the first step, which takes six days, write to me care of the Cochran-Odlum Ranch, Indio, Calif. You might become the first woman astronaut who really earns that name.

Jacqueline Cochran watches as Jan Dietrich takes treadmill test to check physical condition. Equipment measures lung function.

A page from Cochran's April 1961 *Parade* article.

Cochran wasn't an ideal astronaut candidate. Nobody knew her exact birthday—she had given out a few different dates over the years—but she had to be at least fifty years old. That put her way over the cutoff of thirty-five. She suffered from health problems, including a dodgy heart and a handful of other medical issues. But Cochran was determined. She wanted her chance in space. She scheduled a trip to the Lovelace Clinic for her own astronaut examinations.

Shortly after Sarah Gorelick finished her Phase I astronaut tests, a fast-talking storm of a woman barged into the clinic. Jackie Cochran. Gorelick darted out of the way and watched as Cochran marched right into Lovelace's office. The door slammed and before long, muffled shouts echoed through the clinic hallways. Gorelick couldn't make out their conversation, but Cochran sounded furious. It was safe to guess that Lovelace had told her an unfamiliar word: no.

Nineteen women completed their Phase I astronaut tests at the Lovelace Clinic. Of these, thirteen, including Jerrie Cobb, passed their tests with "no medical reservations." The female test subjects had a 68% success rate. This was higher than the success rate of male test subjects. Only 56% of them had passed with the same endorsement. This meant that a group of civilian female pilots had outperformed a troupe of top-notch male military test pilots. In other words, the women beat the men.

Lovelace was onto something.

CHAPTER 14

CORVETTES AND PARTIES

an, I got to pee."

Alan Shepard spoke urgently into the microphone attached to his helmet. His mission was supposed to last only fifteen minutes, but delays kept pushing his launch time back. He'd been strapped into his Mercury capsule, the *Freedom 7*, for over three hours now and the man had to *go*. His space suit didn't have a urine collection system. Things were getting dicey.

The engineers in Project Mercury's Mission Control Center conferenced and came back to him: negative. A bathroom break would take too long. Just getting Shepard into his space suit took a solid fifteen minutes. It was a twenty-pound mess of wires, hoses, and rubber. Then there was the issue of even getting him out of the space capsule, which currently sat on top of an eighty-two-foot-tall rocket, down the elevator, and into a bathroom. No. They didn't have time.

Shepard's bladder ached. He couldn't make it much longer. He started shouting into his radio. The conversation

Alan Shepard prepares to launch, May 5, 1961.

would later be stricken from NASA's public records, but the gist of it was pretty simple: Shepard decided to pee in his suit. After a minute or two, a prolonged "Ahhhhhhhh" sounded over the radio.

As urine pooled around Shepard's lower back, the tension in Mission Control rose to nearly impossible-to-bear levels. The astronaut's body was covered in medical wires that would monitor his health during his mission. The engineers had briefly shut their power off while Shepard urinated, but now the wires had to be powered up again. There was a very real possibility that Alan might be shocked when the live wires met his fresh urine.

Thankfully, Shepard's long underwear quickly soaked up the liquid and saved him from being electrocuted by his own pee.

Finally, at 9:34 a.m., May 5, 1961, Shepard heard the end of the countdown: Three, two, one, zero . . . liftoff!

Medics in mission control watched the astronaut's heart rate spike as his rocket hurtled skyward. In the moments just before launch it had climbed from 80 beats per minute to 126. Now it was up to 132 beats per minute. *Thud, thud, thud, thud.* Adrenaline flooded his body. Shepard did his best to keep up a steady stream of updates for the ground crews. "Fuel is go . . . Oxygen is go."

About sixty seconds after his launch, Shephard fell silent. The ground crew in Mission Control tensed their muscles and nervously puffed on their cigarettes. Five, then ten, then fifteen seconds passed. Still no word from *Freedom 7.*

Shepard's ship tore its way through the thickest part of Earth's atmosphere. This created friction, which, combined with the increasing speeds of the rocket, caused his capsule to shake violently. Engineers called this Max Q. It was one of the trickiest and most dangerous parts of a launch. As the radio silence stretched, fear began to infect some on the ground. Was this the end? Was America's first astronaut about to die?

Shepard rattled around inside his tiny ship so much that he couldn't even see, let alone speak.

Finally, after seventeen seconds of silence, the astronaut spoke. He was okay! It was a miracle! Shepard rattled off a few updates and then, with relief, said, "Okay, it's a lot smoother now. A lot smoother." His capsule had punched through the atmosphere, and the rumbling and shaking stopped. Medics on the ground were relieved to see his heart rate begin to fall. Two minutes later, America's first man in space became weightless. Dust particles floated inside the capsule, and Shepard's body gently pulled against his seat restraints. A single steel washer glided slowly in front of his helmet.

He used his control stick to turn the capsule around in space. How about that? It worked exactly like the MASTIF control. Shepard cranked out the periscope to get a view of Earth below. He could only imagine how beautiful it would be. When he peered inside, everything looked gray. Ugh. Of course! At one point while waiting for launch, he'd put a gray filter over the periscope to shield his view from the bright Florida sun. He'd forgotten to take it off. Shepard reached down to flick the gray filter off and as he did, his thick gloved hand bumped the capsule's abort handle. *Yikes.* He decided to leave the filter on. He gazed down on a gray world below. It looked cloudy over the Bahamas. His voice crackled over the radio: "What a beautiful view."

About seven minutes after he launched, it was time for Shepard to start heading back to Earth. He swung his capsule around so that his heat shield would be the first part of his ship to hit the atmosphere. He needed that heat shield to absorb the searing temperatures of reentry if he wanted to live. It wasn't a glorious way to bring America's first crewed spacecraft down, rump-first and flaming, but it was what NASA had come up with.

Freedom 7 sliced through the foggy gases of the atmosphere. The g-forces built and built and built. Engineers on the ground anxiously watched the numbers tick higher on their monitors.

Nine g's.

Ten g's.

Eleven g's.

Just as he had during launch, Shepard did his best to stay in communication with the ground. The g-forces made it hard for him to talk. He just grunted, "Okay . . . okay . . . okay . . . okay."

And he was okay. The heat shield did its job. Just one foot behind Shepard's back, it absorbed temperatures that blazed at 1,200 degrees Fahrenheit. Everything held together beautifully.

When he was 21,000 feet from Earth, a small parachute popped out from the nose of the capsule. Next, out came the main chute. It caught the wind and spread into a glorious sixty-three-foot-wide lifesaving canopy. Shepard later said that seeing that chute was "the most beautiful sight of the mission."

Fifteen minutes and twenty-eight seconds after he launched, Shepard safely splashed down in the Atlantic Ocean. He'd done it.

A rescue helicopter swooped over the *Freedom* 7 and lowered a horseshoe-shaped floatation device on a cable. Shepard opened his hatch, climbed into the horseshoe, and was pulled into the aircraft. The helicopter crew stared, openmouthed, as the astronaut climbed aboard. They were in awe. A real live space man, gleaming silver space suit and all, had just stepped into their helicopter! Shepard grinned and casually remarked that it was "a beautiful day."

Shepard was a hero. Air force planes flew over his hometown and dropped pounds of brightly colored confetti on crowds celebrating in the streets. A navy jet flew over his house and spelled out the letter *S* for Shepard in white smoke. President John F. Kennedy called him personally to congratulate him on his mission and invite him to the White House. Americans were overjoyed. They felt so confident that the stock market even jumped. The United States had finally become a contender in the Space Race.

NASA filled Shepard's first hours back on Earth with careful tests and interviews to determine just how space had changed him. His eyeballs hadn't exploded and his heart certainly appeared to be working, but they needed to check on his mental health. Had his brief taste of space scrambled his brains?

Shepard was examined and questioned extensively. During one interview, a pretty secretary delivered Shepard a cup of coffee. As she left, one witness reported watching "Shepard's brain get up, leave the room, and follow her down the hall." It seemed that, other than losing about three pounds of urine and sweat, Shepard was "just like he was before . . . only happier."

Over the next few weeks, Shepard's face would grace the covers of countless newspapers and magazines. People couldn't get enough of their brave space explorer. Americans were delighted to celebrate his accomplishment, and Shepard gladly joined the party.

NASA launched its rockets out of Cape Canaveral, Florida. Just down the road from the enormous launch complex sat a rugged little town called Cocoa Beach. It wasn't much, a few ramshackle motels and dinky restaurants. But as the space program grew, Cocoa Beach had grown as well. Clubs and restaurants popped up. Hotels and motels sprouted from the scrubby beachfront. Especially after Shepard's launch, everyone wanted to go to little Cocoa Beach. Gawkers, fans, and groupies rolled into town, hoping to buy an astronaut a cocktail. And most of the Mercury 7 were delighted to oblige.

Plenty of people have guessed at exactly *why* it happened. Some have suggested that you just can't keep test pilots from flying. It makes them stir-crazy. Others have theorized that the drama of the Space Race simply created too much tension for the boys. Still others have wondered if it was the shock of becoming celebrities overnight. Regardless of the cause, the outcome was clear: The astronauts partied. They partied *hard*.

Cocoa Beach transformed into a hotbed for pool parties, beach parties, house parties, and hotel parties. All an astronaut had to do was show up somewhere, and hey! Let's party! They drank too much alcohol and pulled elaborate pranks on one another. They flirted with women who weren't their wives. They climbed onstage at clubs and told jokes.

Many of the most infamous astronaut stunts happened at the Cocoa Beach Holiday Inn. Once, Gordo Cooper dumped a bunch of live fish into the hotel's pool and made a big show out of sitting on the diving board with a fishing pole. Another time, Shepard plopped a four-foot alligator into the same pool, declaring that he'd like to keep it as a pet. Perhaps the astronauts' most elaborate prank occurred after a boat party turned sour. The boys weren't quite ready to call it a night, so they carried the whole boat on over to the Holiday Inn and dropped it into the pool. Then they climbed back on board and continued their merrymaking.

They really liked that pool. And the manager of the Holiday Inn really liked the astronauts. He went to great lengths to keep their parties stocked with alcohol, girls, and food, and free from the press.

The astronauts still weren't flying much. NASA filled their workdays with training and traveling, and their evenings were often chockablock full of parties. But parties weren't enough for the hotshots. They needed to get into the air, and nobody seemed able to squeeze a maintenance flight or two into their schedules. It was agony. They were men who lived and breathed airplanes. It had been months since they'd really flown. They needed time in the cockpit.

Gordo Cooper decided to pull a fast one on the agency. With his country twang and ol' boy antics, nobody expected him to play politics to get his way, but he did. Gordo went right ahead and leaked a story to the press about how frustrated the astronauts were about not getting flight time. This was unheard of. The astronauts were supposed to project an image of teamwork, unity, and pride. They should never complain, especially to the press!

The next thing they knew, the Mercury 7 had a pair of Delta Daggers (F-102), the same type of jet that Jean Hixson had reveled in flying. Schirra was less enthused about them. He deemed the Daggers "marginally supersonic but satisfactory." After a while, the astronauts were given a few Delta Darts (F-106) as well. These jets could get to Mach 2. "Finally," Schirra sniffed, he was "getting back to speed."

Meanwhile, General Motors saw an incredible advertising opportunity in these seven handsome, daredevil rocket boys. Just imagine how much their sales would soar if Americans saw the astronauts cruising around town in GM cars. It was an advertiser's dream. The company offered the astronauts a special deal on brand-new Corvettes. They could lease them for a dollar a year. A dollar!

Shepard, Cooper, Grissom, Schirra, and Slayton all took the deal. They zoomed around in their nearly free sports cars, often engaging in high-speed and highly illegal street racing. Once, while wanting to show off his Corvette's powerful engine to a reporter, Shepard couldn't find a good straightaway to really build up his speed. He called an airfield tower and pulled a few strings. A few minutes later he tore down an airport runway at 100 miles per hour while the reporter in his passenger seat quietly panicked.

John Glenn and Scott Carpenter opted out of the Corvette deal. Carpenter already had a hot little souped-up Shelby Cobra. He didn't need a replacement. Glenn was the outlier. While the rest of the astronauts were screaming down the streets in their sports cars, he happily puttered home in a used economy car that got good gas mileage. Glenn's car preference wasn't the only thing that set him apart from his peers. He didn't party or flirt. He enjoyed a happy marriage to a woman he'd known since his early childhood, and he valued a quiet and stable home life.

Gus Grissom beams from the driver's seat of his new Corvette.

Glenn's straitlaced lifestyle got a little annoying to the other astronauts. After all, how fun is it to get really wild when you've got some fuddy-duddy casting you disapproving looks the whole time? The tension escalated as time went on. It didn't help things at all that the media absolutely adored Glenn. He gave wonderful, heartfelt interviews, where he'd talk about God and country and the rest of it. When asked why he wanted to be an astronaut, Glenn had responded earnestly, "because it is the nearest to heaven I'll ever get." The press lapped it up.

While not all of the astronauts had Glenn's stage presence, they were still happily admired by the much of the media. Shepard's flight had restored the country's faith in the space program, and Americans were back on their team. Rumors floated around that the astronauts were a little wild, that they pranked and drank a bit too much, but most Americans didn't know exactly what happened down in Cocoa Beach. NASA needed to keep the astronaut partying under wraps. If the public knew just how crazy their golden boys could get, the new agency might lose some of the nation's support.

Late one night, an astronaut came to Glenn with a confession: "I think I got myself in trouble." He told Glenn he'd been drinking with a young woman while out one evening. As he flirted, he saw a few flashes out of the corner of his eye and realized someone was taking his photograph. It was a journalist. The astronaut fled quickly, but, he feared, the damage had been done.

Glenn knew this could have a huge fallout. Americans looked up to the astronauts. Any photographs that showed a drunk astronaut getting frisky with a strange woman could seriously hurt the space program. Glenn figured out who the journalist was and called his editor to ask, really beg, that he toss the story in the trash. He told the editor that Americans were in a race with "godless communists" and that he needed the press to help NASA "get back in the Space Race." A scandalous story about NASA would only help the Soviet space program. Glenn's call worked. The story wasn't published.

Glenn never revealed who the astronaut in this story was, but other people close to the astronauts have hazarded a guess: It was probably Alan Shepard.

John Glenn might have saved Shepard's butt, but he wasn't happy about it. The next day, Glenn gathered Mercury 7 into a closed-door meeting and absolutely lit into them. He was the oldest of the group, and his lecture took on the tone of an angry dad. Glenn seethed. He told them to knock it off with the partying, with the street racing, and most of all with the "skirt chasing." He reminded them that they had "worked too hard to get into this program and that it meant too much to the country to see it jeopardized" by reckless flirting.

If Glenn had expected a warm response, he was disappointed. Most of the other astronauts rolled their eyes and huffed in annoyance. They told him to mind his own business. They could do what they wanted. Scott Carpenter was the only one to side with Glenn. He thought the other guys were out of line. The room boiled with barely contained tension.

This wasn't the first time the Mercury 7 had disagreed. The astronauts sometimes argued and occasionally came close to blows as they hashed out the business of pioneering spaceflight. But this fight felt different. They weren't debating whether foot pedals or a hand control would be the best way to steer their capsule. This was personal. They were fighting over how to live their very lives. And they did *not* agree. How could they work together after something like this?

Three weeks after Shepard's flight, President Kennedy stood before a joint session of Congress and made an astounding speech. He said, "I believe that this nation should commit itself to achieving the goal, before this decade is out, of landing a man on the Moon and returning him safely to the Earth."

It looked like everyone at NASA, including the Mercury 7, would need to find a way to get along. They had a job to do.

And while the astronauts were bickering behind closed doors, the nation's most ambitious female pilots were still hard at work, trying their best to navigate the sexist politics of American aviation.

CHAPTER 15

THE WOMEN WHO FOUGHT FOR FLIGHT

It wasn't enough for a woman pilot to simply be talented in the 1950s and 1960s. If she wanted to get work, good work, she had to be savvy, too.

Astronaut test subject Jerri Sloan was as savvy as they came. The petite brunette was funny and flirty. She kept her hair in a curled and stylish bob. She had a handsome husband, two young children, and a house in the suburbs. To the average passerby, she would have looked like any other lovely Texas housewife. But Jerri was much, much more than that.

Jerri Sloan was a pilot and entrepreneur. She was also an adventurer. She liked to fly high and fast and far, and when she wasn't racing airplanes, she was growing her aviation career. In the late 1950s, she had learned that a company called Texas Instruments was looking to hire out test flight work. Some of it was military test flight. Jerri wanted those jobs.

Sloan's test flight ambitions were almost absurdly lofty. Military test flight remained an elite aviation field that was still technically off the table for women. The military forbade it, and the collective American opinion was that women just

Jerri Sloan works the radio in the cockpit of her aircraft.

didn't belong in that world. Test flight was technical, dirty, dangerous, and secretive. It was a job for men like Alan Shepard, who could come preposterously close to crashing a plane and then simply shrug it off with an obscene gesture. Test pilots were *men*.

In spite of all this, Sloan had set her sights on breaking into test flight. She knew she couldn't succeed on her own, as a private female civilian. So, she had decided to start an aviation business to try to get the test flight jobs. But starting a business was difficult to do as a woman. Sloan asked her father and a friend named Joe Truhill for help. Joe signed on as a business partner. Her father cosigned on her bank loans. Armed with two male signatures, Jerri launched Air Services of Dallas in 1959. She soon built it into a thriving business. And then, Sloan accomplished the unthinkable. She nabbed the military test flight jobs.

Jerri gamed the system. She worked a series of loopholes and, at the dawn of the 1960s, often found herself doing top-secret military test flight. She never got to test fly a brand-new type of plane. Rather, she tested aircraft components, such as experimental technologies or weapons. One of these was called Terrain Following Radar (TFR). This radar would eventually help combat pilots to "see" in the dark as they zoomed low over unfamiliar territory. TFR could alert planes to unseen obstacles. This enabled combat pilots to focus their attention elsewhere, on shooting or bombing or dodging fire.

Sloan did many of her TFR test flights in the dead of night, far out over the ink-black waters of the Gulf of Mexico. She would barrel just over the water in the same military bomber Jean Hixson had mastered seventeen years earlier, the B-25, relying only on the radar for guidance. It was risky flying. And Sloan just loved it.

Jerri wasn't a typical test pilot. But she was a great one.

The fact that Sloan worked at all made her unusual. At the time, only about 38% of American women worked outside of the home. Women were often limited in their career options. They were encouraged to take jobs as secretaries, typists, nurses, or teachers, and discouraged from pursuing careers that were considered more intellectual. Women were often thought of as dramatic and too emotional to hold down certain types of jobs. In 1960, only 6% of American doctors were women. One medical school dean explained this tiny number, saying that his school actively refused women applicants: "We do keep women out, when we can. We don't want them here."

That same year, only 1% of engineers in America were women. Wally Funk later learned why. When she tried to apply to an engineering program, she was firmly rebuffed. An administrator told her, "We don't have engineering for girls. You have to go to home ec[onomics]."

These limitations extended beyond medicine and engineering. Many aviation companies didn't want to hire female pilots or executives, either. During her 1958 job interview at Aero Commander, a manager had told Jerrie Cobb that aviation "is a man's industry . . . Aircraft manufacturers' front offices are womanless. And I'm afraid it's going to continue that way." But Cobb didn't give up. She argued that she had a contribution to make. Aero Commander relented, and she got the job. One year later, Cobb flew an Aero Commander to set a new world speed record, darting from Las Vegas to San Diego in five hours, twenty-nine minutes, and twenty-seven seconds. She bested the previous record, held by a Russian pilot, by just twenty-six seconds.

In 1961, Gene Nora Stumbough applied for a job flying and selling Beech aircraft. She dutifully filled out an application and supplied the requested photo. A man soon responded that she could have the job "if you live up to what your background and resume indicate and also, if you are the 'lady' suggested by your photograph." Stumbough took the job, and later obliged when her boss encouraged her to make frequent trips to the beauty salon. He wanted her to keep her hairstyle looking picture perfect.

These experiences weren't extraordinary. Nearly all of the thirteen women could have recalled a time that they had been discriminated against because of their gender. Back in 1952, Jan Dietrich had experienced it when she applied for a chief pilot position at a Cessna dealership. She didn't think she'd get the job. After all, it would involve working as a civilian test pilot, managing the company's flight school, and selling airplanes. Few employers at the time would be open to hiring a woman for the job.

Dietrich was surprised when the interview began very smoothly. "I want to hire a lady pilot," her potential new boss told her. She was pleased and began listing off her credentials: "I have a commercial pilot's license with flight instructor and instrument ratings—"

He cut her off. "What do you wear flying?"

Later, Dietrich showed off a batch of new planes to a group of customers. After the smoothest landing she could manage, one of the prospective buyers exclaimed, "Why, the airplane practically lands itself!"

Dietrich was confused. The airplane didn't land itself. She landed it. She had worked and studied for years to be able to bring the wheels down onto the runway with just a whisper of sound. Obviously the airplane didn't land itself! Then she caught a glimpse of her boss. He was smiling broadly. Dietrich instantly understood: "If a girl does something well, especially a small one who dresses and looks like a girl, it

Jan Dietrich smiles from the cockpit of her aircraft.

looks easy." Dietrich had been hired to prove a point: If a woman can fly a plane, then it must be easy to do.

Some women were able to use this outdated and sexist notion to their advantage. In 1953, when the military needed to boost its recruitment for the Korean War, a few women had been allowed to fly jets as proof that they were easy to handle. It was surely an insulting and irritating premise. But it was still an opportunity, and smart women pilots knew to grab any opportunities they got. When the chance arose for Janey Hart to take one such flight, she pounced. The mother of eight absolutely relished in her hour-long flight in a Thunderbird (F-16).

Of course, once women like Cobb and Dietrich did manage to find work, they weren't paid well for it. In 1961, women earned an average of 59 cents for every dollar earned by a man. In some states, a woman's earnings belonged not to her but to her husband.

Women in the early 1960s weren't just limited in their careers. They faced all sorts of obstacles. They couldn't attend most Ivy League colleges. They couldn't take out a credit card without the permission of their husband. They couldn't get birth control without a parent or husband's approval. In short, women weren't allowed to do much, and they had few legal protections. Discriminating against women wasn't illegal yet.

For women like Jerri Sloan, this gender dynamic presented a vexing issue. Despite her extraordinary skills and ambitions, she was limited by the men in her community. Fortunately, her father and friend Joe were supportive. Unfortunately, her husband was not.

Even as she worked diligently at her flying and astronaut testing, divorce loomed terrifyingly over Sloan's marriage to her husband, Lou. The end of a marriage was scandalous for both genders, but it was especially troublesome for women. A divorced woman might be cast out of her social network because she hadn't been able to make her marriage work. Some divorced women struggled financially, unable to find decent jobs and relying on their ex-husbands for child support. Women facing divorce had to weigh their options carefully: They could remain in an unhappy or even violent marriage, or they could strike out on their own, knowing that it would be very, very difficult.

Lou made this decision for Jerri. She returned from her Phase I astronaut tests to find her house in ruins and divorce papers from her husband. Lou picked up a framed photo of him and his airplane and shattered it over his knee.

"See, I had competed with him," Sloan later recalled with sadness. Her marriage was over.

Juggling marriage with work was often stressful for women, but when their job was something as unusual as flying airplanes, it could be nearly impossible. Myrtle Cagle remembers the struggle. "It took me a while to find a husband because they all wanted me to stop flying," she said. "I had one sweetheart who wanted to marry me and he said he couldn't bear the thought of me flying. I told him: 'I was flying long before I ever saw you and I'll be flying long after.'" Cagle didn't marry him. For other women undergoing Phase I astronaut testing, it often *was* impossible to find love.

Many of these elite women aviators simply chose not

to get married at all. This choice came at a price. Unmarried women in the early 1960s were looked upon as oddballs, weirdos. People called them spinsters and whispered behind their backs.

Irene Leverton remembered watching scores of talented female aviators hang up their flight jackets after they got serious with some boy. "They all got married—and some of them not happy, some happy—but they all quit flying ... Why would you *do* that?"

Myrtle Cagle, 1961.

Leverton chose to remain single, explaining her decision with a joke: "I just say I was too smart to ever do that ... I don't clean and I don't work for anybody else."

Leverton wasn't the only pilot who didn't get married. Wally Funk stayed single. Jerrie Cobb, Jean Hixson, and the Dietrich twins did, too. Married women had so many responsibilities. They had to clean and cook and raise children. Sometimes they worked, too. These duties made it hard to get into the air for an hour or two, let alone the 1,000 flight hours required for female astronaut hopefuls.

The women who managed to eke out enough flight hours to make it to the Phase I astronaut tests in New Mexico were a truly impressive bunch. It wouldn't take much for a military aviator to get 1,000 flight hours in his log. A busy test pilot could hit that number in a year of work. It might take a woman several years to reach that same milestone. Since few women managed to make careers out of flight, most had to get their flight hours in their off time. One thousand hours in the air meant 1,000 hours of babysitters booked, hundreds of dinners prepped and frozen, and countless loads of laundry done late into the night.

Sloan had done it. Her manipulation of the system and tenacity paid off. She made it to the Lovelace Clinic with 1,200 hours in her log.

As Sloan grew accustomed to life as a divorcée, she hoped that she might get to play a bit higher than the clouds someday. And things were looking up for Sloan. She had traded one stale and depressing role—the wife of an abusive alcoholic—for another: potential astronaut.

A letter soon arrived in Sloan's mailbox from Lovelace. It told her that Jerrie Cobb was preparing to take her third and final phase of astronaut tests at the Naval School of Aviation Medicine in Pensacola, Florida. If all went well, Sloan should expect to travel to Florida soon for the next round of her own tests.

Sloan booked childcare and started to train. She *would* pass those tests.

CHAPTER 16

Gus Grissom was drowning.

Salty water streamed into his eyes. It filled his mouth and he coughed, sputtered, choked.

Help me.

He flailed his arms in a desperate wave to the rescue helicopter hovering just above, but the pilot wasn't looking at him. He focused instead on the sinking space capsule just feet away from the thrashing astronaut. A steel cable hung from the chopper's belly and hooked onto the top of the space capsule. The pilot tried to heave his helicopter up and away to lift the capsule out of the water, but it wouldn't budge. It was too heavy. It was sinking. So was Grissom.

His space suit filled with water and pulled him down. Grissom thought bleakly of all the dumb souvenirs he'd packed into the pockets of the silver suit. All those dimes. Tiny model space capsules. They had been part of a hopeful plan; he'd give them away after his spaceflight. Gifts from an astronaut! A dime that had flown in space! But now?

Now they were a collection of weighty knickknacks, dragging him to a waterlogged death.

In between gasps, Grissom could hear the deafening *thump-thump-thump* of helicopter rotors. Three more choppers had arrived on the scene. Arm over arm, Grissom slapped at the water in an exhausted attempt to stay afloat. He feebly tried to signal to the men hovering above him: *Help me! I'm drowning!* The men waved back. They didn't understand! The helicopter blades whipped sea spray into Grissom's eyes. He wondered if he would die, right here in front of everyone. Someone in a helicopter snapped photos.

Then he saw it: One chopper had lowered a horseshoe-shaped life preserver. That was Grissom's lifeline! If he could just get there. A salty swell sent him under again. The chopper pilot swooped in and finally, finally, Grissom got a hold of it. He threaded his head and shoulders through the loop with his arms dangling out front and gave a limp wave to the pilot. *Get me out of here already!*

The chopper dragged Grissom across the surface of the water, his ragdoll body flopping and slapping at the waves before finally being hoisted aloft. Dangling there below that chopper, Grissom didn't look like a heroic space explorer. He looked like a clump of drooping seaweed on the end of some fisherman's line. The helicopter crew hauled him into the aircraft and noticed that the hotshot test pilot, the best and bravest, was shaking.

"I didn't do anything," he croaked. "I didn't touch it. I was just lying there—and it blew."

Gus Grissom is fished out of the water after his space capsule, *Liberty Bell 7*, sinks, July 21, 1961.

Thus began one of the greatest scandals in NASA's history.

On July 21, 1961, Gus Grissom flew *Liberty Bell 7*, the second project Mercury space capsule. His mission essentially mimicked what Shepard had done in *Freedom 7*. Grissom's flight would show that what Shepard had accomplished wasn't a fluke.

Everything went pretty well for Grissom. Until the end. After *Liberty Bell 7* splashed down into the Atlantic and began its bobbing wait for rescue, something happened.

The plan had been clear. After his mission, Grissom would wait inside his capsule for a recovery helicopter to hover overhead and carefully attach a hook to the top of the spacecraft. Once everything was secure, Grissom would hit a button to open his capsule hatch using a set of explosives. The astronaut would crawl out the open hatch and float in the water for a moment or two while the helicopter lowered a horseshoe-shaped floatation device for him. If all went according to plan, Grissom and his capsule would both be out of the water in a flash.

Collecting the capsule was important. Scientists and engineers needed to study it to see what they could learn about its performance in space. Shepard had managed it. His *Freedom 7* ship taught engineers boatloads about its flight and reentry. It showed them what worked and what needed to be improved. After NASA was done with it, the agency donated it to the Smithsonian, where it became a national treasure. It was a symbol of American success.

But something happened inside Grissom's capsule after

its splashdown. The transcripts show that he was hot and ready to get out. Over and over he asked the rescue crews when they would show up. "Give me how much longer it'll be before you get here." "Are you ready to come in and hook on anytime?"

Grissom was hopped up on adrenaline from his mission. When his capsule tipped to one side, the astronaut thought he heard gurgling. Was *Liberty Bell* sinking? He wanted out. Now.

Grissom armed the explosive hatch in preparation. He was ready to hit the button that would blow it open.

He radioed again: "This is *Liberty Bell 7*. Are you ready for pickup?"

A rescue chopper approached in. Before its pilot could attach his hook to Grissom's capsule, he saw the hatch explode out into the frothy sea, followed closely by a silver-suited astronaut. Grissom was in the water! What on earth was he doing? He wasn't following protocol! The chopper pilot watched as water streamed into *Liberty Bell 7*'s open hatch. The capsule started to sink.

The helicopter pilot knew how essential that capsule was. He dropped lower and lower, at one point even dipping all three of his wheels into the choppy waters. Somehow, he managed to hook onto the capsule. He made a few desperate attempts to haul it out of the water, but it was too late. The seawater filling it made it far too heavy. Alarms squealed inside his cockpit. His engine couldn't bear the weight of the waterlogged capsule. Reluctantly, he released the hook. He watched in horror as *Liberty Bell 7* slipped under the water and began its three-mile dive to the bottom of the ocean. It was lost.

Even after releasing the capsule, the rescue chopper was still in trouble. Its engine had five minutes left, maybe less, before it completely burned out. The pilot glanced down at Grissom and saw him wave. He figured the astronaut must be okay. He requested a backup chopper for the astronaut and hightailed it to safety.

Grissom was in the water for about five minutes before the backup chopper collected him. He said it "seemed like an eternity." Normally, swimming in a space suit is pretty easy. They're filled with air and perfectly sealed, which makes them a little like a human-shaped life raft. As long as an astronaut makes sure that their suit is fully cinched and zipped and snapped, they can usually float comfortably for quite a while. But, after his mission, Grissom had forgotten to shut a small valve in his suit. This meant that with every passing moment, the buoyant air inside his suit was replaced by a steady trickle of cool, heavy water. His five-minute swim had been a terrifying, gasping ordeal.

Grissom didn't have much recovery time after his near-drowning. NASA officials were quick to question him about what had happened with the hatch. He stuck to his story. "It just blew." He told them he'd been lying there on his seat, doing exactly what he should, when he heard a bang and looked up to see the bright blue sky. The hatch was gone. He hadn't touched a thing. It wasn't his fault.

Many engineers at NASA didn't buy it. A hatch doesn't just *blow*. Maybe it had been pilot error. He was crammed into a tiny cockpit in a bulky space suit and bobbing around in the waves. Accidents happen. They felt pretty certain: Grissom had hit the button.

This mattered because the capsule was expensive. Just the nuts and bolts of it cost more than $1 million in 1961 currency, which equals somewhere around $8.8 million today. It was important. Grissom's job as a test pilot was to try out a new craft, sure, but that wasn't all. He also had to bring the thing back after his flight.

Grissom himself knew how bad this looked. He later recalled, "In all my years of flying—including combat in Korea—this was the first time that my aircraft and I had not come back together. In my entire career as a pilot, *Liberty Bell* was the first thing I had ever lost."

The loss of *Liberty Bell 7* cast a dark shadow over its gruff pilot. Grissom didn't get the welcome home parties that Shepard had enjoyed. He didn't go to the White House. Nobody dumped confetti over his hometown. Even his wife, Betty, was disappointed in him. During their first phone conversation after his spaceflight, she got right to it:

"I heard you got wet," she said. "Are you all right?"

Grissom said he was fine.

"It wasn't your fault, was it?" she asked.

Grissom said no. Betty responded dully that she was "glad for his sake that he was not to blame."

Despite his claims of innocence, people at NASA still wondered if Grissom was at fault. An agency investigation into the incident didn't prove much. Engineers ran the same type of explosive hatch through different scenarios, trying their best to get it to blow open, but it never did. They just couldn't re-create a situation in which the hatch would pop open on its own, which further raised doubts about Grissom's denial.

NASA's official response was lukewarm. The agency supported Grissom but didn't make him into a Shepard-level hero. They praised his work during his mission and brushed over the loss of the capsule as a sad accident. Oops.

Grissom did his best to make light of the situation. He joked that "there were still a few gaps in our training which we could easily remedy—like how to make sure you don't sink when you get back."

Sixteen days after Grissom lost *Liberty Bell* 7 to the depths of the Atlantic, the Soviets struck again. On August 6, 1961, cosmonaut Gherman Titov flew onboard *Vostok* 2. The mission lasted twenty-five hours and whipped Titov around Earth seventeen times.

It was another crushing blow to the American space program. The Soviets were flinging guys up there for a full day, and the Americans couldn't figure out how to stop their astronauts from destroying their own property!

Shepard and Grissom had been in space for mere minutes. It was child's play compared to what the Soviets could do.

The glory of Alan Shepard's first spaceflight had faded, and now NASA was dealing with the messy reality of being in second place in the Space Race. Again. It was an ugly time. The public pressured NASA to catch up to the Soviets. To work faster and harder. But everyone at NASA was already working as fast and as hard as they could. They scrambled to figure out the capsule door problem that might not have actually been a problem at all. They worked on new procedures to prevent the next guy from pulling another boneheaded screwup. And all the while, they dealt with a group of astronauts who had no idea how to handle their sudden celebrity.

Grissom's maybe-mistake might have been the most visible astronaut issue, but it wasn't the only one. Shepard's booze-fueled hijinks were becoming more public. He'd started jumping onstage at a Cocoa Beach nightclub, sometimes pulling Schirra and Slayton up with him, and performing a racist routine alongside the famous comedian Bill Dana. The act focused on a character named Jose Jimenez, or The Cowardly Astronaut. Dana played Jimenez with a lisping, lilting accent. It was a cruel characterization of both homosexuals and Hispanics, and Shepard thought it was the funniest thing he'd ever seen.

Shepard was lousy onstage. He wasn't much of an actor, and besides, he couldn't stop giggling when he got up there. But his comedy skills didn't really matter. What did matter was that he was coming dangerously close to causing a scandal. A tipsy astronaut sharing the spotlight with a celebrity was a recipe for disaster.

In contrast to female aviators at the time, who often felt pressured to project an image of professionalism, the astronauts were beginning to unravel. Their imperfections were becoming increasingly public. NASA had its boys on a loose leash, but soon, they might run out of slack.

By the summer of 1961, tensions among the astronauts ran high. The Mercury 7 weren't used to playing on a team. They were test pilots, and test pilots spend a lot of time on their own. Flight assignments were a matter of enormous competition and conflict among the men. When the Mercury 7 were told that Shepard would get the first flight, the remaining six men fell into a sulking, stunned silence. Their egos were bruised. Eventually, Glenn snapped himself out of his self-pity and gamely stepped forward to shake Shepard's hand in congratulations. The others half-heartedly followed along. *Nice work, bud. Good luck, Shep.* But none of them meant it. They were devastated to have missed the first flight. Later, the men would realize with some surprise and embarrassment that none of them had taken Shepard out for celebratory drinks that night. They were too upset.

Though Glenn had been the first to step forward and congratulate Shepard, the very next day he quietly wrote a letter to NASA leadership objecting to the decision. Glenn thought he should have been first instead.

The following flight assignments created still more drama for the men. When Deke Slayton learned that he wouldn't have one of the first three flights, he said he was "shocked, hurt, and downright humiliated." He was angry, too. Didn't NASA know what a good pilot he was?

The Mercury 7 weren't behaving like technical, detached aviators. They were emotional, hurt, and even backstabbing. If a group of female pilots had engaged in this behavior, the public might have jumped to criticize them for falling into a negative stereotype about their gender. But the Mercury 7 were men, and everyone let it go.

Even after the early assignments were doled out, tensions simmered among the astronauts. The men teased and pranked each other in public. In private, they gossiped and plotted.

Glenn was too goody-goody. Nobody liked that. The word around NASA was that Shepard needed to rein in the public antics. Grissom had obviously screwed up with the *Liberty Bell*. What an embarrassment. Gordon Cooper thought Shepard was manipulative. He said Shepard "was not to be trusted when it came to anything that he considered in his best interests." Schirra was extremely critical of the way things worked around NASA. He didn't think a lowly bomber pilot like Scott Carpenter should be in the group. He hedged his criticism carefully. "Nothing against Scott," Schirra said, he was "a nice, sweet guy," but he didn't belong. Slayton also thought NASA had a few bad apples on board. Unlike Schirra, he hesitated to call out anyone specifically, but he still made his feelings crystal clear: "we definitely had a couple who didn't belong."

There were plenty of arguments. The Mercury 7 started retreating into private meetings they called séances to settle these disputes away from the spotlight. These séances would later become famously mysterious. The astronauts shouted, snapped, and roared at one another in these shadowy meetings. And then, as if by a miracle, they would

Six of the astronauts clown around for the cameras. From left: Gordon Cooper, Deke Slayton, John Glenn, Alan Shepard, Scott Carpenter, Wally Schirra.

reemerge red-faced but unified. "When we came out of the room, we had an astronaut opinion," Gordo later recalled, though he noted that "some of us were more team players than others."

Outside of NASA, few people knew how rocky the astronauts' relationships were. The space agency did its best to present the Mercury 7 as a united front. It downplayed their shortcomings and emphasized their strengths. Magazines and newspapers detailed how the men supported one another and how they worked together as a team. *LIFE* magazine highlighted the heroics of the astronauts' missions, the danger and the suspense and the nail-biting greatness of it all. And America, so desperate to pull ahead of the Soviets, willingly played along.

On August 4, 1961, *LIFE* ran a story about Grissom's troubled mission. The headline read, "A Hero Admits He Was Scared." A decision had been made. *LIFE* and NASA were standing by their man. He might have lost his capsule, but he was still a hero.

CHAPTER 17

PHASE III TESTING AND A TELEGRAM

I n May 1961, Jerrie Cobb stepped onto the pristine lawn of the U.S. Naval Aviation School of Medicine. The Florida sunshine pressed warmly on her shoulders. It wasn't even 8:00 a.m., but the air was already chokingly muggy. Cobb would spend the next ten days on this campus, undergoing a series of brutal stress tests, physical-fitness checks, and spaceflight simulations that would be similar to those taken by the Mercury 7 at Wright-Patterson Air Force Base two years earlier. This would be Cobb's third and final phase of astronaut testing.

Cobb knew that the stakes for her were high. If she did well on her Phase III astronaut tests, then surely, surely, everyone at NASA would listen. Women could become astronauts. *She* could become an astronaut.

However, Cobb's Phase III tests were troubled before they even began. This phase required sophisticated aero-medical equipment. The tests couldn't just be done anywhere. The male astronauts took their Phase III tests at Wright-Patterson Air Force Base. Cobb had attempted to schedule her testing at the same facility but was refused. The air force had made themselves clear from the start: They didn't want some woman using their equipment.

Dr. Lovelace had asked around, hoping to find someone who knew someone who might be feeling charitable. Finally, he succeeded. The leadership at the naval school in Pensacola, Florida, agreed. Cobb could use their facilities.

Jerrie's time at Pensacola began with thorough medical exams to double-check that she was up for the challenge that lay ahead. When she showed doctors that she was indeed ready, she embarked upon her last marathon of astronaut tests.

The first of these would test Cobb's capacity to think and act at near-toxic altitudes. It took place inside the naval school's high-altitude chamber. This was a room in which the air pressure could be manipulated to simulate flying in an aircraft at different heights. Cobb needed a pressure suit to get through this test. Without it she could be seriously hurt when the air pressure dropped and pulled her fragile, soft body in a ruthless outward yank. Of course, the navy didn't have a pressure suit small enough to fit Cobb, so she spent the ninety minutes leading up to her run in the chamber in a frantic dress fitting of sorts. Navy technicians tucked and cinched and strapped Cobb inside the smallest suit they could find.

Cobb rode in the chamber up to a simulated 60,000 feet. She did well at that towering altitude, even managing to move around and show technicians that her brain wasn't addled by the dizzying height. Then, to see what Cobb could handle, the techs simulated a free fall. The air pressure around her built and built and built and built, just as it would if she were plummeting from a shattered cockpit. Cobb stayed calm. Observers watched through the room's thick glass window as Cobb experienced a 5,000-foot-per-minute tumble, likely wondering how the woman in the oversized pressure suit could possibly handle this trial.

She did just fine. The only emotion she showed was a hint of sadness when the test was over and she had to take off the pressure suit. She wondered if she'd ever get one of her own.

After her run in the altitude chamber, Jerrie moved on to a series of grueling physical fitness tests. For the first time since beginning her work with Dr. Lovelace, Cobb didn't perform well.

The physical fitness testing equipment towered over Cobb. She couldn't reach the chin-up bar, and even when someone hoisted her up she didn't manage a single one. Cobb was furious with herself. A speed agility test challenged her to climb up and over a 6' 6" wall. Cobb ran at it two times before managing to hook her fingertips on top and scramble over. When she finished, she was "scratched, bruised, and breathless."

Next came the spaceflight simulation tests. These results would show Dr. Lovelace, and whomever else was interested, whether Cobb could hack it in space.

The first of these tests required special approval. The navy planned to have Cobb fly a powerful military fighter jet on a series of acrobatic maneuvers to see how her brain held up under high g-forces. Because this meant a civilian woman would pilot a military aircraft, the navy had been required to reach out to the Pentagon for official permission. They wired over a request asking to use a plane as part of Dr. Lovelace's exploration into "the fundamental difference between male and female astronauts." The Pentagon whipped back its joking reply: "If you don't know the difference already, we refuse to put money into the project."

After people at the Pentagon had stopped laughing, they agreed, and Cobb was allowed to take the test. She climbed into the copilot seat of the jet. Technicians stuck eighteen needles into her scalp and wired each to different sensors to monitor her brain's performance during the flight. A camera perched near her helmet to capture her facial expressions.

The jet roared down the runway and into the sky. It was a wild ride. Cobb said "the airplane almost tore itself apart in dives and rolls and loops." The forces of the different maneuvers were so intense that Cobb said her "eyeballs popped in and out with the shifting stresses." However, this was a test she could handle. By the time she brought the jet back down onto the runway, Cobb was perfectly collected. She noted matter-of-factly that it was simply "one more test passed."

To test her ability to withstand motion sickness, Cobb stood inside a giant room that was decorated to look like a shabby apartment. It had a table, chairs, bookshelves, and even a hotplate. But it wasn't an ordinary apartment. It was a spaceflight training device called the Slow-Rotation Room (SRR).

Cobb's first activities inside the SRR took place in a seated position. She answered a few questions and allowed test administrators to check her eyesight. That wasn't so bad. In fact, she felt perfectly fine. Thank goodness! But when they directed her to stand, Cobb nearly toppled over. The sensation was very odd. The room appeared still, but she could feel it moving. A voice crackled over the radio: "Walk heel-and-toe to the center of the room."

Cobb tried to follow the directions but found that she couldn't stop stumbling to the side. A sickly, queasy feeling tugged at her belly. She shook it off. Next, the voice directed her to sit in a chair and operate a series of dials. This was a relief after her staggering, clumsy attempts at walking. The test administrators were clearly pushing her—they had her reaching up, down, and side to side, grabbing this dial and that. It was a set of actions that would have lost the average aviator his lunch. But Jerrie was hanging in there. After that, she was instructed to stand up and throw darts at a dartboard. Now they were testing both her stomach and her brain. Cobb's first two attempts were terrible. The darts landed several feet away from the target. But she didn't give up. She thought about the problem mathematically. The rotation of the room affected where the darts landed. She tried aiming 45 degrees to the left of the target and bingo! A hit!

After thirty minutes of tasks in a room that she said felt like "an amusement park crazy house," Cobb stepped out. Her performance had been exceptional. Test administrators told her she was "markedly less hampered" than a group of male navy flight students who had recently taken the same test.

Later, Cobb trained for a Mercury water landing in a device called a Dilbert Dunker. This was a mock cockpit perched on a set of tracks that led deep into a swimming pool. It looked a little like a tiny, single-seat roller coaster. Cobb strapped herself into the seat and then gritted her teeth as the whole contraption shot down the tracks and plunged underwater before twisting upside down. Cobb's task was relatively simple: She just had to unstrap herself and escape without drowning. However, this was far from easy. Her oversized life jacket and parachute pack fit snugly inside the cockpit, and she didn't have much room to wiggle. Getting out was tricky. *Don't panic just because you're in a headstand under sixteen feet of water. Watch it,* she told herself.

Divers standing nearby sighed in relief when Cobb surfaced. They wouldn't need to rescue her after all.

Cobb soldiered on. She took an ejection seat test. This simulated an explosive aircraft ejection, those events so feared by jet pilots. She settled into a padded chair, got buckled in, and then waited. *BANG!* A .50-caliber shell exploded just under her seat and shot her up into the air on a set of steel tracks. It was a poor approximation of an actual ejection, but it showed who had real guts. Navy test administrators saw that day that Cobb had plenty to spare. They gave her an honorary membership to an elite, if silly and unofficial, aviation group: the Ejection Seat Club.

Jerrie Cobb sits inside an altitude chamber.

Jerrie was happy to be welcomed to this little navy fraternity. But what she wanted much more was a welcome from NASA. And it seemed like she was getting closer. After ten days in Pensacola, Jerrie passed her Phase III tests. It was all so exciting! When word reached the men on the base that a woman had passed her astronaut tests, they threw an impromptu party for her.

Before leaving Florida, Cobb was told that twelve other women who had passed their tests at the Lovelace Clinic would arrive in Pensacola soon to complete Phase III testing of their own. Cobb later said, "That clinched it, I figured. If the Navy itself was willing to cooperate in astronaut testing of female candidates, then we'd reached the top of the ladder. The next step would be—would have to be—an official astronaut training program for women."

On May 27, 1961, Cobb attended NASA's conference on the Peaceful Uses of Space. It was a fancy affair, with 2,000 guests mingling and dining and talking shop. Lovelace gave a speech about his research on women astronaut candidates.

The audience was delighted and entranced. And Cobb, sitting at the main table beside NASA's new administrator, James Webb, was the star. She bubbled with happiness.

Just when it seemed as though Cobb's night couldn't get any better, Webb stood up to give a speech. He gestured to his tablemate and acknowledged her successful completion of astronaut testing. And then he did the unimaginable: Right there in front of everyone, he made her a consultant to NASA and welcomed her aboard.

Jerrie Cobb had a job at NASA! She was thrilled.

Shortly after that fateful night, Cobb traveled to NASA's headquarters and was officially sworn in for the position. As she raised her hand and declared her allegiance to both NASA and the United States, she was hardly able to stop herself from bursting out into great, racking sobs of happiness and relief. It was finally happening.

Cobb hurried home and began thinking about how she could help NASA. She spent her days working as a pilot in Oklahoma City, and her evenings and weekends giving shaky public speeches about her role as an astronaut test subject. The press reported on Cobb's new title excitedly, informing readers about her salary ($50 per day) and also reminding readers of her preferred hairstyle (ponytail).

The Mercury 7 likely knew about Cobb. Her face had appeared in several magazines, she'd given plenty of television interviews, and she was now officially on staff at NASA. But the astronauts didn't talk much about her, to the press at least. It's possible that they thought her mission to join them in space was foolish, or misguided, or simply a nonissue.

Deke Slayton would later mention her dismissively in his memoir, not as an actual contender for spaceflight, but as a sort of odd blip in history. While Cobb and the other female astronaut test subjects were well informed about their male counterparts, it seemed as though the men were going out of their way to ignore the women.

Meanwhile, in the weeks following Cobb's appointment to NASA, a flurry of letters crisscrossed the country. Many came from Cobb herself. She spent hours hunched over her desk, writing extensive letters to NASA that explained her ideas for American women in space. Her plans were thoughtful and thorough. She waited eagerly to hear back from the agency.

In the middle of July, Jackie Cochran wrote letters to the twelve other women who had passed their Phase I tests. She told them to prepare for a trip to Pensacola for further testing. Cochran promised to pay for the women's expenses but also reminded them not to get ahead of themselves: "There is no astronaut program for women as yet." She told them that the tests were "purely experimental and in the nature of research." But she also wrote that "I think a properly organized astronaut program for women would be a fine thing." It seemed that Cochran was urging the women to proceed with caution, but also, perhaps, a little hope.

In August, Lovelace sent letters of his own. These alerted the women that their Phase III testing had been scheduled for September. It was an electrifying update. The wheels were moving! It didn't matter that only Cobb had finished her Phase II tests at this point. Lovelace wasn't particular about the order in which the women completed their tests. They just had to finish all three phases to give Dr. Lovelace a solid set of data to show NASA. Lovelace urged the women to keep the whole thing a secret: "There is to be no publicity whatsoever about these tests or your trip to Pensacola." He also recommended that they prepare themselves as much as possible for the rigorous ordeal they were about to face: "I suggest you study the FAA manual, mathematics, theory of flight, meteorology and things that have to do with design of aircraft and engines." Dr. Lovelace wanted these women to perform well.

While the twelve female aviators waited for their trip to Pensacola, Cobb invited them to Oklahoma City for their Phase II tests. Rhea Hurrle arrived first. Cobb was instantly impressed and a little intimidated by the brown-haired, blue-eyed pilot. At the time, Hurrle was working as a charter pilot and flight instructor in Houston. She had zipped over to Oklahoma City in her boss's private plane. That meant something to Cobb. "Bosses don't lend multi-thousand-dollar airplanes to just any pilot," she mused.

Wally Funk came next. The twenty-two-year-old spitfire flight instructor was quiet, determined, and fiercely talented. Cobb said she "hadn't dreamed" a pilot so young could have met the astronaut testing requirements, but here Funk was, a "long-legged youngster" who might just become the first woman in space.

Cobb did her best to make the experience fun, even decorating her guest bedroom with a space theme. She bought spaceship bedspreads, hung charts of the solar system, and papered the ceiling with stars. She made a banner for

Clockwise from top: Rhea Hurrle, Jerrie Cobb, Wally Funk.

one wall that read, "Have Urge, Will Orbit." Though the women were friendly, they also felt competitive with one another. After all, nobody knew how many women—if any at all—would be allowed to pilot a spaceflight.

The women spent long days at the medical clinic staring at inkblots and answering probing questions. Funk, typically a quiet pilot, did her best to speak confidently and clearly during her many psychological interviews. She stood up when her doctors entered the room and gave firm, strong handshakes. Funk knew that her evaluation wasn't limited to her psychological fitness. Her interviewers wanted to see if she was likable, if she would do well on camera. Funk smiled broadly and laughed at their jokes. She wanted them to see she was exactly the astronaut they were looking for.

Even during their off time, the women didn't rest. They trained in Cobb's backyard. They did sit-ups and push-ups, and eyed one another's performance with equal parts jealousy and admiration.

When it was Hurrle's turn to take the isolation tank test, Cobb and Funk found themselves watching the clock, wondering how long she could possibly last. Cobb had blown everyone away by staying in it for nine hours and forty minutes. It was a record-shattering performance. Hurrle stayed in the water for ten hours. Just a few days later, Funk beat them both with a time of ten hours and thirty minutes.

At the end of Hurrle and Funk's Phase II tests, their performances were assessed. The physician in charge gave them the same endorsement he'd given Cobb. They had "much to recommend them for selection as astronaut candidates." Privately, he told Cobb: "You three share a common characteristic. You are all strong, silent women."

Hurrle, Funk, and Cobb were stoic. They were professional. They would do just about anything for the chance to be part of Project Mercury. In comparison, the Mercury 7 were complaining about their jobs and fighting among themselves. Alan Shepard was clamoring onto nightclub stages, drunkenly giggling racist jokes into the microphones. The contrast was stark. And so far, the tests supported the women's ambitions. They were doing well. Maybe the women could become astronauts after all. It sure looked like they'd do a better job handling the pressure than the men.

After their tests in Oklahoma, Funk and Hurrle flew back to their homes and jobs and began preparing for their upcoming trip to Pensacola. The other women did the same. They bought plane tickets to Florida, packed their bags, and scheduled nannies and babysitters. Several scrambled to get the time off from their jobs.

Sarah Gorelick couldn't convince her employers to give her the time off. It presented a tricky problem for the talented engineer. Should Gorelick stay home and keep her job, or pursue her dreams of spaceflight? Gorelick quit. On September 7, 1961, her coworkers threw her a space-themed going-away party. A photo of the event shows the ambitious pilot beaming while wearing a space helmet with "S. Gorelick" printed across the forehead. Gorelick's head was in the clouds that day. She wasn't worried about the risks she might face as an astronaut. Rather, she focused on the adventures that awaited just ahead: jet flight! And then, maybe even *spaceflight*!

Gene Nora Stumbough worked as a university flight instructor. The tests in Pensacola would take her away from her students during the first two weeks of the fall semester. Her boss didn't want to fool around with losing this valuable instruction time, and so Stumbough was forced to quit as well.

Irene Leverton was working as an air taxi pilot when she got the news that the Pensacola tests were imminent. Her boss had punished her for taking time off for the first round of tests by demoting her to a lower position. When she told him about the next stage of tests, he moved to demote her further. Leverton quit.

It was a major risk, but the women who passed Dr. Lovelace's tests were ready to sacrifice it all for a chance at becoming astronauts. Jerri Sloan lost her marriage. Stumbough, Gorelick, and Leverton were out of work. And Jerrie Cobb, the group's most feverish cheerleader, began to sense that something wasn't right. It had been more than four months since she had mailed NASA her plans for

Sarah Gorelick (bottom left) smiles at her going-away party, September 7, 1961.

women in space, and nobody had responded yet. Then there was another issue: NASA still hadn't paid Cobb.

What Cobb didn't know was that the women's upcoming astronaut tests had raised red flags at a few key organizations. People from the navy, NASA, and the Pentagon were discussing the Pensacola tests with a mix of curiosity and disdain.

Up until this point, Lovelace's testing had been fairly low-key. The women's testing had been staggered and squeezed in where administrators could make it work. This made it look informal, nonthreatening. It was also privately funded by Cochran. Now Lovelace was preparing to bring a whole crew of women into a naval facility for testing on sophisticated aerospace equipment.

In order for the navy to proceed with the women's testing, they needed NASA to provide something called a requirement. It was essentially a permission slip that allowed the navy to spend government money on a project. Though Cochran was paying for the women's travel expenses, the testing still used naval equipment and personnel, which the government had to pay for.

So, the navy requested NASA's requirement. The agency swiftly declined.

Lovelace called Cobb to tell her the news. "Jerrie, I just had a call from Pensacola. The testing is off."

Cobb's heart sank. The phone line was silent for several seconds. Finally, she mumbled, "What happened?"

"I'm afraid that's all I know," he responded. He was just as stunned as she was.

On September 12, 1961, thirteen women received a telegram from Dr. Lovelace:

"Regret to advise arrangements at Pensacola cancelled

Probably will not be possible to carry out this part of program . . ."

Cobb couldn't believe it. She wouldn't. She flew to Washington, D.C., and began talking to anyone who would listen. She begged her case to NASA leaders, U.S. Navy brass, and politicians. She wrote a letter to the other women, whom she called FLATS (Fellow Lady Astronaut Trainees), and kept them informed: "I have talked to everyone from the janitor to [Administrator] Webb at NASA." Unfortunately, their responses were mostly the same: Women can't meet the jet test pilot requirements. Cobb was infuriated. She told the FLATS that it was "unfair discrimination."

Five months after the tests were canceled, Cobb met with Jackie Cochran. The meeting should have been a cordial affair. After all, both women were after the same goal of advancing women in space. Cobb wanted to be an astronaut. Cochran was bankrolling the women's astronaut tests. However, it was an icy encounter. Cochran didn't like how much of a star Jerrie had become. The aging pilot and entrepreneur had spent decades in the spotlight, alone. That was the way she liked it.

Cobb didn't know it yet, but Cochran was planning a bold move. She was about to change the future of female astronautics.

CHAPTER 18

RACE TO THE FINISH

Jerrie Cobb's heart thumped in her chest as the countdown progressed.

T-minus ten seconds. Counting. Eight, seven, six, five, four...

Enormous rocket engines sixty-five feet below the space capsule rumbled to life. A teeth-clanking jolt rocked the capsule. The hold-down clamps must have released. These tethered the rocket to Earth as its power built. They separated just before liftoff. The rumbling grew louder. This was it.

Three, two, one, zero. Liftoff!

The ground around Cape Canaveral shook and crowds of spectators on the nearby beaches gasped. A giant cloud of smoke erupted around the launchpad as the Atlas rocket heaved mightily away from the ground. A plume of fire trailed just behind it, the flames licking the Earth in a white-hot blaze.

Scott Carpenter wished the astronaut good luck over his headset radio: "Godspeed, John Glenn." It was February

20, 1962, and the third Mercury capsule, *Friendship 7*, was on its way to orbit the Earth

Cobb watched the launch from NASA's elite viewing platform along with some of the best minds in rocketry. She wasn't there as an astronaut candidate. No one at NASA was going to call her that. But she was there as an official observer for the National Aeronautic Association, a historic and well-respected aviation organization. She was also there as a friend of Wernher von Braun, that rocket scientist Alan Shepard had angrily cornered a year earlier.

Jerrie's heart ached that day. She said a silent prayer for Glenn's success. At the same time, she deeply, painfully wished she could be in his place.

Glenn remained calm as his capsule ripped through the heavens. Five minutes into the mission, his cool demeanor cracked. He reported, "Zero G and I feel fine." There was joy in his voice. That unflappable marine test pilot was, well, having fun.

Glenn's body gently lifted away from his seat. His limbs floated effortlessly. Tiny specks of dust swam across his cockpit. Loose straps and buckles on his space suit waved lazily. Glenn grasped his control stick and turned the capsule so that he could see Earth below. The astronaut's voice sounded over the radio again, this time rich with satisfaction: "Oh, that view is tremendous."

Friendship 7 included a small window directly above Glenn's head. The astronaut couldn't really move around to stare out the window the way he might have wanted to. His bulky space suit and restraint straps kept him firmly

John Glenn looks at *Friendship 7*'s control panel during his mission, February 20, 1962.

in his seat. All he could manage was to lift his eyes to take in the sights. But that was enough. What he could see was extraordinary. Earth curved away in a graceful, hazy arc. It was a blue-and-green-and-brown marble covered with swirling white clouds. Above it was the darkest night, the blackest ink. White stars pierced the velvety expanse.

About 100 miles up, Glenn entered Earth's orbit, making him the first American to achieve such a feat. The mood in Cape Canaveral was ecstatic. Men exchanged great, back-slapping hugs of relief. America had done it! Their man was in orbit! In the middle of the celebration was the quiet, blonde, overlooked Cobb. She was an island of envy in an ocean of celebration. She was a reject. A loser. Why hadn't it been her?

Meanwhile, things were about to get even better for Glenn. He had always loved sunsets and sunrises. He said he "mentally collected them, as an art collector remembers visits to a gallery full of Picassos, Michelangelos, or Rembrandts." Their stunning colors made him think of his Christian faith and miracles and the mysteries of existence.

Forty minutes into his mission, Glenn watched his first sunset from space. He felt overcome with emotion at the sight. In his later years, he would struggle to describe its beauty: "The sun was fully round and as white as a brilliant arc light, and then it swiftly disappeared and seemed to melt into a long thin line of rainbow-brilliant radiance along the curve of the horizon."

He sailed through the deep dark, and then, just thirty-four minutes later, Glenn remarked: "I can see brilliant blue horizon coming up behind me; approaching sunrise. Over." Orbiting at 17,500 miles per hour made the sun rise and set about eighteen times faster than it would on Earth. A voice over Glenn's radio responded, "Roger, *Friendship 7*. You are very lucky."

"You're right," Glenn said. "Man, this is beautiful."

After two hours of successful flight, a suspicious message came across Glenn's radio. "You haven't heard any banging noises or anything of this type . . . ?"

"Negative," Glenn answered, absently wondering what

that might be about. The astronaut was happy. Things were going pretty darned well up there. What Glenn didn't know was that on the ground, a cluster of men in mission control had just realized that their pilot might not make it home.

A few minutes earlier, a systems controller noticed a blinking light on his console. Officially, the light alerted him to a "Segment 51," but few others in the room knew what that meant. He had to explain it to them: "It's saying that the landing bag deployed."

Men around the room exchanged puzzled looks. *What?*

Friendship 7's landing bag was a large, inner tube–shaped device that sat just under the heat shield. It was meant to pop open just before splashdown. It softened the landing so that the capsule wasn't damaged by slamming into the water. It also made the landing more bearable for the astronaut inside. The landing bag was an important component of the *Freedom 7*, but it definitely shouldn't have popped open in orbit.

Glenn's limited view out the window wouldn't allow him to check for the bag. Engineers on the ground couldn't tell if their warning light was accurate. It was possible that it was just a glitch and that the landing bag was safely stowed, just as it should be. But no one knew.

Men in mission control instantly started discussing the problem. Alan Shepard thought it was a wonky signal. The bag was probably stowed. Others didn't agree. If the landing bag *had* deployed, then the heat shield had come unlatched from its proper position. If this was the case, Glenn was toast.

The mission was over. That heat shield was crucial to a successful reentry. If it wasn't locked into place, Glenn and his ship would burn up as they tore through the atmosphere in the last few minutes of the flight.

Nobody in mission control wanted to tell Glenn about the warning light yet. There was no sense in scaring the socks off the man with something he couldn't control. No, it was best to wait and see if they could figure things out on the ground first. Then they'd tell him.

For the next two hours, engineers anxiously tried to solve the problem. Had some wire gone screwy? It was certainly possible. The *Friendship 7* was crammed full of 750,000 parts and a mind-blowing seven miles of electrical wiring. Maybe something was causing an incorrect signal. Maybe that Segment 51 warning light was wrong. For probably the first time in its short history, mission control was full to the brim with men who were praying for an electrical mistake in their capsule. Unfortunately, there wasn't much the ground crews could do to know for sure.

Finally, four hours and twenty minutes into the mission, it was time to tell Glenn. Gordon Cooper's voice crackled onto the radio and he reported the news in his calm, twanging drawl: The guys down in mission control had a glowing landing bag warning light, but he reassured Glenn, "We suspect this is an erroneous signal." All the same, he told Glenn that the ground crew wanted him to flip the landing bag switch inside the cockpit to see if a light came on. If it did, then they'd have some answers.

Glenn was silent for a few seconds. Finally, he grunted, "Uh, okay, if that's what they recommend, we'll go ahead and try it."

Glenn knew his capsule like the back of his hand. He understood the magnitude of this situation right away. If his landing bag had deployed, then his heat shield wasn't latched. If his heat shield wasn't latched, he was about to become a fireball. His test pilot instincts took over. He had a mission to complete. There was no room for fear or worry. It was time to grip and rip.

He flipped the switch. No light. No answers. Gordo responded, "Roger, that's fine. In this case, we'll go ahead, and the reentry sequence will be normal." But Glenn understood. The guys on the ground weren't sure if his heat shield would stay on. His reentry might be anything but normal.

Scott Carpenter called Glenn's wife, Annie. She was at home, watching the television news coverage of the mission in her living room. Carpenter wanted to be the one to tell her. He couldn't bear it if she found out from the news: John might not survive.

Unlike the Soviets, who kept the details of their spaceflights secret until after they occurred, NASA allowed the press extraordinary access to information before, during, and after each of its missions. It was all part of the hot-and-cold American love affair with their astronauts. The public celebrated space missions as though they were sporting events. They rooted feverishly for success, and despaired at any signs of trouble.

The agency encouraged this enthusiastic fandom. In fact, NASA even allowed the press to set up camp just outside of the Atlas launch complex. This meant that someone from the launch team had only to walk a few paces from his desk to find himself in the glare of dozens of news cameras and spotlights. This setup made it convenient and easy to keep the American public updated. Unfortunately, Glenn's mission required quite the update.

Word spread from the press pool in Florida to newsrooms around the nation. NASA spokesperson Shorty Powers broke the news to television and radio audiences: John Glenn might be in trouble.

Glenn had rehearsed for his mission countless times. He knew exactly what to expect. When he was ready to leave his orbit and reenter Earth's atmosphere, a set of rockets that were strapped over his heat shield would fire. These would slow him down enough to make his capsule fall out of orbit and toward Earth. Then the straps holding the rockets to the capsule would be released, and he would begin his burning, blazing trip home.

Men on the ground had decided that if Glenn's heat shield *was* loose, then they'd just have him keep the empty rockets and straps in place. Maybe, they hoped, the flimsy straps would hold the heat shield on for a few extra seconds of reentry.

Not everyone agreed on this. Chris Kraft, the mission's flight director, thought it was a death sentence for Glenn. If any of the rockets contained any leftover fuel, the heat of reentry would turn them into deadly explosive bombs. Bombs that were *strapped* to Glenn's ship. It was insanity! But no one could come up with a better idea, and so they went with it.

Mission control told Glenn the plan. It was almost funny, all these months of meticulous work, testing and retesting and testing again. And now they were just going to see what happened if they left the straps in place. *Let's try it. Why not?*

"Roger," Glenn responded soberly. "Understand." His rockets fired and *Friendship 7* began plummeting toward Earth. Glenn's eyes flicked up to the window for one last glance at the stars.

As it ripped through Earth's atmosphere, temperatures built up against the capsule's heat shield. The rocket straps caught fire. Glenn stared out his window and watched a flaming strap slap wildly against the capsule before breaking loose and flying off. Orange flames wrapped around the capsule. The inside of the cockpit glowed red, then yellow.

Glenn waited for the heat. It would hit his back first, then in an instant, the flames would be everywhere. His spine tingled. His mind raced: *Is that it? Do I feel it?*

Glenn never felt the heat. *Friendship 7* made it through the atmosphere, and the landing bag deployed right on time. As planned. He splashed down safely in the Atlantic. When he hit the button to blow open the hatch on his capsule, it recoiled and hit his hand. This resulted in Glenn's only injury from his mission: a set of scraped knuckles.

Forty million Americans tuned in to watch Glenn's mission. They spent the four hours and fifty-six minutes of his flight watching and cheering and then praying and fretting as newscasters reported on the landing bag danger. They pleaded for his safety. *Oh please, oh please.*

Americans could hardly contain their joy at his safe return. President Kennedy and Vice President Johnson flew in to congratulate Glenn. Two thousand partygoers ate a giant cake shaped like the *Friendship 7* at a celebration in Cape Canaveral. On March 1, 1962, four million New Yorkers showed up at a parade in his honor, where 3,500 tons of paper streamers were thrown into the air. The nation wrapped Glenn in a delighted embrace. Mercury 7's latest hero.

Over at NASA, the celebrations didn't last long. Engineers were soon back to work planning the next mission and working toward Kennedy's goal of getting a human to the Moon by 1970.

And of course, everyone at the agency still had to handle this pesky business of the Space Race. Rumors circulated that the Soviets were planning to launch a woman soon. This would represent the next step in their space supremacy. They would send the first man *and* woman into space. A Soviet air force general even announced that "Under no circumstances should an American become the first woman in space."

One month after Glenn's mission, five female cosmonauts began training for spaceflight in the Soviet Union.

Cobb, still chewing on the best way to change NASA's unfair policies, feared that the Soviets would succeed in their mission. She wrote a letter to the agency urging it to consider women astronauts once more: "The public interest

John and Annie Glenn ride with Vice President Johnson in the backseat of a convertible during their ticker tape parade in New York City, March 1, 1962.

in putting a woman in space is overwhelming—no other space achievement at this time would attract more admiration and respect throughout the world. Russia will not delay in their eagerness to reap this acclaim—but let us not wait for their challenge!"

She went on, suggesting that the agency send a "qualified, tested and capable woman" into space, "thereby earning the world's admiration and respect for the United States . . ." Cobb was so desperate to go to space that she was willing to use the tiresome, sexist idea that had plagued women pilots for decades. She reminded the agency that a woman's flight would "prove the safety, dependability and simplicity of our spacecraft systems. If a woman can do it—it *must* be safe and simple!"

Cobb proposed that NASA begin training a woman pilot on the Mercury procedures trainer, and then, just as soon as she was ready, pop her into the next Mercury mission. Why not? But there were countless reasons this plan wouldn't work. The Mercury 7 had trained for months for their flights. They had whole teams of engineers backing them up that knew exactly how they acted, what they liked, and how they responded to crises. Their space suits were custom fitted. Their seats were precisely sculpted to fit their bodies. Every mission was expertly planned for individual astronauts. A new player couldn't just be thrown into the mix. And NASA had already scheduled the remaining flights. How would Gordon Cooper respond if he was sidelined so a *girl* could take his place? Nobody wanted to even speculate about that.

Plus, everyone over at NASA was just too busy to mess with the idea of women astronauts. After Project Mercury would come Gemini, a series of two-man flights. Then it would be time for Project Apollo, the three-man ships that would hopefully go all the way to the Moon.

Contrary to what Cobb had written to NASA, most Americans didn't really care about female astronauts. Gender equality was still two years from becoming a major part of the national conversation. Few people troubled themselves with the issue of getting American women in space. Cobb's astronaut dreams were an interesting news story, a topic for dinnertime conversation. Nothing more. Most people didn't take her seriously.

Dr. Lovelace had a subdued response to the Pensacola cancellation. He wrote a single, politely worded letter to NASA, explaining his project and its importance. And then he fell strangely quiet on the matter. This would have been the perfect time for him to chime in. The Soviets were hot on their tails! It's time for an American woman in space! But Lovelace knew that people at NASA weren't interested in his pet project. He was earning more influence at NASA and, perhaps out of a desire to stay involved at the agency, he didn't push the issue.

Around this time, NASA introduced a new message to the American public. It wasn't about a Space *Race* anymore. The Americans weren't in competition with anyone, not even the Soviets. Now the agency was interested in progress just for the sake of progress. This new line took the heat off of NASA to match each of the Soviets' advances.

This was especially handy because NASA *couldn't* match everything the Soviets had done without falling behind on their own goal of going to the Moon. And this message made the United States sound civilized, mature, and unbothered by any potential competitors.

Of course, not everyone was satisfied with this new stance. Some Americans still wanted to see their country match the Soviets in a punch-for-punch fight to the finish. But NASA had a plan, and it was sticking to it. First Mercury, then Gemini, then Apollo. Women need not apply.

On May 24, 1962, NASA inched forward with its plan. Scott Carpenter launched on board the fourth Mercury capsule, *Aurora 7*. His mission, which was intended to mimic Glenn's, was riddled with errors and mishaps. Carpenter got distracted in space. He used too much fuel and ignored directions from mission control. He fired his reentry rockets late, which caused him to splash down a laughable 250 miles off target. It took rescue crews an hour to get to him, and when they finally arrived on the scene, they found Carpenter lounging in a life raft near his bobbing capsule. The astronaut was eating a candy bar.

Carpenter's first post-mission words to a reporter were, "I didn't know where I was, and [NASA] didn't either." The agency was furious. NASA knew exactly where Carpenter had splashed down. It just took them a while to get to the dingbat.

"Shut this guy up!" yelled James Webb, the agency's administrator. Still, through gritted teeth, he reminded everyone of NASA's official stance on each of their astronauts: "He's a hero and that's what we're telling the world."

And so, NASA cleaned up Carpenter's story. They coached him on how to discuss his sloppy flight. He was to explain that he'd had some equipment problems but that the experts on the ground had brought him down safely. His job now was to convince the world that his mission marked another triumph for NASA. It worked. Most Americans bought his story. They welcomed him into the tiny and elite fraternity of space heroes.

But NASA knew the truth. They'd given Carpenter the chance of a lifetime, the opportunity thirteen women pilots were dying to have, and he'd blown it.

Scott Carpenter never flew in space again.

Scott Carpenter poses for a photograph in his space suit.

CHAPTER 19

THE FIGHT GOES TO WASHINGTON

I n the spring of 1962, just after John Glenn's historic Earth orbit, Jerrie Cobb's hardscrabble fight to get an American woman into space finally became a matter of national interest. What had begun as a quiet research question— would women make good astronauts?—had transformed into something bigger, something more important. And now, two years into the project, Americans were becoming legitimately curious as well. They scratched their heads in earnest wonder: *Well,* should *a woman be next in space?*

Americans were intrigued by the issue because Cobb had, in a fit of desperation, or determination, or both, embarked upon a media blitz. No longer content to wait for NASA to come around to the idea, she realized her only option was to force the agency into a decision.

Cobb teamed up with another test subject, Janey Hart, whose political connections and experience lent the duo an air of credibility. The two met with scores of reporters. They argued that women deserved a chance in space. They reminded the journalists of their skills as aviators.

They discussed their performance in their astronaut tests. But the women didn't stop there. They also attacked NASA. They claimed the space agency didn't take women candidates seriously.

Hart wrote to politicians arguing that NASA was discriminating against women. She pointed to the agency's requirements that astronauts must have experience as military test pilots and in jet flight. She reminded her readers that these requirements were impossible for women to meet.

In March 1962, the women's work paid off. They found themselves sitting across the desk from none other than the vice president of the United States, Lyndon B. Johnson. He was the head of President Kennedy's Space Council. If they could get Johnson on their side, well, then maybe NASA would pay attention.

Johnson politely listened to the women's appeal. Cobb repeated the message she'd already delivered in public countless times before: Women weighed less, they ate less, they breathed less. They were easier and more accommodating space travelers. It just made sense to send them into space. Hart took a different approach. She argued that women wanted access to a full spectrum of careers, not just the same old jobs their mothers and grandmothers had worked. She said NASA was discriminating against women by not giving them the chance to become astronauts.

Hart's arguments were savvy. The same day that Glenn had orbited Earth, President Kennedy announced a Commission on the Status of Women. It would investigate discrimination based on gender. Kennedy said that "women are entitled to equality of opportunity for employment in Government and in industry." He urged the nation to "take steps to see that the doors are really open for training, selection, advancement and equal pay" for women.

The vice president leaned back in his chair and appeared to consider the women's arguments. He told them he liked women pilots. Really, he did. But this was a tricky subject. The government was getting pressured to allow minorities into NASA, too. If he opened the door for women astronauts, a flood of applications would come pouring in from Black, Chinese, and Mexican astronaut hopefuls. Cobb and Hart asked why that would be a problem. Johnson changed the subject.

Both women urged Johnson to consider the Soviet threat. The Soviets were going to send a woman into space soon. Americans couldn't let them accomplish this feat first. Johnson sighed. The issue was out of his hands, he told them. This was really a decision for NASA to make, not the vice president. He then picked up his phone, signaling the end of the meeting.

Johnson's secretary was on Cobb and Hart's side. Just before their meeting, she neatly typed up a letter for Johnson and placed it on his desk. It was addressed to NASA's administrator, James Webb, and it politely questioned whether the agency had a reason to keep women out of their astronaut corps. It didn't demand action from NASA. It simply gave a gentle nudge. Consider women, it urged. Just give them a chance. The letter was *right there*. Johnson just needed to sign it.

After Cobb and Hart left his office, Johnson did indeed write something along the signature line of the letter. His secretary would later read his scrawled message to her: "Let's stop this now!" She never mailed it.

What Cobb and Hart didn't understand was that their mission was being steadily undercut by a woman who should have been their ally: Jackie Cochran. The very woman who had funded their testing was now sabotaging their chances at going to space.

Cochran had begun quietly but effectively campaigning against Cobb and the twelve other women who passed their tests at the Lovelace Clinic. Her powerful connections to politicians in Washington, D.C., and military leaders made her opinions important. Men listened to Cochran.

One man listened to Cochran with particular interest: the vice president. Fourteen years earlier, in May 1948, Cochran saved Lyndon B. Johnson's life. He was in Dallas, campaigning for the Senate, when a kidney stone brought him to his knees. Pneumonia followed. Suddenly, it looked as though the promising young politician was at death's door.

Cochran knew a doctor at the Mayo Clinic in Minnesota who performed a treatment that could save Johnson's life. She whisked the dying man out of his hospital room and into her plane. He soon passed out from pain and exhaustion. Cochran roared down the runway and took to the skies.

Somewhere over America's heartland, a howl pierced the silence inside Cochran's airplane. She switched on the plane's autopilot and raced back to see Johnson struggling to stand. Sweat poured from his face. The man was out of his mind from pain and sickness. Cochran stood there, taking in the scene for a moment. She sure hoped her plane's autopilot worked.

Cochran hurried to Johnson and attempted to hold him steady as she injected him with a painkiller. He began to retch. Cochran tried, with little success, to catch his vomit in a pan. When his gagging passed, she wrapped him in blankets and gingerly helped him lie back down. Years later, she would recall the story with a laugh: "I may be one of the few women in the world to have been vomited on by a future president of the United States."

Cochran got Johnson to the Mayo Clinic, and his treatments there saved his life. Her quick thinking and ability to fly had made all the difference. The two became close friends.

Right around the time when Cobb and Hart sat across from the vice president, asking for his help in moving their astronaut testing program forward, he received a letter from his good pal Cochran. Interestingly, the letter was not addressed to him. It was addressed to Jerrie Cobb. Cochran had written the letter for Cobb, but then made several copies of it. She shrewdly sent these out to many important men involved in the space program. This strategy gave her a wide audience. It also put her in a position of power. Recipients of her letters might wonder: *Who else is reading this?*

Cochran's letter was ruthless. It stated that NASA

shouldn't waste its resources to try to beat a Soviet with the first woman in space. It warned that a "hastily prepared flight by a less than completely trained woman could backfire." It also reminded Cobb (and all the other intended readers) of the historic role women had held in aviation: "Women for one reason or another have always come into each phase of aviation a little behind their brothers. They should, I believe, accept this delay and not get into the hair of the public authorities about it."

Cobb and Hart ignored Cochran's letter and continued fighting. They kept their story in the press. They wanted the world to know that a group of talented aviators was being denied the chance to become the first women in space. Their voices were loud and grating and, in the end, effective. The House of Representatives' Committee on Science and Astronautics agreed to hold a special hearing to determine whether NASA was discriminating against women in July 1962.

NASA got all of its money from Congress. If this special hearing determined that NASA was, in fact, discriminating against women, then the agency might be forced to change its policies or face losing its financial support. The American space program was incredibly expensive. NASA needed D.C. on its side.

The special hearing would proceed a little like a court case. Experts would testify on both sides of the issue, arguing that NASA was or was not discriminating against women. Then a committee would make a decision.

Cobb would testify. So would Hart, Cochran, and a handful of people from NASA, including John Glenn and Scott Carpenter. Dr. Lovelace was not invited. His absence was significant but hard to explain. Some think he might have been overlooked. Others suspect he wanted to stay out of the limelight in case the trial hurt his career at NASA. Whatever the reason for his omission, it had a significant impact. The women's primary champion, the man behind it all, wouldn't be there to show his support.

The weeks leading up to the special hearing were a flurry of activity. A recent development seemed to favor the women's cause. In April 1962, NASA had issued a call for a new class of astronauts. It needed ten to fifteen more pilots. And that wasn't all. It had officially dropped the requirement that they come from the military. The women were one step closer!

Jackie Cochran prepared to testify by putting her thoughts to paper. She wrote down what she planned to say during the hearing and, just days beforehand, she mailed it out to people at NASA, the air force, the navy, and to Lovelace. She wanted everyone to know exactly how she felt.

On July 17, 1962, the hearing began. Cobb testified first, repeating her arguments about the scientific reasons women should go into space. Then, for the first time, she made public the full list of women who had passed their Phase I astronaut tests. Up until now, Cobb and Lovelace had kept the list closely guarded. Now it was time to let the world meet the rest of the women.

JAN AND MARION DIETRICH

Single | both 35 years old | 5' 3" | 103 pounds
Jan worked as a pilot for a large company and had 8,000
flying hours. Marion was a pilot and aviation journalist with
1,500 hours.

RHEA HURRLE

Married | 31 years old | 5' 7" | 120 pounds
Worked as an executive pilot and had 1,500 flight hours.

IRENE LEVERTON

Single | 35 years old | 5' 8" | 145 pounds
Worked as an executive pilot and had 9,000+ hours.

BEA STEADMAN

Married | 36 years old | 5' 7" | 140 pounds
Owned and operated an aviation service and had
8,000+ hours.

JEAN HIXSON

Single | 38 years old | 5' 4" | 125 pounds
Schoolteacher, Air Force Reserves captain,
and pilot with 4,500 flight hours.

GENE NORA STUMBOUGH

Single | 25 years old | 5' 7" | 120 pounds
Professional pilot with aircraft company with 1,450 flight hours.

JERRI SLOAN

Divorced | 31 years old | 5' 3" | 103 pounds
Owned an aviation company and had 1,200+ flight hours.

MYRTLE CAGLE

Married | 36 years old | 5' 2" | 110 pounds
Pilot and mechanic with 4,300 flying hours.

SARAH GORELICK

Single | 28 years old | 5' 5" | 130 pounds
Engineer and pilot with 1,800 flight hours.

WALLY FUNK

Single | 23 years old | 5' 8" | 125 pounds
Flight instructor with 3,000 hours.

Cobb reminded the committee, "There were women on the *Mayflower* and on the first wagon trains west, working alongside the men to forge new trails to new vistas." Then she implored, "We ask that opportunity in the pioneering of space."

When questioned about the requirement for astronauts to have jet test experience, Cobb explained that she did not think it was necessary. She felt that years of flying prop aircraft offered the women in the group equivalent experience. "What counts is flawless judgment, fast reaction, and the ability to transmit that to the proper control of the craft. We would not have flown all these years, accumulating thousands and thousands of hours in all types of aircraft without accumulating this experience. This experience is the same as acquired in jet test piloting," she said.

After Cobb, Hart testified. Her speech was passionate, angry, and forceful. She told the committee, "It is inconceivable to me that the world of outer space should be restricted to men only, like some sort of stag club." Then she continued with her most important point: "I'm not arguing that women be admitted to space merely

Jerrie Cobb (left) and Janey Hart testify at the U.S. House of Representatives, July 17, 1962.

so that they won't feel discriminated against. I'm arguing that they be admitted because they have a real contribution to make." Hart went on to say that women deserved a chance to try out new careers outside of the home. "If girls elect to be homemakers, excellent," she acknowledged. But then she quipped, "Let's face it: For many women, the PTA just is not enough."

Hart's testimony struck a chord. Committee members nodded and scratched down notes.

Suddenly, in burst Jackie Cochran. Jaws dropped as the blonde dynamo marched into the room. A brief recess was called so that Cochran could get settled and everyone could take a break before continuing.

When the hearing reconvened, it was Cochran's turn to testify. After briefly introducing herself, she launched into an all-out assault on Cobb and Hart's arguments. In fact, Cochran did *not* support their effort to be tested as astronaut candidates.

Cochran proposed a new, more in-depth, larger study of women as astronaut candidates. She thought Dr. Lovelace's group was too small and selective. She claimed that large numbers of women would drop out of the program when they got married or had children. Cochran wanted to see hundreds of women tested to better absorb these losses. She thought a larger group would also ensure that whatever findings came from the research, they represented the female gender accurately. Cochran even suggested that she might have the perfect person to run this new program: herself. After this revised and enlarged testing program had been completed, Cochran acknowledged, women *might* be considered for spaceflight.

Jackie Cochran wasn't worried about a Soviet woman getting into space before an American. She said it would be better to follow the Soviets than to have American women "fall flat on their faces" trying to be first when they simply weren't ready.

Her testimony was a gut punch. Cobb and Hart reeled. *What?* But the damage had been done. Her thoughts were already familiar to many of the people in the room. She'd mailed them out in advance.

Cochran's arguments were attractive to NASA. She wasn't ruling out women astronauts. She was just advising everyone to slow down. Wait till Project Mercury was done and dusted. Let the men go first, then, when everyone is good and ready, maybe women can follow. By adhering to Cochran's plan, NASA could sidestep accusations that it was discriminating against women. The agency wasn't saying no women. It was just saying no women *yet*. Things only got worse for Hart and Cobb from there.

After Cochran, a NASA official took the stand. He argued that the agency's jet flight and test flight requirements were, in fact, necessary. Their astronauts needed to be professional aviators who could think on their toes, and test flight and jet flight were two excellent ways to hone those skills. He also claimed that NASA was not discriminating against women. If any women could meet the test flight and jet flight requirements, he said he'd happily welcome them aboard. Of course, this statement dodged the issue at hand. Women could not meet those requirements.

He went on to say that even if the agency did decide to open up its requirements further to allow women into the program, they weren't needed. NASA only planned for "perhaps 40 or 50 space pilots" in the "near future," and they already had a large pool of test pilots who matched the requirements. Adding women into the mix would simply take time and resources away from a project that was already working at full bore.

The second day of the hearing brought the real stars: the astronauts. Glenn and Carpenter were both asked about NASA's astronaut requirements. In addition to jet flight and test flight, the agency also wanted its astronauts to have college engineering degrees or the equivalent. Neither Glenn nor Carpenter had their diploma when they joined Project Mercury. This made it clear that the agency had bent the rules for the right candidates. Their lack of actual degrees had been overshadowed by their aviation skills. Nobody cared that they hadn't finished college. They were the best!

Glenn spoke at length that day. He did not argue against prejudice against women. Rather, he simply commented on *why* he thought it existed. He said it had to do with "the way our social order is organized . . . It is just a fact. The men go off and fight the wars and fly the airplanes and come back and help design and build and test them. The fact that women are not in the field is a fact of our social order."

Perhaps sensing that his statement might ruffle some feathers, Glenn added a quick thought: "It may be undesirable."

The astronauts were asked if they thought the women's thousands of flight hours gave them enough experience in aircraft to roughly equal their own jet test experience. Glenn said no. He said he didn't care "how many thousands of hours" a person had in a "light plane or transports." ". . . It is just not the same type of flying." Carpenter agreed: "A person can't enter a backstroke swimming race and by swimming twice the distance in a crawl, qualify as a backstroker."

Glenn then noted that the fact that thirteen women had passed Dr. Lovelace's medical tests didn't mean they were suddenly ready to become astronauts. He said "the tests mainly are run to see if there is anything wrong with a person physically . . . A real crude analogy might be: We have the Washington Redskins football team. My mother could probably pass the physical exam they give preseason for the Redskins, but I doubt if she could play too many games for them."

This argument ignored all the work the women had done before their tests to become some of the nation's most accomplished aviators. They weren't a bunch of old ladies trying to play football. They were a group of pilots who wanted admission into the highest level of American aviation: astronautics.

Glenn and Carpenter were fawned over during the hearings. One committee member even gushed, "We as Americans are very proud of you and the wonderful job you have done." He went on, noting that Glenn had been a "stellar" witness. The special hearing committee was utterly swayed by their two star witnesses. Hart and Cobb didn't stand a chance.

More men from NASA testified. They discussed jets, space capsules, and the possibility that the agency might consider a parallel program for women somewhere down the line. Everyone seemed to agree, though, that the country shouldn't do anything to slow NASA in its hurried dash to the Moon. And diverting funds and resources to women astronauts would most certainly throw a wrench in the agency's work.

Glenn emphasized that he was not "'anti' any particular group." He was simply "pro space" and wanted the very best people to become astronauts. He then noted that he still hadn't been convinced that it would be better to send a woman into space than a man. "The only thing we have seen thus far is women coming in space just by the very fact that they are women . . . to spend many millions of dollars to additionally qualify other people, whom we don't particularly need, regardless of sex, creed or color, doesn't seem right, when we already have these qualified people."

After Glenn finished his testimony, the committee chairman stood up with a few remarks. He congratulated the astronauts on their achievements and praised the committee for their hard work. Then, with a "thank you, gentlemen" and the bang of a gavel, the hearing adjourned.

Cobb and Hart stared at one another, baffled. That was it? The hearing was over? The two women quietly collected their things and shuffled out of the building. Holding their purses tightly, Cobb and Hart brushed past a crowd of congressmen. The politicians were eagerly waiting to catch a glimpse of Glenn and Carpenter.

In September 1962, NASA announced its second class of astronauts: the New Nine. They were all male test pilots. Two, Neil Armstrong and Elliot See, were civilians.

The following month, the Committee on Science and Astronautics issued its official recommendation in a written report. It said that NASA's astronaut selection program was "basically sound" and "should continue to be maintained." It also noted that an investigation of women astronauts could be considered at "some time in the future."

That was it. NASA wasn't going to let the women go to space anytime soon.

Jerrie Cobb refused to accept this. She wrote letters to politicians and people at NASA. She begged to speak with President Kennedy. She embarked upon a speaking tour where she criticized the space agency for being slow to act: "NASA says it has no need for women astronauts . . . With that kind of attitude, it's no wonder we're second in the Space Race." She also wondered aloud why she had been hired as a consultant in the first place. She told a crowd at the Air Force Association convention that she was "the most unconsulted consultant in any government agency today."

In December 1962, Cobb was fired as a special consultant to NASA. Six months later, the agency hired Jackie Cochran to replace her.

CHAPTER 20

OF COURSE, NO WOMEN

A mid the chaos of Cobb's visit to Congress, NASA was busily preparing Wally Schirra for his own Mercury launch. Schirra refused to fly his capsule, the *Sigma 7*, in "chimp mode." That was what he called it when the engineers on the ground preprogrammed everything for the astronauts. He thought it wasted fuel, but also, it didn't seem very fun.

When he launched on October 3, 1962—just as NASA was issuing its final statement on Cobb's appearance—the agency gave him the go-ahead to fly the capsule on his own. And he sure did. He turned the *Sigma 7* this way and that but made sure not to waste too much fuel in the process. He later said, "I fired my thrusters sparingly, in small bursts that I like to call micromouse farts." It worked. When he landed his ship in the Atlantic Ocean nine hours and thirteen minutes after launch, he still had more than half of his fuel left over. The previous Mercury capsules had used all or nearly all of their fuel.

After splashing down, Schirra waited for rescue helicopters to arrive and hoist his capsule to safety before blowing his hatch to exit. When he hit the button to pop his door open, the explosive blast injured his arm. This reminded him that John Glenn had also been injured when he'd hit the button to open his capsule door. It was a funny little badge of astronaut honor—a matching set of bonked arms.

Then something occurred to Schirra: Gus Grissom hadn't been injured when his hatch opened. Could that mean that he hadn't actually hit the button to blow the door open? That was how both Schirra and Glenn had been hurt. If Grissom didn't have an arm injury, then that had to clear his name. He couldn't have intentionally opened the door! Those stories of a panicked astronaut fleeing his hot and rocking capsule were baloney! Right?

He pleaded his case to NASA. The agency still couldn't know for sure what happened to Grissom's hatch, but many people were happy to believe Schirra's argument. It cleared Grissom's name and helped restore the reputation of a talented pilot.

Finally, on May 15, 1963, Gordo Cooper launched on board the final Mercury 7 mission: a thirty-four-hour, twenty-two-orbit flight on board *Faith 7* that very nearly ended in disaster. On his nineteenth orbit, Gordo's capsule suffered from what mission control called a "total power failure" and he'd been forced to fly it completely on his own, without the help of computer navigation. Luckily, his instincts kicked in and Gordo stayed calm, even managing to bring

A sweaty Gordon Cooper smiles at rescue crews following his thirty-four-hour flight on board *Faith 7*, May 16, 1963.

his capsule down impressively close to its target. Glenn told others Gordo had brought it in "right on the old gazoo." Gordo just grinned happily, a good ol' country boy happy to be back on his home turf.

Gordo's tense mission brought Project Mercury to a shaky close. The only member of the Mercury 7 who hadn't been up in space yet was Deke Slayton, but it wasn't looking good for old Deke. Doctors had discovered a defect in his heart and the man was grounded until they could decide what to do with him.

Exactly one month after Gordo splashed down, the Soviets launched their first woman into space. Valentina Tereshkova spent three days in outer space and orbited the Earth forty-eight times. She spent more time in space than all of the American crewed flights combined. After she landed, Soviet leader Nikita Khrushchev pointed to her and shouted to a crowd of admirers, "There is your weaker sex!" The Soviets had shown that they believed in women aviators. Did the United States?

Tereshkova was disdainful of the American attitude toward women pilots. Remarking on Jerrie Cobb's struggle to get women into space, she said, "I sincerely sympathize with her. She seems to be a daring and courageous woman. I am sorry that American leaders put her in such an awkward position. They shout about their democracy but declare they will not put a woman into space. Why, this is obvious inequality of rights."

Some feminist groups shared Tereshkova's criticisms and rallied in support of Cobb. Clare Booth Luce, a writer at *LIFE* magazine, penned a lengthy response to Tereshkova's flight and comments. She pointed a finger directly at the men at NASA and blamed them for being shortsighted. She quoted one agency employee who had even admitted that the idea of a woman astronaut made him "sick at [his] stomach." Booth didn't stop there. She went further, praising the Soviet Union for the way they included women in their space program. She said Tereshkova's flight "symbolizes to Russian women that they actively share (not passively bask, like American women) in the glory of conquering space."

Valentina Tereshkova, the first woman to fly in outer space, smiles happily for a photo 1963.

And then *LIFE* gave

the thirteen women pilots their due: a two-page spread, featuring each of their photos and qualifications. The women shone brightly in their grainy black-and-white pictures.

There it was, the magazine that padded the pockets of the Mercury 7, offering not just a scathing criticism of NASA's sexism but also a clear alternative. Thirteen willing, able, and enthusiastic pilots. Ready to launch.

NASA ignored these taunts and stayed focused on their plans to send men to the Moon. Then, tragically, in November 1963, President John F. Kennedy was assassinated in Dallas, Texas.

The nation wept.

Kennedy had represented such hope and promise and a sense of something new. In Kennedy, people saw a little something of the American dream. He was willing to chase greatness, no matter how impossible it might seem. In a 1962 speech, he had told the American public that "we choose to go to the Moon in this decade and do other things, not because they are easy, but because they are hard . . ." Kennedy had whipped Americans into a frothy mass of excitement and hope. His death hardened the nation's resolve to get to the Moon.

Meanwhile, the thirteen women did their best to return to life as it was before their astronaut testing. Some fared well, chalking it up to a frustrating loss. Others stumbled around in a daze of disappointment and confusion and mourning. They were embarrassed, too. Their testing, which had begun in a flurry of secrecy and seriousness, had evolved into something of a national joke. Newspapers ran cartoons making fun of the women. One, printed a year earlier, showed then–Vice President Johnson looking away as a space capsule, bedecked with curtains and flowers, whizzed by in the background.

People within NASA enjoyed a good laugh at the idea of women in space, too. Robert Voas, the astronaut training officer, gave a 1963 speech where he cracked several jokes about what would happen if the agency ever accepted female astronauts. He said that the agency could save weight on trips by asking female astronauts to leave their purses at home. He also joked that they could get away with fewer rations for female astronauts by telling them they looked fat before launch. That way, the women would be sure to diet in space.

The male astronauts seemed happy with the outcome of the Committee on Science and Astronautics' hearing. Gordo, fresh from his own mission, said "all this talk" of "dames in space is bunk." He just didn't think they belonged in the space program. "To date there have been no women—and I say absolutely zero women—who have qualified to take part in our space program." Like so many others at the agency, Gordo was satisfied with the agency's requirements of jet flight and test flight. Alan Shepard and Deke Slayton agreed. While discussing astronaut selection in a 1994 book, they noted those first requirements that were set out back in 1959: 1,500 flight hours, an engineering degree, jet flight, and test flight. Then they added, "And of course, no women, thank you."

For a group of women who had already overcome

countless obstacles—elbowing their way into flight lessons when few thought they could fly; cobbling together careers in the air when nobody wanted to pay them fairly; competing in air races, despite the common notion that they had no business in the cockpit in the first place; and performing well on a series of grueling astronaut tests—this was a hard pill to swallow.

They'd gotten their answer. They wouldn't be going to space.

CHAPTER 21

AFTER MERCURY

Project Mercury ended after Gordon Cooper's rocky flight. But the stories of the Mercury 7 did not. Their lives traced different paths across history, some long and fortunate, some short and tragic.

Gus Grissom didn't wallow in the shadow of his sunken space capsule for long. With Schirra's assurances about the hatch accident, NASA soon forgave the talented pilot and promised him more work on future missions. He flew on board *Gemini 3* in 1965, and soon after, quiet rumors began buzzing around the agency that Grissom would be the first man to walk on the Moon. But, in 1967, Grissom's life came to a fiery end. He and two other crew members, Ed White and Roger Chaffee, were killed during a practice launch when a spark caught inside their *Apollo 1* space capsule. The three men burned to death right there on the launchpad, while dozens of ground crew members sputtered and coughed and tried frantically to claw the capsule door open. Today, a plaque sits on the site of the *Apollo 1* disaster. It reads *"ad astra per aspera,"* Latin for "A rough road leads to the stars."

Gordon Cooper went back into space in 1965 on *Gemini 5*. His second space trip lasted 190 hours and 56 minutes and brought his total space time to 225 hours and 15 minutes. This was higher than the number held by any Soviet, and so it won a small victory for Americans in the Space Race. In his later years, Cooper retired from the air force and space agency and went into private business. He also wrote an autobiography in which he described his belief in UFOs, several of which he said he'd seen while flying planes. Cooper divorced his first wife, Trudy, and married Suzan Taylor in 1972. He died in 2004.

After Deke Slayton's heart condition took him out of the running for a Mercury mission, he stayed at NASA in different leadership roles. He supervised astronaut training and helped select space crews. But he never gave up on his dream. He wanted to fly in space. In 1971, Slayton's health improved, and he was allowed back in the astronaut corps. In 1975, he flew on board the *Apollo-Soyuz* mission, in which an American spacecraft docked with a Soviet spacecraft. It was a highly technical mission, but it was also symbolic. The two nations were finally ready to work together. The Space Race was over.

Slayton later retired from NASA and worked for Space Services, a privately funded American space company. In 1983, Slayton divorced his first wife, Margie. He married Bobbie Osborne later that year. Slayton died in 1993.

American and Soviet space crews float together during the *Apollo-Soyuz* mission.

Scott Carpenter's Mercury flight was his last space mission. But it was not his last exploration into the unknown. In 1965, he spent a month living 205 feet under the ocean as part of Project Sealab. This made him the first man to be both an astronaut and an aquanaut. After this, he returned to NASA and helped design underwater spacewalk training programs for future astronauts. He retired from the navy as a commander in 1969. Carpenter became interested in environmental issues in his later years. He also wrote two novels.

Carpenter's home life became rocky in the years after Project Mercury. He divorced his first wife, Rene, in 1972, and then married three additional times. He died in 2013.

Wally Schirra went on to become the only astronaut to fly in all three of NASA's first crewed space programs: Mercury, Gemini, and Apollo. He later reflected on his time in space, telling a reporter, "Mostly it's lousy out there." He said space travel was a lot like sitting in "a flying Thermos bottle." Schirra retired from NASA and the navy in 1969, and went on to work in finance. He died in 2007.

Alan Shepard said that his flight on board *Freedom 7* was "just the first baby step" for the American space program. He was right. Shepard returned to space on board *Apollo 14*, where he famously golfed on the Moon.

Shepard's behavior during the Mercury years has drawn plenty of attention from historians and biographers. Some have portrayed him as a cutthroat competitor, a man who would do anything to get what he wanted. Others think of him in a kinder light. They remember him as a profoundly driven individual who was fiercely bright and motivated. John Glenn, the astronaut who probably had the most difficult relationship with Shepard, called him "a highly intelligent, dedicated leader." Shepard died in 1998.

Glenn left NASA in 1964 to work in private industry and try his hand at politics. He served four terms as a Democratic senator from his home state of Ohio before an unsuccessful run for president in 1984. Then on October 29, 1998,

Scott Carpenter just after his 1965 Sealab mission, in which he spent thirty days living and working underwater.

seventy-seven-year-old Glenn went back to space. He flew on board the space shuttle *Discovery* (STS-95) as part of a study on how space affects aging humans.

Glenn's time in space and politics placed him firmly among the nation's greatest heroes. He didn't think he deserved the spotlight. Glenn said, "I don't think it was about me. All of this would have happened to any-one who happened to be selected for that flight." Of course, he meant that first orbital flight back in 1962, when his cool test pilot demeanor helped him stay calm in the face of death.

Aviation coursed through Glenn's blood even until his very last years. He finally sold his twin-engine propeller plane in 2012 when it got too hard for him and his wife, Annie, to climb into. Glenn died in 2016. He and Annie had been married for seventy-three years.

It is hard to describe the impact these seven men had on American history. In 1998, Schirra tried his best to put it

John Glenn enjoys his time in zero g once again on board the space shuttle *Discovery* (STS-95), 1998.

into words: "The brotherhood we have will endure forever."
He was right.

But there is also a sisterhood to remember.

CHAPTER 22

PICKING UP THE PIECES

When NASA changed its astronaut requirements in the spring of 1962, it could have been a game changer for Jerrie Cobb and the twelve other women astronaut test subjects. This tiny shift in policy, which now allowed civilian aviators to become astronauts, meant that the women were one step closer to their dream. And, as they'd seen with Carpenter and Glenn, the agency had relaxed its requirements for really great pilots in the past. It accepted both men despite their lack of engineering degrees. Was it possible that NASA might show a little flexibility again in the future?

Several of the women came close to fitting NASA's revised requirements. Janey Hart and Wally Funk had flown jets. Gene Nora Stumbough, Jan Dietrich, Jerri Sloan, and Bea Steadman had done test flight. Jerrie Cobb and Jean Hixson ticked both of these boxes during their careers. Sarah Gorelick was an engineer. Despite the overwhelming odds against them, these women were close. Very close.

Funk enthusiastically applied to join the 1962 class of astronauts. NASA rejected her. Its official reason was that she was not an engineer. The twenty-four-year-old pilot took the news surprisingly well. "I wasn't discouraged," she said, "I just believed it would come. If not today, then in a couple of months."

The majority of the women weren't as optimistic as Funk. They could see that this wasn't about any official set of requirements, not really. It was their gender. It had always been their gender. Accepting women as astronauts would mean that NASA—and all its feverish fans—would be forced to acknowledge that female aviators could do exactly what male aviators could do. And that might threaten the heroic, ultramasculine, tough-guy status the astronauts enjoyed. If a pilot in a housedress could fly a spacecraft just as well as a muscle-bound macho man, well, then maybe the whole social order that dictated who could do what and when and how might just crumble.

In 1964, a glimmer of hope shone through the darkness.

That year, Dr. Lovelace was appointed NASA's director of space medicine. This title gave him incredible influence within the agency. It was possible that he could use his new role to argue once again for women in space. In fact, it looked like that was exactly what he had planned.

Then, tragedy struck. In 1965, Dr. Lovelace and his wife were killed when their plane crashed in the mountains of Colorado. In that instant, the women's last shaky ties to NASA were cut. They were cast adrift. Their advocate, the man who'd believed in them all along, was gone. They had also lost a dear friend.

Randy Lovelace was remembered by the women as exceptionally kind, generous, and gentle. He gave them all an incredible gift: a brief period spent in hopeful dreaming that they might one day fly among the stars. The excitement and urgency and secrecy of this time had been magical. For a few years, thirteen ambitious pilots had filled their empty moments with dazzling fantasies of spaceflight.

Historians have since noted that Lovelace likely didn't envision women as hotshot space pilots. He probably didn't picture women-only astronaut crews bravely exploring the inky depths of outer space, firing their rockets and gritting their teeth through mounting g-forces. Instead, it appears that Lovelace thought women should go into space in subservient roles. He thought they should fly alongside male pilots and work as secretaries or scientists. He imagined them as assistants rather than leaders. This idea wasn't as progressive as some might have hoped, but it still represented a giant leap in the way people thought about women at the time. The mere fact that Lovelace was willing to entertain the idea of women flying in space at all made him an innovator. He stuck his neck out with this idea. Some people thought it made him look like a fool. Others thought it made him a hero.

After Lovelace's death, the women involved with his astronaut testing took different paths. Jackie Cochran spent the mid-1960s pushing for her own large-scale female astronaut testing program. It never came to be, but Cochran remained involved in the space program for years after. She even attended two Gemini launches. In 1971, Cochran became the first living woman to earn a place in the Aviation Hall of Fame. In 1975, she told the *Washington Post* that she had never experienced discrimination. She said, "I think the women complaining they've been discriminated against are the ones who can't do anything anyway." She said claims of discrimination were "baloney." Cochran died in 1980.

Janey Hart ferociously disagreed with Cochran's stance on discrimination. Her passionate testimony at the special hearing was a mere glimpse into her future as an activist for women's rights. In 1966, she was one of nine women who founded the National Organization for Women (NOW), an advocacy group that pushed for equal rights. Today, NOW is the biggest organization of feminist grassroots activists in America.

Hart spent the years after the special hearing juggling family life, flight, politics, and a new passion for a spunky little yellow motorcycle. When the Vietnam War erupted, Hart was one of its most outspoken critics. In 1969, she was even arrested for participating in an antiwar protest inside the Pentagon.

Hart gave up flying as she grew older, claiming that it was "too expensive." In its place, she took up sailing, even managing to sail a boat across the Atlantic Ocean at the age of seventy-three. Hart died in 2015.

Three of the women left their jobs in order to be

available for the Phase III tests. Gene Nora Stumbough, Sarah Gorelick, and Irene Leverton found themselves not just disappointed with the special hearing's decision but also unemployed. Stumbough bounced back quickly, landing a job as a demonstration pilot for a new type of plane called a Musketeer and embarking on a cross-country adventure to show it off.

About one week after John Glenn testified that he just hadn't seen a woman who deserved a spot in space, Stumbough flew a Musketeer in formation for the first time. This is an incredibly difficult task. Planes, crowded together in different geometric shapes, must maintain precise speeds and altitudes. If one pilot makes a mistake, she could kill herself and the pilots in the rest of her formation.

Eight days after learning this skill, Stumbough flew in a diamond-shaped formation through the Grand Canyon. She kept one hand firmly on her control yoke and the other on her throttle. She dodged the uneven canyon walls as they jutted out in spikes and blocks, all the while being careful not to clip a neighboring plane's wing or tail or nose. Her heart pounded in her chest the whole time. It was, in Stumbough's words, "the best job ever, anywhere."

Stumbough later married Robert Jessen and the two started an aircraft dealership near their home in Boise, Idaho. Today, she writes books about the history of aviation and cares for her husband.

Sarah Gorelick went to work for her family's company as a bookkeeper. The job allowed her to use her mathematics degree and also paid enough to finance her true passion:

aviation. She later married Roy Ratley and learned to fly a helicopter. Today, Gorelick lives just outside of Kansas City. She still flies with friends in a rented Cessna 172.

Irene Leverton struggled in the years after her astronaut testing. She worked as a flight instructor, forest service pilot, and as a commuter pilot. But the jobs didn't last. She continued to face that familiar resistance from men who didn't like to see a woman fly a plane. "I was used to that kind of thing," Leverton said. Men just didn't want her in the cockpit. Leverton eventually clawed her way into a career as an aviation consultant in Arizona. She died in 2017 with a staggering 25,762 hours in her flight log. To put this in perspective, Gordon Cooper's log topped out at about 7,000 hours.

Several of the women returned to the aviation careers they'd held before their testing. Myrtle Cagle went back to Georgia to resume her work as an airplane mechanic and pilot. After that, she got a job as an airplane mechanic at Robins Air Force Base. While there, she took her first flight in a jet. She remembers the experience with overwhelming joy: "the air was fluid, and the clouds were like little bubbles. I could roll it left, roll it right, like through water . . . That was one of the highlights of my life." Cagle can still be found poking around an airplane engine near her home in Georgia.

Bea Steadman returned to Michigan and picked right up where she left off, running a thriving aviation business with her husband, Bob. She kept racing, even managing to win the International Women's Air Race in 1963 and the AWTAR in 1966. She was inducted into the Michigan Aviation Hall of Fame in 2002 and the Michigan Women's Hall of Fame in 2003. Steadman died in 2013.

Jerri Sloan returned to her aviation business in Texas and married her business partner, Joe Truhill. In 1964 she became the spokeswoman for a brand-new type of fabric called Lycra. She wore a baby-pink Lycra flight suit and flew a matching pink plane on a publicity tour for the new miracle material. After that, she went on to take leadership positions at two air companies. She died in 2013.

Jean Hixson went back to her job as a schoolteacher and remained active with the Air Force Reserves. She continued to stay involved in aerospace studies, even researching life support equipment needed for female pilots. In 1984, she received the Meritorious Service Medal for the aerospace research she did with the air force. She died later that year.

Rhea Hurrle worked for a while at an aircraft company after her astronaut testing, but when she married Len Woltman in 1972, he asked her to stop flying. She did. "I loved flying," she said, "but I loved him more." This is not to imply that she settled into a quiet life. She spent the following years learning to hang glide, hunting large game such as polar bears and walrus, collecting classic cars, riding motorcycles, and hula-hooping. The only thing she has left to do is go to outer space. "It's a little late," she says, "but we're still ready."

After the astronaut testing came to a halt, Marion Dietrich went back to work as an aviation writer and part-time pilot. She and her sister continued to believe that they may have

Jerri Sloan models her pink Lycra suit, 1964.

Irene Leverton.

a shot at space in the near future. They hoped that Jackie Cochran's women's astronaut testing program might pan out for them but eventually realized it wouldn't happen. When Marion died in 1974 from cancer, Jan brought her ashes up with her in her airplane and then lovingly scattered them over the Golden Gate Bridge.

Jan Dietrich returned to her job as a corporate pilot, ultimately racking up 12,000 flight hours in her log. She was one of the few women in the country to hold the highest aviation certification, an Airline Transport Pilot Rating. This is the rating needed to fly for a commercial airline, such as Delta or American Airlines. Despite this, Jan was never able to land a job as a large commercial airline pilot. She suspected this was because of her gender. In 1968, she sued an airline after being denied a job she felt she deserved. The lawsuit was long and expensive, and eventually Jan dropped it. She seethed at the memory of being told "that the image of an airline captain was a tall, gray-haired man."

In her later years, Jan dealt with health problems. She lost her vision and hearing. But before all that happened, she told a friend, "I was the best damn pilot there ever was." Jan died in 2008.

Wally Funk spent the years after the special hearing working furiously to get herself into space. She applied to four separate astronaut classes but was denied each time for not meeting the requirements. She wasn't discouraged. She just kept trying.

Funk took it upon herself to complete the third and final phase of astronaut testing on her own. She *would* show NASA what she was made of. She wrote letters to different aviation facilities around the country and asked for permission to use their equipment as a test subject. She rode a centrifuge at the University of Southern California, did the altitude chamber test at El Toro Marine Base, and completed still other tests at the Federal Aviation Administration in Oklahoma City. In 1991, Funk rode a MASTIF trainer that was just like what Cobb and the Mercury 7 had ridden. It took Funk thirty years to complete her astronaut testing, but she did it. She finished all three phases.

While she busily worked her way through her astronaut tests, Funk also became one of the most respected female aviators in the United States. She became the first female inspector for the Federal Aviation Administration and then one of the first women accident investigators at the National Transportation Safety Board. Today, her flight log boasts more than 19,600 hours.

Funk attended a Russian astronaut training course in 2000 and has invested in private space companies who hope to bring civilians into space in the near future. Despite everything that happened, Funk still looks to the stars with hope. She's ready for her mission.

The news that the women would not become astronauts was hard on everyone, but it was shattering for one woman in particular. Jerrie Cobb had devoted herself entirely to this singular mission. She spent the three years that followed the special hearing arguing that she'd been slighted, that NASA was on the wrong side of this issue. She didn't make any progress. NASA plodded ahead with Project Gemini and looked hopefully toward Apollo. Nobody was interested in going back to the sticky politics of Project Mercury. Finally, in 1965, in a muddled mix of fatigue and sadness and disgust, Cobb accepted the truth. She wasn't going to space.

Cobb had always had a strong faith, but this devastation renewed her beliefs and made her think about how to use her skills and religion to help others. She applied to become a missionary pilot, but no one would hire her. Even missionary groups turned their noses up at the idea of a woman in the cockpit. Once again, Cobb's dreams were being crushed by the fact of her gender. It was absurd! She was volunteering to help, and even that wasn't enough!

And so, as she had in so many other pivotal moments in her life, Jerrie decided to just go it alone. She bought a twin-engine plane and flew into the heart of the Amazon jungle, hoping to figure out a way to be of service once she arrived. Her first years were rocky. She had to contend with malaria, explosive tropical storms, and language barriers. But if anyone was used to adversity, it was Jerrie Cobb. Slowly, slowly, she carved a tiny place for herself there in the jungle. She worked hard to help the native populations, using her plane to deliver goods, medicines, and seeds to isolated regions.

But even as she filled her days with jungle transport flights, Cobb never really got over the disappointment of missing her chance to go into space. In the summer of 1969, while buzzing the dense green treetops, Cobb received a call on her airplane radio. The crackled message was unbelievable: Man had landed on the Moon! NASA had done it! At first, she was overjoyed at the update. "Wow! That's wonderful news!" she responded.

But later that night, after making camp near a tribal settlement, her mood shifted. Jerrie climbed up onto her airplane's wing and gazed up at the blue-white moon. "Congratulations, fellow pilots . . ." she said quietly. "You are fulfilling my deepest dream." Somewhere in the distance, a jaguar growled.

"*Vaya con Dios*, my brothers," she said. Go with God.

Cobb stayed in the Amazon, flying and helping, for forty-eight years. While she was gone, Americans grew to recognize the importance of her work in aviation and as a missionary. In 1973, President Richard Nixon gave her the Harmon Trophy, an honor that named her "the world's best woman pilot." In 1981, her missionary work earned her a

Nobel Peace Prize nomination. The award went to someone else that year, but Cobb wasn't discouraged. She just kept working—flying and helping.

While Cobb was soaring over treetops in the Amazon, NASA's stance on women in space slowly began to evolve. In 1978, the agency welcomed its first female astronaut trainees. In 1983, Sally Ride flew on board the space shuttle *Challenger* (STS-7), not as a pilot, but as a mission specialist. It wasn't what Cobb and the other women had wanted, but it was progress. An American woman was in space!

In the 1990s, the story of the thirteen women who had originally tested to become astronauts was once again in the press. A journalist dubbed them the Mercury 13, a nod to the male astronauts, and a gesture of validation. They weren't just a bunch of women who chased a dream. They were Mercury women now. The Mercury 13.

Finally, in 1995, air force test pilot Eileen Collins piloted the space shuttle *Discovery* (STS-63). Seven of the Mercury 13, including Cobb, traveled to Cape Canaveral, Florida, to watch Collins's launch. After the space shuttle streaked into the sky, the aging women aviators were treated to fabulous receptions, parties, and warm welcomes from NASA. It was a bittersweet day. They cheered and cried with joy for Collins, while also feeling the deep pangs of opportunities lost.

Then, in 1998, NASA announced a plan to have John Glenn fly on board the space shuttle *Discovery* (STS-95) as part of a study on how space affects an aging person's body. This news propelled Cobb back into the national spotlight. Feminist groups rallied around the aging aviator

Seven of the Mercury 13 gather to watch Eileen Collins's historic launch in 1995. From left, Gene Nora Jessen (née Stumbough), Wally Funk, Jerrie Cobb, Jerri Truhill (née Sloan), Sarah Ratley (née Gorelick), Myrtle Cagle, Bea Steadman.

and proposed that she be sent up, too. Thousands of letters poured into NASA, arguing that Cobb had more than earned her seat on the mission.

Cobb was caught up in the momentum of it all. "It feels so right," she told a reporter. "I'm going to get to go."

In a sad echo of the events of 1962, NASA once again brushed Cobb aside. At 2:19 p.m. on October 29, 1998, the space shuttle thundered into the heavens while Cobb's feet remained firmly on the ground.

Jerrie Cobb died on March 18, 2019, exactly one week before the first-ever all-female spacewalk was cancelled for a reason that would have sounded painfully familiar to the aging aviator: NASA hadn't prepared enough space suits in the women's sizes.

EPILOGUE

THE ULTIMATE GLASS CEILING

It's easy to look back on the story of the Mercury men and women as a sad example of how sexism affected the first several years at NASA. After all, none of the Mercury 13 made it into space. They were laughed at, then ignored, while their male peers flew higher, faster, and farther than any humans before. The men soared while the women were sent back home.

But this story is bigger than that. It tells us how the Mercury 13 created the first faint crack in the ultimate glass ceiling: the arcing, hazy line that distinguishes Earth from space. They weren't able to punch through it, but the crack they created was lasting. Over the years, more female aviators created cracks of their own by flying high and fast and far. Other women fractured it further by becoming renowned scientists and engineers. Dr. Mae Jemison combined medicine and astronautics when she became the first woman of color to fly in outer space on board the space shuttle *Endeavour* (STS-47) in 1992. Three years after Jemison's pioneering flight, Eileen Collins delivered that old ceiling its final thump and brought the whole thing crashing down in a sparkling shower. The glass shards, sharp and painful reminders of the sexism that stunted so many dreams, fell like rain or tears or both.

Today, over 360 Americans have flown in space. Of those, more than 50 are women. Female astronauts have served a variety of roles in space. They've been scientists, educators, engineers, and aviators. They've performed essential tasks in order to further the human understanding of what, exactly, space has in store for us.

Despite this rise in female participation in the American space program, there is still work to do. As of the publication of this book, only three women have piloted American space missions. Eileen Collins, Pamela Ann Melroy, and Susan Kilrain have flown two space missions each Collins and Melroy have also acted as space shuttle commanders, the highest rank for astronauts on a mission. There have been 179 American crewed spaceflight missions. This means that a measly 3% of American crewed space missions have had a female in the driver's seat, and just 1.6% have had a woman in charge.

Much has changed since those first nail-biting space missions, in which a single, white, testosterone-soaked test pilot squeezed into a cramped capsule with less computing power than a modern smartphone, and then blasted through the atmosphere. Now our technology is better. Our computers are infinitely smarter. Today, astronauts fly in diverse, mixed-gender teams. NASA's twelve-member Astronaut Class of 2017, which was selected from more than 18,000 applicants, contains five women and people from a variety of racial backgrounds. Private companies, such as SpaceX, have burst onto the scene and shocked everyone with their powerful, light, reusable rockets. The industry of spaceflight is, quite literally, on the rise. It's a field of immeasurable growth, where starry-eyed dreamers are welcomed.

There wasn't a place for women in the space industry of the past. Men enjoyed all the firsts: the first spaceflight, the first spacewalk, and the first footsteps on the Moon. But the future is bright. Mars beckons. Who knows? Maybe the next set of firsts will belong to women, not because it's their turn, but because they will be the best.

A NOTE ABOUT THE
WOMEN'S TEST SCORES

Many of the Mercury 13 left their astronaut testing believing that they had outperformed the men who preceded them. Bea Steadman and Wally Funk were told as much by test administrators. Jerrie Cobb was even given a specific number: She'd performed in the top 2% of all test subjects. We do know that a greater percentage of women passed their tests with no medical reservations than men. However, beyond that, the picture remains murky.

The test scores and rankings of the nineteen women who underwent Mercury astronaut tests were never released in their entirety. In fact, the full group's only surviving test results come from the bicycle test. The doctor who supervised this exam passed his notes on to a colleague, who then preserved them carefully. These figures show that the male astronaut test subjects had, in general, better fitness than the women. However, the performance of the top four females (Jan Dietrich, Rhea Hurrle, Wally Funk, and Jerrie Cobb) was on par with the average performance of the male test subjects.

Jerrie Cobb made her own test results public by submitting them to the special subcommittee in the days after her hearing. They were later published along with the committee's official report. These test results included favorable comments from physicians involved in all three phases of her testing.

Sifting through the remaining test results would provide a clearer picture of just how the two groups of pilots stacked up against each other. Unfortunately, this is an impossible task. The full collection of the women's test results was never published, and at some time over the last sixty years, the majority of the records went missing. When asked where they might have gone, Lovelace Foundation and Clinic historian Dr. Jake Spidle Jr. replied that they're probably lost. He says they might have been destroyed, or that if he had to guess, they're probably "deep in a landfill somewhere."

In 1964, a single scientific paper about the Mercury 13's testing was published. It didn't include any of their test scores but instead discussed the potential for a woman's period to affect her ability to fly a spacecraft.

GLOSSARY

Altimeter: a gauge inside an aircraft that displays altitude, or distance from the ground

Biplane: a fixed-wing aircraft with two sets of wings, one stacked on top of the other

Centrifuge: a large training device that exposes passengers to increased g loads to mimic some types of flight

Flak: antiaircraft fire

G: the unit used to measure g-force

G-force: the measurement of acceleration relative to Earth's gravity

Meteorology: the study of Earth's atmosphere and weather

Mission specialist: an astronaut who works alongside the commander and pilot to maintain their spacecraft, manage experiments, and perform other necessary duties in space

Rating: a certification given to aviators when they become qualified to operate a type of aircraft or under certain conditions. For example, an instrument rating certifies a pilot to fly under poor visibility conditions, when they must rely on their instruments rather than sight

Reconnaissance: military observation

Sonic boom: the explosive noise created by an object traveling faster than the speed of sound

Squadron: a military group or unit

Swept wing: a type of wing that projects away from an aircraft's body on an angle, rather than straight out to the sides

Vertigo: the sensation of dizzying motion. Vertigo can occur due to problems in the inner ear or brain

BIBLIOGRAPHY

BOOKS

Ackmann, Martha. *The Mercury 13*. New York: Random House, 2004.

Baker, Philip. "Science, and a Little Golf." *Footprints in the Dust: The Epic Voyages of Apollo, 1969–1975*. Lincoln, NE: University of Nebraska Press, 2010.

Bradley, James. *Flyboys*. New York: Little Brown, 2003.

Burgess, Colin. *Faith 7: Gordon Cooper, Jr., and the Final Mercury Mission.* Chichester, UK: Springer, 2016.

——————. *Liberty Bell 7: The Suborbital Mercury Flight of Virgil I. Grissom.* Chichester, UK: Springer, 2014.

——————. *Sigma 7: The Six Mercury Orbits of Walter M. Schirra, Jr.* Chichester, UK: Springer, 2016.

Burgess, Colin, and Kate Doolan. *Fallen Astronauts: Heroes Who Died Reaching for the Moon*. Lincoln, NE: University of Nebraska Press, 2003.

Burrows, William E. *This New Ocean: The Story of the First Space Age*. New York: Random House, 1998.

Carpenter, Scott M., L. Gordon Cooper Jr., John H. Glenn Jr., Virgil I. Grissom, Walter M. Schirra Jr., Alan B. Shepard Jr., and Donald K. Slayton. *We Seven*. New York: Simon & Schuster, 1962.

Carpenter, Scott, and Kris Stoever. *For Spacious Skies: The Uncommon Journey of a Mercury Astronaut*. New York: Harcourt, 2002.

Catchpole, John. *Project Mercury: NASA's First Manned Space Programme*. Chichester, UK: Praxis Publishing, 2001.

Chaikin, Andrew. *A Man on the Moon*. New York: Penguin, 2007.

Cobb, Jerrie. *Solo Pilot*. Sun City Center, FL: Jerrie Cobb Foundation, 1997.

——————. *Woman into Space*. Englewood Cliffs, NJ: Prentice Hall, 1963.

Cochran, Jacqueline, and Maryann Bucknum Brinley. *Jackie Cochran: The Autobiography of the Greatest Woman Pilot in Aviation History*. New York: Bantam Books, 1987.

Cooper, Charlie, and Ann Cooper. *Tuskegee's Heroes*. Osceola, WI: MBI Publishing, 1996.

Cooper, Gordon, and Bruce Henderson. *Leap of Faith: An Astronaut's Journey into the Unknown*. New York: HarperCollins, 2000.

Doolan, Kate, and Colin Burgess. "Women and the Challenge of Space Flight." *Electronic Australia*, September 1997.

Douglas, Deborah G. *American Women and Flight since 1940*. Lexington, KY: University Press of Kentucky, 2004.

Erickson, Lance K. *Space Flight: History, Technology, and Operations*. Plymouth, UK: Scarecrow Press, 2010.

Gibson, Karen Bush. *Women Aviators: 26 Stories of Pioneer Flights, Daring Missions, and Record-Setting Journeys*. Chicago: Chicago Review Press, 2013.

—————. *Women in Space: 23 Stories of First Flights, Scientific Missions, and Gravity-Breaking Adventures*. Chicago: Chicago Review Press, 2014.

Glenn, John, and Nick Taylor. *John Glenn: A Memoir*. New York: Bantam Books, 1999.

Grissom, Betty, and Henry Still. *Starfall*. New York: Crowell, 1974.

Grissom, Virgil. *Gemini! A Personal Account of Man's Venture into Space*. New York: Macmillan, 1968.

Hallion, Richard P. *Silver Wings, Golden Valor: The USAF Remembers Korea*. Air Force History and Museums Program, 2006.

Haynsworth, Leslie, and David Toomey. *Amelia Earhart's Daughters*. New York: William and Morrow, 1998.

Kraft, Chris. *Flight: My Life in Mission Control*. New York: Dutton, 2001.

Lathers, Mary. *Space Oddities: Women and Outer Space in Popular Film and Culture 1960–2000*. New York: Continuum International Publishing Group, 2010.

Leopold, George. *Calculated Risk: The Supersonic Life and Times of Gus Grissom*. West Lafayette, IN: Purdue University Press, 2016.

Lovell, Jim, and Jeffrey Kluger. *Apollo 13*. New York: Houghton Mifflin, 1994.

Maher, Neil M. *Apollo in the Age of Aquarius*. Cambridge, MA: Harvard University Press, 2017.

Merryman, Molly. *Clipped Wings: The Rise and Fall of the Women Airforce Service Pilots (WASPS) of World War II*. New York: NYU Press, 1998.

Nolen, Stephanie. *Promised the Moon: The Untold Story of the First Women in the Space Race*. New York: Thunder's Mouth Press, 2002.

O'Brien, Keith. *Fly Girls: How Five Daring Women Defied All Odds and Made Aviation History*. New York: Houghton Mifflin, 2018.

Pearson, P. O'Connell. *Fly Girls: The Daring American Women Pilots Who Helped Win WWII*. New York: Simon & Schuster, 2018.

Rankin, William H. "The Man Who Rode Thunder." *Into the Blue: American Writers on Aviation and Spaceflight*. New York: Library of America, 2011.

Schirra, Wally, and Richard N. Billings. *Schirra's Space*. Annapolis, MD: Naval Institute Press, 1988.

Shayler, David J., and Colin Burgess. *NASA's Scientist-Astronauts*. New York: Praxis, 2006.

Shepard, Alan, Deke Slayton, and Jay Barbree. *Moon Shot: The Inside Story of America's Moon Landings*. Atlanta, GA: Turner Publishing, 1994.

Slayton, Donald K., and Michael Cassutt. *Deke!—U.S. Manned Space: From Mercury to the Shuttle*. New York: Tom Doherty Associates, 1994.

Southern, Neta Snook. *I Taught Amelia to Fly*. New York: Vantage Press, 1974.

Steadman, Bernice Trimble, and Jody M. Clark. *Tethered Mercury: A Pilot's Memoir: The Right Stuff but the Wrong Sex*. Traverse City, MI: Aviation Press, 2001.

Thomas, Shirley. *Men of Space: Profiles of the Leaders in Space Research, Development, and Exploration*, vol 3. Philadelphia: Chilton Press, 1961.

Thompson, Neal. *Light This Candle: The Life & Times of Alan Shepard*. New York: Crown Publishers, 2004.

Townley, Alvin. *Fly Navy: Discovering the Extraordinary People and Enduring Spirit of Naval Aviation*. New York: St. Martin's Press, 2011.

Weitekamp, Margaret A. *Right Stuff, Wrong Sex: America's First Women in Space Program*. Baltimore, MD: Johns Hopkins Press, 2004.

Wolfe, Tom. *The Right Stuff*. New York: Picador, 1979.

Yelen, Emily. *Our Mothers' War: American Women at Home and at the Front During World War II*. New York: 2004.

MAGAZINES

Cochran, Jackie. "Jerri and Marion Dietrich: First Astronaut Twins." *Parade*. April 30, 1961.

"Commander 680F Record Breaker." *Flying Magazine*, December 1969. pg. 84

Kocivar, Ben. "The Lady Wants to Orbit." *Look Magazine*, February 2, 1960.

Luce, Clare Booth. "She Orbits Over the Sex Barrier." *LIFE*. June 28, 1963.

Schanche, Don. "The Astronauts Get Their Prodigious Chariot: The Spacemen's Cramped Capsule Can Almost Think for Itself." *LIFE*. December 14, 1959.

WEBSITES

"FAA Certified Pilots 1929–2011." AOPA.org. March 25, 2011. Digital. https://www.aopa.org/about/general-aviation-statistics/faa-certificated-pilots.

Nelson, Craig. *Rocket Men: The Epic Story of the First Men on the Moon*. New York: Viking, 2009. https://books.google.com/books?id=LWMivGgbM7kC&pg=PT150&dq.

"Qualifications for Astronauts." *House of Representatives Special Subcommittee on the Selection of Astronauts, Committee on Science and Astronautics*. July 17, 1962.

Roach, Mary. *Packing for Mars: The Curious Science of Life in the Void*. London: OneWorld Publications, 2011. https://books.google.com/books?id=SUbFAQAAQBAJ&pg=PT37&dq.

Ukockis, Gail. *Women's Issues for A New Generation: A Social Work Perspective*. New York: Oxford University Press, 2016. https://books.google.com/books?id=2kUnDAAAQBAJ&pg=PT84&lpg=PT84.

Deffree, Suzanne. "1st US Satellite Attempt Fails, December 6, 1957." EDN.com. Accessed December 6, 2016. http://www.edn.com/electronics-blogs/edn-moments/4402889/1st-US-satellite-attempt-fails--December-6--1957.

"KC-135 A Stratotanker Refueling a B-52 Stratofortress." BoeingImages. com. Digital. Accessed April 20, 2017. http://www.boeingimages.com/ archive/KC-135AStratotanker-Refueling-a-B-52-Stratofortress-in-Flight-2JRSXLJMESCG.html.

"The ZPG-2 Airship Snowbird Sets Unrefueled Flight Time and Distance Records." BlimpInfo.com. Digital. Accessed June 20, 2017. http://www.blimpinfo.com/ history-2/this-mo-in-hist/this-mo-in-hist-mar-2/zpg-2-snowbird-records/.

"Eisenhower Takes First Presidential Ride in a Helicopter." History.com. 2009. Digital. Accessed June 2017. http://www.history.com/this-day-in-history/ eisenhower-takes-first-presidential-ride-in-a-helicopter.

Achenbach, Joel. "50 Years Ago, Launch of a New World." *Washington Post*. October 2, 2007. Digital. Accessed June 20, 2017. http://www.washingtonpost.com/ wp-dyn/content/article/2007/10/01/AR2007100101678_2.html?hpid=topnews.

Silver, Alexandra. "Kaputnik." Time.com. April 19, 2010. Digital. Accessed June 20, 2017. http://content.time.com/time/specials/packages/ article/0,28804,1982672_1982673,00.html.

Endres, Kathleen. "Jean Hixson." UAkron.edu. September 11, 2014. Digital. Accessed June 20, 2017. https://blogs.uakron.edu/womenshistory/2013/09/11/ jean-hixson-1922-1984/.

DeLand, Dave. "Rhea's Story Is Out of this World." SCTimes.com. May 16, 2015. Digital. Accessed June 20, 2017. https://www.sctimes.com/story/news/ local/2015/05/16/deland-column-rheas-story-world/27463857/.

"Medical Testing." NASA.gov. Digital. Accessed June 20, 2017. https://history.nasa. gov/SP-4003/ch5-4.htm.

Keim, Brandon. "Right Stuff, Wrong Sex: NASA's Lost Female Astronauts." Wired.com. Accessed October 6, 2009. Digital. Accessed June 20, 2017. https://www.wired.com/2009/10/mercury-13/.

"Project Mercury Overview." NASA.gov. November 30, 2007. Digital. Accessed June 20, 2017. https://www.nasa.gov/mission_pages/mercury/missions/astronaut.html.

"Mercury Astronauts Presentation." Youtube.com. Digital. Accessed June 20, 2017. https://www.youtube.com/watch?v=fuXXw5Jggvg.

Ratley, Sarah Lee Gorelick. "Sarah Lee Gorelick Ratley." AirandSpace.si.edu. Digital. Accessed June 29, 2017. https://airandspace.si.edu/support/wall-of-honor/ sarah-lee-gorelick-ratley.

"Wally Funk." Ninety-nines.org. 2017. Digital. Accessed June 29, 2017. https://www. ninety-nines.org/wally-funk.htm.

"Jan & Marion Dietrich." Mercury13.com. Digital. Accessed June 29, 2017. http://www.mercury13.com/jan.htm.

"Sarah Ratley." Mercury13.com. 2012. Digital. Accessed July 1, 2017. http://www. mercury13.com/sarah.htm.

"Myrtle 'Kay' Cagle." GAAviationHallofFame.com. Digital. Accessed July 2, 2017. https://www.gaaviationhalloffame.com/hall-of-fame/.

"Jerri Truhill." Mercury13.com. 2013. Digital. Accessed July 2, 2017. http://www. mercury13.com/jerri.htm.

"About CAP." GoCivilAirPatrol.com. Digital. July 2, 2017. http://www.gocivilairpatrol. com/about/.

Rickman, Sarah Byrn. "A History of the Women Airforce Service Pilots." WASPmuseum.org. Digital. Accessed July 2, 2017. http://waspmuseum.org.

"Amelia Earhart as an Aviator." AmeliaEarhartmuseum.org. Digital. Accessed July 2, 2017. http://www.ameliaearhartmuseum.org/AmeliaEarhart/AEAviator.htm.

"Sigma VII." WallySchirra.com. Digital. Accessed February 2, 2018. http://www.wallyschirra.com/mercury.htm.

"Deke Slayton." Nasa.gov. Digital. Accessed February 2, 2018. https://www.jsc.nasa.gov/Bios/htmlbios/slayton.html. [Content removed from website]

Malnic, Eric. "Walter M. 'Wally' Schirra Jr., 84; flew in three NASA programs." LATimes.com. May 4, 2007. Digital. Accessed February 2, 2018. http://articles.latimes.com/2007/may/04/local/me-schirra4.

White, Mary C. "Detailed Biographies of Apollo I Crew—Gus Grissom." NASA.gov. Digital. Accessed February 2, 2018. https://history.nasa.gov/Apollo204/zorn/grissom.htm.

"Big News from the Air Race Classic!" Ladieslovetaildraggers.com. June 27, 2011. Digital. Accessed February 2, 2018. http://www.ladieslovetaildraggers.com/blog/big-news-from-the-2011-air-race-classic/.

"Scott Carpenter." NASA.gov Digital. Accessed February 2, 2018. https://www.jsc.nasa.gov/Bios/htmlbios/carpenter-ms.html. [content removed from website]

"Women in Air Racing." Ninety-Nines.org. Digital. Accessed February 2, 2018. https://www.ninety-nines.org/women-in-air-racing.htm.

"Geraldine 'Jerri' Sloan Truhill." UWosh.edu. May 22, 2012. Digital. Accessed February 2, 2018. http://www.uwosh.edu/library/Wlio/truhill,php.

"The Powder Puff Derbies." Aerofiles.com. Digital. Accessed February 2, 2018. http://www.aerofiles.com/powderpuff.html.

"Republic F-84E Thunderjet." NationalMuseum.af.mil. May 4, 2015. Digital. Accessed February 2, 2018. http://www.nationalmuseum.af.mil/Visit/Museum-Exhibits/Fact-Sheets/Display/Article/196111/republic-f-84e-thunderjet/.

"Historical Snapshot." Boeing.com. Digital. Accessed February 2, 2018. https://www.boeing.com/history/products/f-86-sabre-jet.page.

Joiner, Stephen. "The Jet that Shocked the West." AirSpaceMag.com. December 2013. Digital. Accessed February 2, 2018. https://www.airspacemag.com/military-aviation/the-jet-that-shocked-the-west-180947758/?page=3.

White, Mary C. "Detailed Biographies of Apollo I Crew—Gus Grissom." NASA.gov. Digital. Accessed February 2, 2018. https://history.nasa.gov/Apollo204/zorn/grissom.htm.

"Profile of John Glenn." NASA.gov. Digital. Accessed February 2, 2018. https://www.nasa.gov/content/profile-of-john-glenn.

"Scott Carpenter." NASA.gov. Digital. Accessed February 2, 2018. https://www.jsc.nasa.gov/Bios/htmlbios/carpenter-ms.html. [content removed from website]

"Leroy Gordon Cooper, Jr." NASA.gov. Digital. Accessed February 2, 2018. https://www.jsc.nasa.gov/Bios/htmlbios/cooper-lg.html. [content removed from website]

Bailey, Ron. "The Flying Coopers Are Full of Dad's Spirit." LIFE. May 17, 1963. Digital. Accessed February 2, 2018. https://books.google.com/books?id=2kgEAAAAMBAJ&pg=PA92&dq.

Waxman, Olivia B. "The Hidden Risk Faced by Female Pilots During World War II." Time.com. September 7, 2017. Digital. Accessed February 2, 2018. http://time.com/4923054/world-war-ii-sugar-engines/.

"Navy Fighter Sets Record Crossing U.S." The Mercury (Pottstown, Pennsylvania). July 17, 1957. Digital. Accessed February 2, 2018. https://www.newspapers.com.

"Why Do We Really Need Pressure Suits?" NASA.gov. Digital. Accessed February 2, 2018. https://www.nasa.gov/sites/default/files/atoms/files/dressing_for_altitude.pdf.

"Historical Snapshot." Boeing.com. Digital. Accessed February 2, 2018. http://www.boeing.com/history/products/a3d-a-3-skywarrior.page.

"Test Pilot." WallySchirra.com. Digital. Accessed February 2, 2018. https://www.wallyschirra.com/test_pilot.htm.

Paur, Jason. "Oct. 14, 1947: Yeager Machs the Sound Barrier." Wired.com. October 14, 2009. Digital. Accessed February 2, 2018. https://www.wired.com/2009/10/1014yeager-breaks-mach-1/.

Young, James. "Mach Buster." ChuckYeager.com. Digital. Accessed February 2, 2018. http://www.chuckyeager.com/1945-1947-mach-buster.

Taylor Redd, Nola. "Breaking the Sound Barrier: The Greatest Moments in Flight." Space.com. September 29, 2017. Digital. Accessed February 2, 2018. https://www.space.com/16709-breaking-the-sound-barrier.html.

Waterhouse, Helen. "Akron Teacher-Flier Cracks Sonic Barrier." *The Akron Beacon Journal*. March 6, 1957. Digital. Accessed February 2, 2018. https://www.newspapers.com.

Creech, Gray. "Mach 2 Milestone Anniversary." NASA.gov. November 19, 2003. Digital. Accessed February 2, 2018. https://www.nasa.gov/vision/Earth/improvingflight/mach2_anniversary.html. [content removed from website]

United States Air Force. *F-86 Sabre Pilot's Flight Operating Manual*. Digital. Accessed February 2, 2018. https://books.google.com/books?id=Fdeo9ZVg6dAC.

Blair, Clay. "The Last Flight of the X-2." AirForceMag.com. Digital. Accessed February 2, 2018. http://www.airforcemag.com/MagazineArchive/Pages/1957/March%201957/0357last.aspx.

"A Lady Proves She's Fit for Space Flight." *LIFE*. August 29, 1960. Digital. Accessed February 2, 2018, pg. 73. https://books.google.com/books?id=EU8EAAAAMBAJ&printsec=frontcover.

Whitehouse, David. "First dog in space died within hours." BBC.co.uk. October 28, 2002. Digital. Accessed February 2, 2018. http://news.bbc.co.uk/2/hi/science/nature/2367681.stm.

Greenfield Boyce, Nell. "After 50 Years, Space Monkeys Not Forgotten." NPR.org. May 28, 2009. Digital. Accessed February 2, 2018. https://www.npr.org/templates/story/story.php?storyId=104578202.

Myler, Joseph. "Monkeys Pave Way in Space." The Tennessean. May 31, 1959. Digital. Accessed February 2, 2018. https://www.newspapers.com.

"Space Chimpanzee and Handler, Number 2." Oaktrust.library.tamu.edu. Digital. Accessed February 2, 2018. http://oaktrust.library.tamu.edu/handle/1969.1/161791.

Hanser, Kathleen. "Mercury Primate Capsule and Ham the Astrochimp." AirandSpace.si.edu. November 10, 2015. Digital. Accessed February 2, 2018. https://airandspace.si.edu/stories/editorial/mercury-primate-capsule-and-ham-astrochimp.

Gray, Tara. "A Brief History of Animals in Space." NASA.gov. 1998. Digital. Access February 2, 2018. https://history.nasa.gov/animals.html.

"Fragments, Capsule, Mercury MA-1." AirandSpace.si.edu. Digital. Accessed February 2, 2018. https://airandspace.si.edu/collection-objects/ fragments-capsule-mercury-ma-1.

"Pioneer Space Probes." HistoricSpacecraft.com. Digital. Accessed February 2, 2018. http://historicspacecraft.com/Probes_Pioneer.html.

"Irene Leverton." Mercury13.com. Digital. Accessed February 2, 2018. http://www. mercury13.com/irene.htm.

"Postlaunch Report for Mercury-Redstone No. 3." JSC.nasa.gov. June 16, 1961. Digital. Accessed February 2, 2018. https://www.jsc.nasa.gov/history/mission_trans/ MR03_TEC.PDF.

Ryan, Kathy, and Dr. Jack Loeppky, et al. A Woman in Space. "A Forgotten Moment in Physiology: The Lovelace Women in Space Program (1960–1962)." *Advances in Physiology Education.* June 2009. Digital. Accessed July 24, 2019. https:// www.physiology.org/doi/pdf/10.1152/advan.00034.2009.

"Myrtle Cagle." TheMercury13.com. Digital. Accessed February 2, 2018. http://www. mercury13.com/myrtle.htm.

Penn, Tandy. "A History of Terrain-Following Radar." TheAtlas.org. October 15, 2005. Digital. Accessed February 2, 2018.

"1960–1961." BLS.gov. Digital. Accessed February 2, 2018. https://www.bls.gov/opub/ uscs/1960 61 pdf

"The Civil Rights Act of 1964 and the Equal Employment Opportunity Commission." Archives.gov. Digital. Accessed February 2, 2018. https://www.archives.gov/ education/lessons/civil-rights-act.

Scullio, Maria. "'Mad Men' Series Inaccurately Depicts Difficulties of Divorce for Women in '60s." Post-Gazette.com. July 25, 2010. Digital. Accessed February 2, 2018. http://www.post-gazette.com/ae/tv-radio/2010/07/25/Mad-Men-series-inaccurately-depicts-difficulties-of-divorce-for-women-in-60s/ stories/201007250142.

"Capsule, Mercury MR-3." AirandSpace.si.edu. Digital. Accessed February 2, 2018. https://airandspace.si.edu/collection-objects/capsule-mercury-mr-3.

"Mercury 4." Spacelog.org. Digital. Accessed February 2, 2018. http://mercury4. spacelog.org/00:00:23:30/.

Grissom, Virgil. "It Was a Good Flight and a Great Float." *LIFE.* July 28, 1961. Digital. Accessed February 2, 2018. https://books.google.com/ books?id=nlQEAAAAMBAJ&pg=PA27.

"Liberty Bell Tolls." History.Nasa.gov. Digital. Accessed February 2, 2018. https:// history.nasa.gov/SP-4201/ch11-8.htm.

"NSSDCA/COSPAR ID: 1961-109A." NASA.gov. Digital. Accessed February 2, 2018. https://nssdc.gsfc.nasa.gov/nmc/spacecraftDisplay.do?id=1961-019A.

Grissom, Virgil. "A Hero Admits He Was Scared." *LIFE.* August 4, 1961. Digital. Accessed February 2, 2018. https://books.google.com/books?id=XFQEAAAAMB AJ&q=grissom#v=snippet&q=grissom&f=false.

"Mercury 6." Spacelog.org. Digital. Accessed February 2, 2018. http://mercury6. spacelog.org/page/00:00:05:04/.

"An American in Orbit." History.Nasa.gov. Digital. Accessed February 2, 2018. https://history.nasa.gov/SP-4201/ch13-4.htm.

"The Moonwalkers Who Could Have Been." UMD.edu. Digital. Accessed February 2, 2018. http://users.umiacs.umd.edu/~oard/apollo/poss_moonwalkers.html.

"The Apollo 1 Tragedy." NASA.gov. Digital. Accessed February 2, 2018. https://nssdc.gsfc.nasa.gov/planetary/lunar/apollo1info.html.

Wald, Matthew L. "Gordon Cooper, Astronaut, Is Dead at 77." NYTimes.com. October 5, 2004. Digital. Accessed February 2, 2018. https://www.nytimes.com/2004/10/05/obituaries/gordon-cooper-astronaut-is-dead-at-77.html.

Wilford, John Noble. "Deke Slayton Dies at 69; Was One of First Astronauts." NYTimes.com. June 14, 1993. Digital. February 2, 2018. https://www.nytimes.com/1993/06/14/obituaries/donald-slayton-dies-at-69-was-one-of-first-astronauts.html.

Fay, Martha. "Ex-Astronaut Wife Rene Is the Carpenter in the News Now." People.com. April 7, 1975. Digital. Accessed February 2, 2018. http://people.com/archive/ex-astronaut-wife-rene-is-the-carpenter-in-the-news-now-vol-3-no-13/.

Goldstein, Richard. "Scott Carpenter, One of the Original Seven Astronauts, Is Dead at 88." NYTimes.com. October 10, 2013. Digital. Accessed February 2, 2018. https://www.nytimes.com/2013/10/11/us/scott-carpenter-mercury-astronaut-who-orbited-earth-dies-at-88.html?searchResultPosition=4.

Goldstein, Richard. "Walter M. Schirra Jr., Astronaut, Dies at 84." NYTimes.com. May 4, 2007. Digital. February 2, 2018. https://www.nytimes.com/2007/05/04/us/04schirra.html.

Wilford, John Noble. "Alan B. Shepard Jr. Is Dead at 74: First American to Travel in Space." NYTimes.com. July 23, 1998. Digital. Accessed February 2, 2018. https://archive.nytimes.com/www.nytimes.com/learning/general/onthisday/bday/1118.html.

Wilford, John Noble. "John Glenn, American Hero of the Space Age, Dies at 95." NYTimes.com. December 8, 2016. Digital. Accessed February 2, 2018. https://www.nytimes.com/2016/12/08/us/john-glenn-dies.html.

Goldstein, Richard. "Walter M. Schirra Jr., Astronaut, Dies at 84." NYTimes.com. May 4, 2007. Digital. Accessed February 2, 2018. https://www.nytimes.com/2007/05/04/us/04schirra.html.

Grimes, William. "Jane Hart, Activist and Nearly an Astronaut, Dies." NYTimes.com. June 12, 2015. Digital. Accessed February 2, 2018. https://www.nytimes.com/2015/06/13/us/jane-hart-activist-and-nearly-an-astronaut-dies-at-93.html.

"Ninety-Nine News." Ninety-nines.org. March 1970. Digital. Accessed February 2, 2018. https://www.ninety-nines.org/pdf/newsmagazine/197003.pdf.

Evans, Ben. "From 'Greasy Grissom' to 'Gruff Gus': The Story of America's Second Man in Space (Part 2)." AmericaSpace.com. July 21, 2013. Digital. Accessed February 19, 2018. http://www.americaspace.com/2013/07/21/from-greasygrissom-to-gruff-gus-the-story-of-americas-second-man-in-space-part-2/.

"Seven Astronauts-in-Training." History.nasa.gov. Digital. Access March 20, 2018. https://history.nasa.gov/SP-4201/ch8-4.htm.

"Death of Bernice Steadman." Tributes.com. Digital. Accessed March 20, 2018. http://www.tributes.com/obituary/read/Bernice-Steadman-102301839.

"Truhill, Geraldine." NorthDallasFuneralHome.com. Digital. Accessed March 20, 2018. http://www.northdallasfuneralhome.com/obituary/8682/?.

Lopez, Cory. "Bay Area Pilot Janet Christine Dietrich Dies." SFGate.com. June 17, 2008. Digital. March 20, 2018. https://www.sfgate.com/bayarea/article/Bay-Areapilot-Janet-Christine-Dietrich-dies-3209399.php.

Kennedy, John. F. "Text of President John Kennedy's Rice Stadium Moon Speech." JSC.NASA.gov. September 12, 1962. Digital. Accessed March 30, 2018. https://er.jsc.nasa.gov/seh/ricetalk.htm.

Bennett, Jay. "Everything You Need to Know about Ejecting From a Fighter Jet." PopularMechanics.com. April 25, 2017. Digital. Accessed March 30, 2018. https://www.popularmechanics.com/military/aviation/a26193/how-pilots-eject-from-fighter-jet/.

Loff, Sarah. "Liftoff of John Glenn's Friendship 7, Feb. 20, 1962." NASA.gov. November 30, 2016. Digital. Accessed March 30, 2018. https://www.nasa.gov/image-feature/liftoff-of-john-glenns-friendship-7-feb-20-1962.

"F8F Bearcat." NavalAviationMuseum.org. Digital. Accessed March 30, 2018. https://www.navalaviationmuseum.org/aircraft/f8f-bearcat/.

"Our History." TheNinety-Nines.org. Digital. Accessed March 30, 2018. https://www.ninety-nines.org/our-history.htm.

"Woman Sets Flight Record." *The Salina Journal*. May 26, 1957. Digital. Accessed March 30, 2018. https://www.newspapers.com.

"650 Feeds and Speeds." IBM.com Digital. Accessed March 30, 2018. https://www-03.ibm.com/ibm/history/exhibits/650/650_fs1.html.

Voas, Robert. "Mercury Project Summary." History.NASA.gov. Digital. Accessed March 30, 2018. https://history.nasa.gov/SP-45/ch10.htm.

Tarantola, Andrew. "Why the Human Body Can't Handle Heavy Acceleration." Gizmodo.com. October 1, 2014. Digital. Accessed March 30, 2018. https://gizmodo.com/why-the-human-body-cant-handle-heavy-acceleration-1640491171.

Low, George. "Status Report No. 4, project Mercury." January 12, 1959. Digital. Accessed March 30, 2018. https://history.nasa.gov/SP-4001/p2a.htm.

Low, George. "Status Report No. 13, Project Mercury." May 6, 1959. Digital. Accessed March 30, 2018. https://history.nasa.gov/SP-4001/p2a.htm.

Jones, Jack. "AF Here Stars at Miami Panorama." September 2, 1959. Digital. Accessed March 30, 2018. https://www.newspapers.com.

Kennedy, John F. "Excerpt from an Address Before a Joint Session of Congress." JFKLibrary.org. May 25, 1961. Digital. Accessed March 30, 2018. https://www.jfklibrary.org/Asset-Viewer/xzw1gaeeTES6khED14P1Iw.aspx.

"Cobb, Geraldyn 'Jerrie' M." NationalAviation.org. Digital. Accessed March 30, 2018. https://www.nationalaviation.org/our-enshrinees/cobb-geraldyn-jerrie-m/.

"About." NOW.org. Digital. Accessed March 30, 2018. https://now.org/about/.

Jessen, Gene Nora. "Irene Leverton." Ninety-Nines.org. July 23, 2017. Digital. Accessed March 30, 2018. https://www.ninety-nines.org/NH-Irene_Leverton_8.htm.

"Mercury-Atlas 130-D Rollout." Archives.gov. Digital. Accessed April 20, 2018. https://catalog.archives.gov/id/68810.

"MR-1: The Four-Inch Flight." History.nasa.gov. Digital. Accessed April 20, 2018. https://history.nasa.gov/SP-4201/ch9-7.htm.

"Eileen Marie Collins." JSC.NASA.gov. Digital. Accessed April 20, 2018. https://www.jsc.nasa.gov/Bios/htmlbios/collins.html. [Content removed from website]

"STS-95." NASA.gov. November 23, 2007. Digital. Accessed April 20, 2018. https://www.nasa.gov/mission_pages/shuttle/shuttlemissions/archives/sts-95.html.

Warren-Findley, Janelle. "The Collier as Commemoration: The Project Mercury Astronauts and the Collier Trophy." History.nasa.gov. Digital. Accessed April 30, 2018. https://history.nasa.gov/SP-4219/Chapter7.html.

"Mikoyan-Gurevich MiG-17 (Fresco)." MilitaryFactory.com. Digital. Accessed April 30, 2018. https://www.militaryfactory.com/aircraft/detail.asp?aircraft_id=31.

Dunn, Marcia. "50 Years Later, Stamp Honors America's First Astronaut." NBCNews.com. May 4, 2011. Digital. Accessed May 20, 2018. http://www.nbcnews.com/id/42905083/ns/technology_and_science-space/t/years-later-stamp-honorsamericas-first-astronaut/#.WwLfnS-ZOL8.

Tuttle, Dwight. "Sheppard Field: The Early Years." Sheppard.af.mil. November 9, 2006. Digital. Accessed August 10, 2018. https://www.sheppard.af.mil/News/Article-Display/Article/369709/sheppard-field-the-early-years/.

Badger, Tony. "How Did Kennedy's Assassination Change the World?" CNN.com. November 22, 2013. Digital. Accessed September 20, 2018. https://www.cnn.com/2013/11/22/opinion/opinion-kennedy-world-badger/index.html.

"Mae C. Jemison (MD)." NASA.gov. Digital. Accessed September 20, 2018. https://www.jsc.nasa.gov/Bios/htmlbios/jemison-mc.html. [Content removed from website]

Jordan, Gary. "Your 2017 Astronaut Class." NASA.gov. July 14, 2017. Digital. Accessed September 20, 2018. https://www.nasa.gov/johnson/HWHAP/your-2017-astronaut-class.

"Edson's Washington Column." *Arizona Republic*. September 9, 1941. Digital. Accessed September 20, 2018. https://www.newspapers.com.

"Flight Training on the Eve of WWII." NationalMuseum.af.mil. April 10, 2015. Digital. Accessed September 20, 2018. https://www.nationalmuseum.af.mil/Visit/Museum-Exhibits/Fact-Sheets/Display/Article/196919/flight-training-on-the-eve-of-wwii/.

"Bessie Coleman." PBS.org. Digital. Accessed September 20, 2018. https://www.pbs.org/wgbh/americanexperience/features/flygirls-bessie-coleman/.

"Negro Aviatrix to Tour the Country." *The Evening News*. November 29, 1921. Digital. Accessed September 20, 2018. https://www.newspapers.com.

"100 Most Influential Women in the Aviation and Aerospace Industry." WAI.org. Digital. Accessed September 20, 2018. https://www.wai.org/pioneers/100womenscript.

Campbell, Lilian. "Miss China Goes Aloft." *The Courier-News*. April 13, 1932. Digital. Accessed September 20, 2018. https://www.newspapers.com.

"Women Involved in Aviation." Ninety-Nines.org. Digital. Accessed September 20, 2018. https://www.ninety-nines.org/women-in-aviation-article.htm.

"Aerial View of Sheppard Air Force Base." Airforce-technology.com. Digital. Accessed September 20, 2018. https://www.airforce-technology.com/projects/sheppard-afb/attachment/sheppard-afb1/.

Demuth, Gary. "Women in History—Olive Ann Beech." Salina.com. March 10, 2017. Digital. Accessed September 20, 2018. http://www.salina.com/796c378f-5b1b-5c0f-8736-88fdc63c4dc8.html.

Gray, Tara. "L. Gordon Cooper, Jr." History.Nasa.gov. Digital. Accessed September 20, 2018. https://history.nasa.gov/40thmerc7/cooper.htm.

"Deaths by Country." NationalWW2Museum.org. Digital. Accessed September 20, 2018. https://www.nationalww2museum.org/students-teachers/student-resources/research-starters/research-starters-worldwide-deaths-world-war.

"Warner, Emily Howell." NationalAviation.org. Digital. Accessed September 20, 2018. https://www.nationalaviation.org/our-enshrinees/warner-emily-howell/.

Pace, Eric. "Navy Puts 1st Woman in Pilot Training." NYTimes.com. January 11, 1973. Digital. Accessed September 20, 2018. https://www.nytimes.com/1973/01/11/archives/navy-puts-1st-woman-in-pilot-training.html.

"Walter 'Wally' Marty Schirra." History.Navy.Mil. November 16, 2016. Digital. Accessed September 20, 2018. https://www.history.navy.mil/research/histories/biographies-list/bios-s/Schirra-Walter.html.

Carlson, Michael. "Scott Carpenter Obituary," *Guardian*. October 11, 2013. Digital. Accessed September 20, 2018. https://www.theguardian.com/science/2013/oct/11/scott-carpenter-obituary.

"Odom Dies in Speed Race; 2 Killed in Ohio Home." *The Ithaca Journal*. September 6, 1949. Digital. Accessed September 20, 2018. https://www.newspapers.com.

Waterhouse, Helen. "Akron Names Queen for Air Race." *The Akron Beacon Journal*. August 22, 1949. Digital. Accessed September 20, 2018. https://www.newspapers.com.

Foster, Robert. "Girls Win Honors at First Annual Air Race." *The Times* (San Mateo, California). September 15, 1947. Digital. Accessed September 20, 2018. https://www.newspapers.com.

"Marion Dietrich." *99 News*. March 1975. Digital. Accessed September 20, 2018. https://www.ninety-nines.org/pdf/newsmagazine/197503.pdf.

"1949 Survey of Consumer Finances." Freser.Stlouisfed.org. November 1949. Digital. Accessed September 20, 2018. https://fraser.stlouisfed.org/files/docs/publications/FRB/pages/1945-1949/30288_1945-1949.pdf.

Johnson, Kaci. "Klingensmith, Florence 'Tree Tops.'" MNOpedia.com. Digital. Accessed September 20, 2018. http://www.mnopedia.org/person/klingensmith-florence-tree-tops-1904-1933.

"Youthful Pilot Dies in Air Race." *The Pantograph*. August 12, 1950. Digital. September 20, 2018. https://www.newspapers.com.

"News letter." Ninety-Nines.org. July 15, 1953. Digital. Accessed September 20, 2018. https://www.ninety-nines.org/pdf/newsmagazine/195307.pdf.

"Ohio Pilot First In Aerial Race, Sooner is 11th." *The Daily Oklahoman*. May 21, 1956. Digital. Accessed September 20, 2018. https://www.newspapers.com.

"News letter." Ninety-Nines.org. July 15, 1953. Digital. Accessed September 20, 2018. https://www.ninety-nines.org/pdf/newsmagazine/195307.pdf.

"Rhea Woltman." CoGreatwomen.org. Digital. Accessed September 20, 2018. http://www.cogreatwomen.org/project/rhea-woltman/.

"I.A.R. Results." *Ninety-Nine News*. Ninety-Nines.org. June 1964. Digital. Accessed September 20, 2018. https://www.ninety-nines.org/pdf/newsmagazine/196406.pdf.

"News letter" and "Official Results: Dallas Doll Derby, September 13, 1958." Ninety-Nines.org. October 1958. Digital. Accessed September 20, 2018. https://www.ninetynines.org/pdf/newsmagazine/195810.pdf.

Millet, Allan R. "Korean War." Britannica.com. Digital. Accessed September 20, 2018. https://www.britannica.com/event/Korean-War.

Hoversten, Paul. "Could You Fly a Sabre?" AirSpacemag.com. November 2011. Digital. Accessed September 20, 2018. https://www.airspacemag.com/military-aviation/could-you-fly-a-sabre-76642301/.

Mather, Paul D. "Mind If I Borrow It?" AirSpacemag.com. November 2011. Digital. Accessed September 20, 2018. https://www.airspacemag.com/military-aviation/mind-if-i-borrow-it-76518363/?page=1.

Burrows, William. "It Had the Body of a Fighter and a Bomber's Soul." AirSpacemag.com. August 2013. Digital. Accessed September 20, 2018. https://www.airspacemag.com/military-aviation/thunderjet-307269/.

Benedict, Howard. "He Once Outflew a Pursuing Missile." *The Morning Call*. October 4, 1962. Digital. Accessed September 20, 2018. https://www.newspapers.com.

"John Glenn." SuccessfulMarines.com. Digital. Accessed September 20, 2018. http://successfulmarines.com/tag/air-medals/.

"Mercury 7 Astronaut Gordon Cooper Discusses New Book." CNN.com. August 6, 2000. Digital. Accessed September 20, 2018. http://transcripts.cnn.com/TRANSCRIPTS/0008/06/sm.06.html.

"Fairchild F-24." Planeandpilotmag.com. October 21, 2008. Digital. Accessed September 20, 2018. https://www.planeandpilotmag.com/article/fairchild-f-24/.

"Virgil I. Grissom." Nasa.gov. December 1997. Digital. Accessed September 20, 2018. https://www.jsc.nasa.gov/Bios/htmlbios/grissom-vi.html. [Content removed from website]

Gray, Tara. "L. Gordon Cooper, Jr." History.Nasa.gov. Digital. Accessed September 20, 2018. https://history.nasa.gov/40thmerc7/cooper.htm.

"Pretty Blonde, Expert Pilot, Delivers Planes." *The Gazette*. March 16, 1955. Digital. Accessed September 20, 2018. https://www.newspapers.com.

Ferrell, Don. "State's Flying Ambassador Ends Record Hop Still Fresh." *The Daily Oklahoman*. May 26, 1957. Digital. Accessed September 20, 2018. https://www.newspapers.com.

"Boomtown 1 Speeds to New Record." *The Daily Oklahoman*. May 26, 1957. Digital. Accessed September 20, 2018. https://www.newspapers.com.

Coffey, Ivy. "Pilot Adds Another 'First' To Career." *The Daily Oklahoman*. October 20, 1959. Digital. Accessed September 20, 2018. https://www.newspapers.com.

"Astronautess Sets a Record." *Springfield Leader and Press*. September 21, 1960. Digital. Accessed September 20, 2018. https://www.newspapers.com.

"Lady Astronaut Sets Record Altitude Mark." *Index-Journal*. September 21, 1960. Digital. Accessed September 20, 2018. https://www.newspapers.com.

"Navigating in Nylons." *Ironwood Daily Globe*. April 10, 1961. Digital. Accessed September 20, 2018. https://www.newspapers.com.

Hendry, Erica R. "Today in History: Jackie Cochran Breaks the Sound Barrier." Smithsonianmag.com. May 18, 2010. Digital. Accessed September 20, 2018. https://www.smithsonianmag.com/smithsonian-institution/today-in-history-jackie-cochran-breaks-the-sound-barrier-130780022/.

Chisholm, Shirley. "Equal Rights for Women." GOS.sbc.edu. May 21, 1969. Digital. Accessed September 20, 2018. http://gos.sbc.edu/c/chisholm.html.

"Project Mercury Overview—Astronaut Selection." NASA.gov. November 20, 2006. Digital. Accessed September 20, 2018. https://www.nasa.gov/mission_pages/mercury/missions/astronaut.html.

"Jerrie Cobb Begins Chores." *Fort Lauderdale News*. May 20, 1961. Digital. Accessed September 20, 2018. https://www.newspapers.com.

Dark, Joan. "Jerrie Cobb May be First Space Woman." *Boston Globe*. June 4, 1961. Digital. Accessed September 20, 2018. https://www.newspapers.com.

"The 'Mercury 13' Were They the First Ladies of Space?" AOPA.org. February 5, 2017. Digital. Accessed September 20, 2018. https://www.aopa.org/news-and-media/all-news/1997/february/pilot/the-mercury-13.

"MA-6 Orbit 3." Science.KSC.NASA.gov. Digital. Accessed September 20, 2018. https://science.ksc.nasa.gov/history/mercury/ma-6/sounds/ma-6-transcriptaudio-0.html.

Posten, Bruce. "Female Astronaut Hopes for Second Chance." *Indiana Gazette*. July 20, 1993. Digital. Accessed September 20, 2018. https://www.newspapers.com.

"Warsaw Aviatrix is Killed." Monash.edu.au. August 20, 1929. Digital. Accessed September 29, 2018. http://www.ctie.monash.edu.au/hargrave/crosson.html.

"Akronite Co-Pilot in Race." *Akron Beacon Journal*. June 17, 1957. Digital. Accessed January 2, 2019. https://www.newspapers.com.

"News letter" and "4th Annual Small Race: Prizes and Trophies." Ninety-Nines.org. September 1959. Digital. January 2, 2019. https://www.ninety-nines.org/pdf/newsmagazine/195909.pdf.

"Geraldyn M. Cobb." NationalAviation.org. Digital. Accessed January 2, 2019. https://www.nationalaviation.org/our-enshrinees/cobb-geraldyn-jerrie-m/.

Collins, Eileen. "Eileen Collins." Linkedin.com. Accessed January 2, 2019. https://www.linkedin.com/in/eileen-collins-8a582351/.

"Statistics of Income from Returns of Net Income for 1921." IRS.gov. 1923. Digital. Accessed January 2, 2019. https://www.irs.gov/pub/irs-soi/21soirepar.pdf.

"Amelia Earhart." AirandSpace.si.edu. Digital. Accessed January 2, 2019. https://airandspace.si.edu/explore-and-learn/topics/women-in-aviation/earhart.cfm.

"News letter." NinetyNines.org. November 1961. Digital. Accessed January 2, 2019. https://www.ninety-nines.org/pdf/newsmagazine/196111.pdf.

"Employment Outlook for Air Transportation." StLouisFed.org. 1951. Digital. January 2, 2019. https://fraser.stlouisfed.org/files/docs/publications/bls/bls_1128_1953.pdf.

"Solo Flier Wins Powder Puff." *The Times* (San Mateo, California). July 15, 1961. Digital. Accessed January 2, 2019. https://www.newspapers.com.

"News letter." Ninety-Nines.org. July 15, 1953. Digital. Accessed January 2, 2019. https://www.ninety-nines.org/pdf/newsmagazine/195307.pdf.

"Ponca City Pilot Wins Flying Derby." *The Lawton Constitution and Morning Press.* June 15, 1958. Digital. Accessed January 2, 2019. https://www.newspapers.com.

"Alan Bartlett Shepard, Jr." History.Navy.mil. November 16, 2016. Digital. Accessed January 2, 2019. https://www.history.navy.mil/research/histories/biographieslist/bios-s/shepherd-alan/Shepard-Alan-Text.html.

"The Sonic Boom Explained." Military.com. December 12, 2011. Digital. Accessed January 2, 2019. http://www.military.com/video/military-aircraft-operations/supersonic-flight/the-sonic-boom-explained/1323853761001.

Nichols, Ruth. "Famed Flyer Ruth Nichols Undergoes Astronaut Test." *Tyrone Daily Herald.* November 11, 1959. Digital. Accessed January 2, 2019. https://www.newspapers.com.

"Recruiting Opens for 10–15 New Astronauts." NASA.gov. June 12, 1963. Digital. Accessed January 3, 2019. https://spaceflight.nasa.gov/outreach/SignificantIncidents/assets/space-news-roundup!-vol.-2%2C-no.-17.pdf.

"Brigadier General Robert L. Cardenas." AF.mil. Digital. Accessed January 3, 2019.

"F11F Tiger." NationalAviationMuseum.org. Digital. Accessed January 3, 2019. https://www.navalaviationmuseum.org/aircraft/f11f-tiger/.

"Inflation Calculator." Dollartimes. Digital. Accessed January 3, 2019. https://www.dollartimes.com/inflation/inflation.php?amount=300&year=1960.

"Mercury Project Summary Including Results of the Fourth Manned Orbital Flight May 15 and 16, 1963." NASA.gov. October 1963. Digital. Accessed January 3, 2019. https://spaceflight.nasa.gov/outreach/SignificantIncidents/assets/summary_fourth_manned_orbital.pdf.

"May 24, 1962–Scott Carpenter on the Way to Mercury-Atlas 7 Launch Site." NASA.gov. May 25, 2017. Digital. Accessed January 3, 2019. https://www.nasa.gov/image-feature/may-24-1962-scott-carpenter-on-the-way-to-mercury-atlas-7-launch-site.

Stewart, Roy P. "Jerrie Gets in Soviet Paper." *The Daily Oklahoman.* July 28, 1963. Digital. Accessed January 3, 2019. https://www.newspapers.com.

Dunn, Marcia. "Alan Shepard Recalls Pioneering Flight as 'the First Baby Step' in Space." LATimes.com. April 28, 1991. Digital. Accessed January 3, 2019. http://articles.latimes.com/1991-04-28/news/mn-1463_1_alan-shepard.

Weigand, Virginia. "Jean Hixson, Flier, Former Teacher, Dies." *The Akron Beacon Journal.* September 23, 1984. Digital. Accessed January 3, 2019. https://abj.newspapers.com.

"Women's Place in Space." AirandSpace.si.edu. June 18, 2010. Digital. Accessed January 3, 2019. https://airandspace.si.edu/stories/editorial/womens-place-space.

"NASA, Space Community Remember 'Freedom 7.'" NASA.gov. May 5, 2011. Digital. Accessed January 4, 2019. https://www.nasa.gov/topics/history/features/50_freedom7.html.

"Phase 3: Reentry." Spacelog.org. Digital. Accessed January 4, 2019. http://mercury3. spacelog.org/page/00:00:07:06/.

"Inflation Calculator." Dollartimes.com. Digital. Accessed January 4, 2019. https:// www.dollartimes.com/calculators/inflation.htm.

"People in the News." *Central New Jersey Home News*. September 21, 1960. Digital. Accessed February 2, 2019 https://www.newspapers.com.

"Sputnik and The Dawn of the Space Age." NASA.gov. 2007. Digital. Accessed March 20, 2019. https://history.nasa.gov/sputnik/.

"Jerrie Cobb." WAI.org. Digital. Accessed March 20, 2019. https://www.wai.org/ pioneers/2000/jerrie-cobb.

Sherrod, Robert. "The Strenuous Selection Process." History.NASA.gov. Digital. Accessed March 21, 2019. https://history.nasa.gov/SP-350/toc.html.

"Biographical Data." JSC.NASA.gov. Digital. Accessed March 21, 2019. https://er.jsc. nasa.gov/seh/shepard.htm.

"Dressing for Altitude." NASA.gov. 2012. Digital. Accessed March 21, 2019. https://www. nasa.gov/sites/default/files/atoms/files/dressing-for-altitude-ebook_tagged.pdf.

"David Clark MC-3 Partial Pressure Flying Suit." NationalMuseum.af.mil. June 2, 2015. Digital. Accessed March 21, 2019. https://www.nationalmuseum. af.mil/Visit/Museum-Exhibits/Fact-Sheets/Display/Article/197600/ david-clark-mc-3-partial-pressure-flying-suit.

"Press Conference Introducing 7 Mercury Astronauts, Part 1/3." YouTube.com. April 9, 2009. Digital. Accessed March 21, 2019. https://www.youtube.com/ watch?v=FXiFlo_QUOM&t=564s,

INTERVIEWS, E-MAILS, AND MISCELLANEOUS SOURCES

Funk, Wally. Personal interview. January 10, 2018.

Funk, Wally. Personal interview. April 4, 2018.

Ratley, Sarah Gorelick. Personal interview. November 16, 2018.

Dean, Brandi K. "Astronaut Question from Scholastic Writer." Email message to the author. November 7, 2018.

Cagle, Myrtle. "99s Questionnaire." 1951.

PHOTO CREDITS

Images; 121: Bettmann/Getty Images; 124, 128: NASA; 135: A. Y. Owen/The LIFE Picture Collection/Getty Images; 138: Bill Bridges/The LIFE Images Collection/Getty Images; 144: NASA; 153: Bettmann/Getty Images; 156: Science History Images/Alamy Images; 159: Len Collection/Alamy Images; 167: courtesy Parade Magazine; 168: courtesy Parade Magazine; 171: Bettmann/Getty Images; 179: Ralph Morse/Getty Images; 184: Courtesy of the TWU Libraries Woman's Collection, Texas Woman's University, Denton, TX; 188: Shel Hershorn/The LIFE Images Collection/Getty Images; 191: Donald Uhrbrock/The LIFE Images Collection/ Getty Images; 195: Bettmann/Getty Images; 204: Ralph Morse/The LIFE Picture Collection/Getty Images; 212: Bill Bridges/The LIFE Images Collection/Getty Images; 216: Carl Iwasaki/The LIFE Images Collection/Getty Images; 219: Netflix/Everett Collection; 224: JSC/NASA; 232, 236: Ralph Morse/The LIFE Picture Collection/Getty Images; 246: Bettmann/Getty Images; 255: RGB Ventures/SuperStock/ Alamy Images; 256: Everett Collection Historical/Alamy Images; 262: NASA;264: Cci/REX/Shutterstock; 265: NASA; 273: courtesy of the International Women's Air & Space Museum, Cleveland, Ohio; 274: Don Cravens/The LIFE Images Collection/Getty Images; 279: NASA.

INDEX

Note: Page numbers in *italics* refer to illustrations.

A3D bombers, 66
Aero Commander, 78, 186
aircraft carriers, 47
Air Force Reserves, 60, 70
Air Knockers, 34–35
airline industry, women working in, 11
Air National Guard, 16
air pressure, low, 71
air races
    All-Women's Transcontinental Air Race, 28–30, *29*, 35, 36
    bottled oxygen used in, 30
    Chico–San Mateo Air Race (1947), 24–26
    dangers of, 27–28
    and expectations for female pilots, 30–31
    high costs of, 36
    sponsored by Cochran, 31
    supportive community in, 32–33
    using vacation time for, 35
    women competing in, 28, 29–30

Air Services of Dallas, 184–85

Akron Beacon Journal, 81

All-Women's Transcontinental Air Race (AWTAR), 28–30, *29*, 35, 36

altitude, records for, 77–78

altitude chamber tests, 91–92, 207–8

animals in test flights, 149–52, *150*, *153*, 154–55

Apollo 1 disaster, 260–61

Apollo 14 mission, 263

Apollo-Soyuz mission, 261, *262*

Apt, Mel, 70

armed forces

  and combat missions, 38–39, 41–45

  gender barriers in, 47

  and jets, 38–40

  and showboating, 43

  and Women Airforce Service Pilots (WASP), 9, *10*, 52–55

Armstrong, Neil, 252

Arnold, Henry "Hap," *80*

Asian American pilots, 7

astronauts

  first class of (*see* Mercury 7)

  gender assumptions in selection of, 95–96

  New Nine class of, 252

  recruitment of, 86–90, 243

  requirements for becoming (*see* requirements for astronauts)

Atlas rockets

  Cooper's graffiti on, 145–46

  failures and explosions of, 88, 118–19, 148–49

  and NASA's plans for space flight, 86

Aurora 7 mission, 235–36

B-25 bombers, 53–54
Banshee (F2H-2), 62
Barr, Norman, 95
beauty expectations for female pilots, 30–31
Beech aircraft, 186–87
Bendix Air Race (1935), 28
bicycle test, 111–12, *112*, 162, 283
Black American pilots, 6–7
Bonney, Walt, 143
Boomtown 1, 76
Boomtown II, 78
Braun, Wernher von, 126, 223
bravery of pilots, 41–42

Cagle, Myrtle, *191*
    air racing of, 36
    aviation experience of, 11
    and first American woman pilot in space, *279*
    flight hours of, 245
    and interviews, 164–65
    post–space program life of, 271
    and romantic relationships, 190
Cape Canaveral, Florida
    and Cocoa Beach, 176–77, 178–81
    failed Atlas rocket launch at, 118–19
    and *Friendship 7* mission, 222, 224, 231
capsule design
    early stages of, 97–99
    and engineering backgrounds of astronauts, 117
    and individual responsibilities of astronauts, 117–18
    and landing of capsules, 99
    prototype of, *121*

capsule design (*Cont.*)
  and reentry of capsules, 98–99, 120
  small size of, *98*, 119
  training in mockup of, 125
  weight considerations in, 101
  and window, 119–20, 223–24
Carpenter, Scott, *85*
  ambitions of, 23
  and *Aurora* 7 mission, 235–36, *236*
  and capsule design, 117
  and congressional hearing, 243, 249, 250–51
  family commitment of, 44
  flight training of, 21
  and *Friendship* 7 mission, 222, 228
  in Korean War, 44
  low-and-slow flight skills of, 44–45
  and NASA's requirements for astronauts, 93, 249, 266
  and partying of colleagues, 181
  post–Project Mercury life of, 262–63, *264*
  in psychological testing, 133
  recruited to space program, 85–86, 88, 89–90, 93,
    94, 95
  Schirra's criticisms of, 203
  showboating of, 66
  sports car of, 178
  as test pilot, 64, *65*, 66
centrifuge, training in, 114–16, *115*, 122
Chaffee, Roger, 260
Challenger space shuttle, 278
Cheung, Katherine Sui Fun, 7
Chico–San Mateo Air Race, 24–26, 28
Civilian Air Patrol (CAP), 8–9

Civilian Pilot Training Program (CPTP), 7–8

Cobb, Jerrie

administering testing, 215–17, *216*

advocacy for women astronauts, 231, 233

air racing of, 32–33

and astronaut testing, Phase I, ix–x, 107, 109–13, *110*, 127–30, *128*, 169

and astronaut testing, Phase II, 132–36, *135*

and astronaut testing, Phase III, 192, 206–12, *212*

and astronaut testing, results of, 135–36, 169, 283–84

aviation experience of, 75–76

and cancellation of testing, 220–21

changing clothes in the cockpit, 75

and Cochran, 221, 240

and congressional hearing, 242, 243, *246*, 246, 248, 251–52

death of, 284

and Discovery space shuttle, 270 79

employment of, 132–33

as "Female, Unit 1," 107

and first American woman pilot in space, *279*

first flight lesson of, 1–3, 12

and *Friendship 7* mission, 222–23, 225

and gender discrimination, 59, 186

Goodyear blimp piloted by, 157

and Harmon Trophy, 277

jet flight of, 104–5

Johnson's meeting with, 238–40

NASA consultant position of, 213–14, 218–19, 252

and NASA's requirements for astronauts, 266

at Peaceful Uses of Space conference, 212–13

post–space program life of, 276–79

press coverage of, 130–32, 136, 140, 159, 237–38

Cobb, Jerrie (*Cont.*)
    records set by, 76–78, *78*, 136–41, *138*, 186
    recruited to WISE project, 102–5
    rejected at copilot job interview, 58
    and salaries, 189
    sexual objectification of, 132, 140
    as single woman, 191
    and Soviets' woman cosmonauts, 231, 233
    speech impediment of, 77, 131
    spin recovery training, 127–30, *128*
    Tereshkova's sympathies for, 256
    test flights performed by, 75
Cochran, Jackie
    and air racing, 28, 31
    ambitions of, 168–69
    Cobb undermined by, 221, 240, 241–42
    and congressional hearing, 242, 247–48
    on discrimination claims, 269
    and funding of women's program, 158–59, 219
    involvement in program, 166–68, *167*, *168*
    Johnson's relationship with, 240–41
    leadership of WASPs, 55
    NASA consultant position of, 252
    on Phase II testing, 214
    piloting jets, 158–59, *159*
Cocoa Beach, Florida, 176–77, 178–81
Cold War with Soviet Union, 77, 126
Coleman, Bessie, 6–7
Collins, Eileen, 278, 280–81
combat missions, 38–39, 41–45
Commander 680F, 137–40, *138*
Commission on the Status of Women, 238–39

consciousness, g-induced loss of, 97–98
Continental Trophy Race in Detroit, 27
Cooper, Leroy Gordon "Gordo," *121*
   ambitions of, 23
   and capsule design, 117–18
   centrifuge training, 114–15
   Corvette of, 178
   Faith 7 mission, 254–55, *255*
   flight hours of, 271
   flight training of, 21–22
   and *Friendship* 7 mission, 227–28
   friendship with Grissom, 70–71
   and graffiti on Atlas rocket, 145–46
   and partying in Cocoa Beach, 176
   piloting jets in Germany, 46
   post–Project Mercury life of, 261
   and press look on lack of airtime, 177
   recruited to space program, 90, *94*, 95
   on Shepard, 203
   as test pilot, 70–72
   on women astronaut candidates, 258
Corvettes of Mercury 7 astronauts, 178
costs of flying, 5–6, 10, 36
Crossfield, Scott, 68
Crusader (F-8), 73–74, *74*

Dallas Air Championship, 34
Dallas Doll Derby, 36
Dana, Bill, 201
dangers in aviation
   in air racing, 27
   and ejecting from jets, 69, 72

dangers in aviation (*Cont.*)
  of high-altitude flight, 71–72
  for test pilots, 61, 70, 71–72, 88
  for women serving in WASP, 54
DC-3s, 76
Delta Daggers (F-102), 71, 81, 177–78
Delta Darts (F-106), 178
Dietrich, Jan
  and astronaut testing, Phase I, 162, 166
  and astronaut testing, results of, 283
  aviation experience of, 11, *25*
  at Chico–San Mateo Air Race, 24–26
  as chief pilot at Cessna dealership, 187,
    188, 189
  flight hours of, 161, 244
  and NASA's requirements for astronauts, 266
  and *Parade* magazine article, 166, *167*, *168*
  post–space program life of, 272, 274–75
  and salaries, 189
  as single woman, 191
Dietrich, Marion
  and astronaut testing, Phase I, 166
  aviation experience of, 11, *25*
  at Chico–San Mateo Air Race, 24–26
  flight hours of, 244
  and *Parade* magazine article, 166, *167*
  post–space program life of, 272, 274
  as single woman, 191
Dilbert Dunker tests, 211
Discovery space shuttle, 278
divorce, scandal of, 190
doctors, women as, 185–86

Earhart, Amelia, 6, 30
ear testing, 109, 111
Edwards Air Force Base, 67–72
Eisenhower, Dwight D., 82, 83
ejecting from planes, 69, 72, 211
electrical pulse tests, 111, 163
employment of women
    in airline industry, 11
    and attitudes about women's abilities, 187, 189
    balancing marriages with, 190
    and competition with men for jobs, 26
    limited options, 26, 185–86
    and sacrifices of women candidates, 218
    and salary disparities, 189
engineering
    background of astronauts in, 117
    women blocked from education in, 186
equal opportunities for women, 238–39
expertise achieved by women pilots
    and ambitions of female pilots, 52
    and attitudes toward female aviators, 57
    and gender discrimination, 59
    and penalization of women, 56
    in WASPs program, 52–54

F11F-1, 64, 66
F8F Bearcats, 18–19
Fairchild airplanes, 49
Faith 7 mission, 254–55, 255
family lives of women, 191–92
fatalities in aviation
    in air racing, 27

fatalities in aviation (*Cont.*)
   among test pilots, 61, 70
   among women serving in WASP, 54
   due to sabotage, 55
"Female, Unit 1," 107. *See also* Cobb, Jerrie
femininity and social expectations for female pilots, 30–31
Flickinger, Donald, *101*
   and Project WISE, 100, 102–5
   role at NASA, 95
   and selection of Mercury 7, *94*
   and urgent pace of NASA, 100
flight hours
   and family lives of women, 192
   of Glenn, 161
   of Mercury 13 candidates, 161, 244–45
   paying for, 10
flight instructors
   and expenses of flying, 6
   and minority populations, 6–7
   Steadman, 50–51
   women as, 11, 26–27
flight/pressure suits, 71–72, 106, 127, 207, 284
Freedom 7 mission, 170–75, *171*, 179, 196
Friendship 7 mission, 222–31
   Americans' watching, 230–31
   and first American in orbit, 222–25, *224*
   and landing bag crisis, 225–30, 264
   and sunset seen from space, 225
Funk, Wally
   ambitions of, 33–34
   applications to astronaut program, 267, 275
   and astronaut testing, Phase I, 162

and astronaut testing, Phase II, 215, *216*, 216–17
and astronaut testing, Phase III, 275
and astronaut testing, results of, 283
aviation experience of, 12
background of, 33–34
and engineering school, 186
and first American woman pilot in space, *279*
flight hours of, 245, 275
and NASA's requirements for astronauts, 266
and parents' presence at testing clinic, 161
post–space program life of, 275–76
as single woman, 191
The Fun of It (Earhart), 6

Gagarin, Yuri, 155–57, *156*
Gemini 3 mission, 260
Gemini 5 mission, 261
gender barriers and discrimination
    in armed forces, 47
    and attitudes about women's abilities, 57, 58, 187, 189
    in commercial aviation settings, 274
    congressional hearing on NASA's, 242–43, *246*, 246–52
    in education, 185–86, 189
    in employment arenas, 185–87
    and expectations for appearance, 30–31, 186–87
    and interviewer's rejection of Cobb, 58
    and jets, 39–40, 81, 102, 238
    in missionary piloting, 276
    and NASA's criteria for astronauts, 221
    and test pilots, 64, 73, 74, 102, 184
    women's response to, 59
gender equality, 234

General Motors, 178
Germany, U.S. military in, 45–46
Glenn, Annie, *232*
Glenn, John
  ambitions of, 22
  on astronaut testing, 107
  and capsule design, 117, 119
  celebrity of, 142, 264
  and congressional hearing, 243, 249–51
  on *Discovery* space shuttle, 264, 278
  flight hours of, 161
  Friendship 7 mission, 222–31, *224*, 264
  and intervention in potential scandal, 180
  in Korean War, 43–44, *44*
  as Marine Corp pilot, 14–15
  medals awarded to, 44
  and medical testing for space program, *91*, 162
  military service in World War II, 13–14, 17
  and NASA's requirements for astronauts, 93, 249–50, 266
  objection to flight assignment, 202
  and partying of colleagues, 178–81
  post–Project Mercury life of, 263–64, *265*
  and press, 179, 180
  and Project Bullet transcontinental flight, 73–74, *74*, 82
  in psychological testing, 133
  quieter lifestyle of, 178–79
  recruited to space program, 86, 90, 93, *94*, 95
  on Shepard, 263
  and Soviets' success, 156
  on spin recovery training, 122
  stunt flying of, 15
  and sunset seen from space, 225

and tension on team, 203
as test pilot, 73–74
ticker tape parade honoring, *232*
on urination in flight suits, 125
weight of, 93
on women astronauts, 249–50, 251
Goodyear blimp piloted by Cobb, 157
Gorelick, Sarah
  air racing of, 11, 35
  and Cochran's ambitions, 169
  credentials of, 164
  and first American woman pilot in space, *279*
  flight hours of, 245
  and interviews, 164
  and NASA's requirements for astronauts, 266
  post–space program life of, 270–71
  quitting job to stay in program, 217–18, *219*, 270
gravity and g's endured by astronauts, 97–98, 114–17, 174,
  208–9
Grissom, Virgil "Gus"
  ambitions of, 23
  bravery of, 42
  and capsule design, 117, 119–20
  celebrity of, 143, 146
  Corvette of, 178, *179*
  early years of, 19–20
  friendship with Cooper, 70–71
  in Korean War, 38–39, *41*, 42
  Liberty Bell 7, 193–200, *195*, 201, 203, 205, 254
  medals awarded to, 39
  post–Project Mercury life of, 260–61
  quiet nature of, 146

Grissom, Virgil "Gus" (*Cont.*)
  recruited to space program, 90, *94*, 95
  and rocket failure close-up, 157
  as test pilot, 70–72
  youthful dreams of flying, 19–20
gunnery practice missions, 52

Hart, Jane Briggs, *33*
  and astronaut testing, Phase I, 165
  aviation experience of, 11, 57
  background of, 32
  and congressional hearing, 242, *246*, 246–47, 248,
    251–52
  helicopter pilot's license of, 57–58
  Johnson's meeting with, 238–40
  media blitz of, 237–38
  and NASA's requirements for astronauts, 266
  post–space program life of, 269
  as test pilot, 189
Hart, Phil, 57–58, 165
high-altitude flight, 71
Hixson, Jean
  air racing of, 35
  ambitions of, 11
  and Arnold, Army General, *80*
  aviation experience of, 79
  and B-25 bombers, 53–54, 185
  and breaking the sound barrier, 78–80
  flight hours of, 244
  and gender discrimination, 59
  and NASA's requirements for astronauts, 266
  piloting a jet, 81

post–space program life of, 272
as single woman, 191
test flights performed by, 53–54, 64
WASP service of, 11, 52–53
Hurrle, Rhea
air racing of, 36
ambitions of, 11
and astronaut testing, Phase II, 215, *216*, 216–17
and astronaut testing, results of, 283
flight hours of, 244
post–space program life of, 272

Illinois Women's Air Meet, 35–36
income disparities, 189
instrument ratings, 160
International Air Race, 36
irolation toото, 133 35, *135*, 216 17

Jemison, Mae, 280
jets
of American armed forces, 40
and attitudes about women's abilities, 189
Cobb's first flight in, 104–5
Cochran's piloting of, 158–59, *159*
ease of flying, 40
ejecting from, 69, 72, 211
and gender barriers, 39–40, 81, 102, 238
and Hixson, 81
in Korean War, 38–40
of Mercury 7 astronauts, 177–78
and NASA's requirements for astronauts, 89, 102, 105, 221,
    246, 248–49

Johnson, Lyndon B.
  Cobb and Hart's meeting with, 238–40
  Cochran's relationship with, 240–41
  and Glenn's *Friendship* 7 mission, 231, *232*
  in political cartoon on women candidates, 258
  on Soviet threat, 82

Kennedy, John F.
  assassination of, 257
  on equal opportunities for women, 238–39
  and Glenn's *Friendship* 7 mission, 231
  and mission to land on the moon, 181–82
  and Shepard's *Freedom* 7 mission, 175
Khrushchev, Nikita, 255
Kilrain, Susan, 281
Korean War, 38–39, 40–46, 189
Kraft, Chris, 229–30

landing of capsule, 99, 123–25, *124*
Langley Aeronautical Laboratory, 117, *118*
Leverton, Irene, *57*
  air racing of, 35–36
  attempt to join WASPs, 55
  aviation experience of, 11
  fired from cargo plane position, 56–57
  flight hours of, 161, 244, 271
  as flight instructor, 26–27
  on marriage, 191
  post–space program life of, 271, *274*
  quitting job to stay in program, 218, 270
Liberty Bell 7 mission, 193–200
  and blown-hatch controversy, 194, 196, 197, 198–200, 254, 260

LIFE magazine on, 205
loss of capsule, *195*, 197–99
near drowning of Grissom, 193–94, 198
and tensions on team, 203
LIFE magazine
on Cobb, 130
feature on women candidates, 256–57
on *Liberty Bell 7* mission, 205
on Mercury 7 astronauts, 143, 204–5
on NASA's shortsightedness, 256–57
Lovelace, William Randolph "Randy," III
ambitions of, 130
and astronaut testing, Phase I, 161–62, 169
and astronaut testing, Phase II, 133
and astronaut testing, Phase III, 207, 214–15
and cancellation of testing, 219–20, 234
and Cobb's participation, 102–5, 129–30
and Cochran's ambitions, 109
and congressional hearing, 243
death of, 267–68
"Female, Unit 1," 107 (*see also* Cobb, Jerrie)
and Flickinger's exit from Project WISE, 105
and funding of program, 158, 159
going public with findings, 130
and NASA's disinterest in women astronauts, 107, 234
and Project WISE, 100
recruitment of candidates, 160
requirements of candidates, 159–60
role at NASA, 95–96
secrecy encouraged by, 215
selection of candidates, 159–60
speech on women astronaut candidates, 212–13

Lovelace, William Randolph "Randy," III (*Cont.*)
   and success rate of women, 169
   vision for women in space, 268
Lovelace Clinic in Albuquerque, New Mexico
   and success rate of women, 169
   testing of female candidates, 107, 109–13, *110*,
      160–63, 165–69
   testing of male candidates, 90
Luce, Clare Booth, 256
Luft, Ulrich, 111–12

Mach 1, 68
marriage, challenges of, 189–91
Melroy, Pamela Ann, 281
menstruation, questions about, 102, 284
Mercury 7
   and animals in test flights, 152
   antics and partying of, 176–77, 178–81, 201, *204*
   astronauts, *94*, 94–95, *144* (*see also individual astronauts*)
   brotherhood of, 265
   and capsule design, 97–99, *98*, 101, 117–18, 119–20
   celebrity of, 142–43, 145–46
   and Cobb's astronaut testing and training, x, 213–14
   Corvettes of, 178
   engineering backgrounds of, 117
   and flight assignments, 202–3
   individual responsibilities of, 117–18
   and landing of capsule, 123–25, *124*
   and lecture program, 117, *118*
   medical testing for, 90–92, *91*, 107
   and piloting jets, 177–78
   and piloting of spacecraft, 87, 146–47

press conference introducing, *94*, 94–95
press coverage of, 142–43, 175, 179, 228–29
psychological testing for, 92, 133–34
public's love affair with, 142–43, 176, 228–29, 230–31
recruitment of, 86–90
séances (private meetings) of, 203–4
selection of, 93
and Skelton, 106
status at NASA, 145
teasing and wisecracks aimed at, 154–55
tension among, 179, 181, 182, 202–4
and test pilots' derision, 146–47, 152
training (*see* training of astronauts)
urination in flight suits, 125, 170–71
and women astronaut candidates, 243, 249–51, 258
Mercury 13 (women astronaut candidates), 244–45
   and animals in test flights, 150
   and astronaut testing, Phase I, ix–x, 105–7, 109–13, *110*,
      127–30, *128*, 161–69, *168*
   and astronaut testing, Phase II, 132–36, 215, *216*, 216–17
   and astronaut testing, Phase III, 192, 206–12, *212*, 214–17, 275
   and astronaut testing, results of, 135–36, 169, 250, 283–84
   bias against, 101–2
   and cancellation of testing, 219–20
   criteria for, 160
   and crowd appeal, 164
   and first American woman pilot in space, *279*
   flight hours of, 192, 244–45, 250
   flight/pressure suits for, 106, 127, 207
   friendly competition among, 216
   and funding of program, 158, 219
   and Glenn's testimony on, 250

Mercury 13 (*Cont.*)
  legacy of, 280
  and Lovelace's death, 267–68
  and NASA's requirements for astronauts, 102, 238, 243,
    249–50, 266–67
  natural advantages of, 100–101, 130, 131, 238
  origins of term, 278
  public mockery of, 257–58
  recruited for testing, 160–61
  relationship statuses of, 189–92
  return to life after candidate testing, 257–58
  sacrifices made by, 218
  and selection of candidates, 159–60
  spin recovery training, 127–30, *128*
  success rate of, 169
MiGs (Soviet fighter jets), 38–39, 40–41, 42–43, 63
minority populations, 6–7
motion sickness, ability to withstand, 209–11
Multi-Axis Space Training Inertial Facility (MASTIF), 122–23,
    127–30, *128*, 173

National Advisory Committee for Aeronautics
    (NACA), 83
National Aeronautic Association, 223
National Aeronautics and Space Act (1958), 83
National Aeronautics and Space Administration (NASA)
  and animals in test flights, 149–52, *150*, *153*, 154–55
  Apollo 1 disaster, 260–61
  astronaut testing of women cancelled by, 219–20
  and celebrity of astronauts, 143, 145
  and Cobb and Hart's media blitz, 238
  and Cobb's advocacy for women astronauts, 231, 233
  Cobb's consultant position with, 213–14, 218–19, 252

on Cobb's training, 136
Cochran's consultant position with, 252
and congressional hearing on discrimination, 242–43, *246*,
    246–52
craft for manned space flight (*see* capsule design)
creation of, 83
disinterest in women astronauts, 107, 136, 233–34, 256
and first American in orbit, 222–25
and first American women in space, 278, 280–81
first class of astronauts (*see* Mercury 7)
man-on-the-moon goal of, 182, 231, 257
mission of *Aurora 7*, 235–36
mission of *Faith 7*, 254–55, *255*
mission of *Freedom 7*, 170–75, *171*, 179, 196
mission of *Friendship 7*, 222–31, *224*, 264
mission of *Liberty Bell 7*, 193–200, *195*, 201, 203,
    205, 254
mission of *Sigma 7*, 253–54
and New Nine class of astronauts, 252
and Peaceful Uses of Space conference, 212–13
and Project Apollo, 234
and Project Gemini, 234
and Project Mercury (*see* Project Mercury)
recruitment of astronauts, 86–90, 243
requirements of (*see* requirements for astronauts)
and rocket failures, 88, 118–19, 148–49, 157
and Skelton with Mercury 7, 106–7
and Soviets' success, 155–56
Space Race goals revised by, 234–35
and unknowns of spaceflight, 99, 149
urgent pace of, 100, 126, 154, 200–201, 251
women accepted into program, 278
and women's roles in space flights, 281

National Air Races in Akron, Ohio, 35
Naval Ordnance Test Station at China Lake,
     California, 66–67
Nichols, Ruth, 7
  and astronaut testing, 105
  and cancellation of WISE project, 106
  and high costs of flying, 5
  pilot's license of, 5
Ninety-Nines, 4–5, 7
Nixon, Richard, 277
nonstop long-distance flight in a light propeller plane, records
     for, 76–77
North, Warren J., 86–87

Odlum, Floyd, 158
Odom, Bill, 27
Oklahoma City Veterans Affairs, 133

Parade magazine, 166, *167*
Patuxent River, Maryland, test pilot school at, 61, 64, 66, 67, 73
Peaceful Uses of Space conference, 212–13
Pentagon, 85–86, 219
pilot's licenses, 5, 7–8
Powder Puff Derbys, 30
Powers, Shorty, 155, 229
press
  access to mission status updates, 228–29
  on appearances of female pilots, 77
  and Cobb's astronaut training, 130–32, 136
  and Cobb's record-beating flights, 77, 140
  and Cooper's leak on lack of airtime, 177
  and *Friendship* 7 crisis, 228

and Glenn, 179
and Hixson's breaking of sound barrier, 80
on Laika, Soviet test dog, 149
and media blitz of Cobb and Hart, 237–38
mockery of women candidates, 258
and public's love affair with astronauts, 228–29
and Shepard's *Freedom 7* mission, 175
and Soviets' success, 155–56
treatment of women air racers, 29–30
procedures trainer, 125
Project Apollo, 234
Project Bullet transcontinental flight, 73–74, *74*, 82
Project Gemini, 234
Project Mercury
    astronauts of, *94*, 94–95 (*see also* Mercury 7)
    closing of, 260
    mission of *Aurora 7*, 235–36
    mission of *Faith 7*, 254–55, *255*
    mission of *Freedom 7*, 170–75, *171*, 179, 196
    mission of *Sigma 7*, 253–54
    See also Friendship 7 mission; *Liberty Bell 7* mission
Project Sealab, 262
Project WISE (Women in Space Earliest)
    and bias against women astronauts, 101–2
    cancellation of project, 105–6
    first test subject for, 102–5 (*see also* Cobb, Jerrie)
    launch of, 100
    and NASA's criteria for astronauts, 102
    and natural advantages of women, 100–101
    pushback against, 102
    testing in, 105, 106
propeller planes, speeds of, 39–40

race issues, 6–7, 64

Rankin, William, 72

records setting

for altitude in light twin-engine plane, 77–78,
136–41, *138*

for continuous flight, 73–74, 82

for nonstop long-distance flight in a light propeller plane,
76–77

for speed, 76, 186

Redstone rockets, 148

reentry of capsule, 98–99, 120, 173–74

refueling, midair, 73–74, 81, 82

relationships statuses of women astronauts, 189–92

renting airplanes, 5–6

requirements for astronauts

basics of, 89

and civilian aviators, 243, 266

jet flight and test flight, 89, 102, 105, 221, 238,
246, 248–49, 258

relaxed in specific circumstances, 93, 249, 266

and selection of Mercury 7, 93

and women candidates, 102, 221, 238, 266–67

Ride, Sally, 278

rocket failures, 88, 118–19, 148–49, 157

sabotage of women pilots, 54–55

Sabre (F-86), 38, 40, 41, 45–46

salary disparities, 189

satellite launches, 82–83, *84*

Schirra, Wally

ambitions of, 22

background of, 17–18, *18*

on brotherhood of Mercury 7, 264–65

and capsule design, 117

Corvette of, 178

criticisms of NASA, 203

in flight school, 19

flying careers of parents, 17–18

in Korean War, 42–43

medals awarded to, 43

and medical testing for space program, 162

and partying in Cocoa Beach, 201

and piloting jets, 178

post–Project Mercury life of, 263

recruited to space program, 86, 90, *94*, 95

showboating of, 43

Sigma 7 mission, 253–54

on spin recovery training, 122

as test pilot, 66–67

See, Elliot, 252

Shepard, Alan

ambitions of, 22, 47

antics and partying of, 176, 180, 201, 203, 217

in centrifuge, *115*

Cooper's criticisms of, 203

Corvette of, 178

expertise of, 62

first flight assignment given to, 202

and *Freedom* 7 mission, 170–75, *171*, 179, 196

Glenn on, 263

impatience of, 155

military service in World War II, 19

morning routine of, 46–47

on NASA's jet flight and test flight requirements, 258

Shepard, Alan (*Cont.*)
  on *Oriskany* aircraft carrier, 47
  post–Project Mercury life of, 263
  on procedures training, 125
  recruited to space program, 90, *94*, 95
  selected as first astronaut, 154
  and Soviets' success, 156
  in spin recovery training, 123, 129
  stunt flying of, 62
  as test pilot, 46, 60–62, *63*, 184
  and test pilots' derision, 147
  on urgency of mission, 126
  urination in flight suit, 170–71
  on women astronauts, 258
Sheppard Field, 2
Shooting Star (P-80), 40
Sidewinder missiles, 66–67, *67*
Sigma 7 mission, 253–54
Skelton, Betty, 106, *108*
Slayton, Deke
  ambitions of, 22
  background of, 15–17
  and capsule design, 117–18
  celebrity and, 143
  on Cobb, 214
  Corvette of, 178
  criticisms of colleagues, 203
  and flight assignments, 202
  grounded for heart defect, 255, 261
  and medical testing for space program, 90
  on NASA's jet flight and test flight requirements, 258
  and partying in Cocoa Beach, 201

piloting jets in Germany, 45–46
post–Project Mercury life of, 261
recruited to space program, 90, *94*, 95
and technicians at NASA, 145
as test pilot, 68–70
on women astronauts, 258
Sloan, Jerri (later Truhill), *184*
air racing of, 34
and Air Services of Dallas, 184–85
ambitions of, 183–84
and astronaut testing, Phase I, 163
and astronaut testing, Phase III, 192
aviation experience of, 11
family life of, 183
and first American woman pilot in space, *279*
flight hours of, 192, 245
and marriage difficulties, 165, 66, 190, 218
and NASA's requirements for astronauts, 266
post–space program life of, 272, *273*
as test pilot, 183–85
youthful ambitions to fly, 34
Slow-Rotation Room (SRR), 209–11
sound barrier, breaking, 68, 78–80
Soviet Union
and *Apollo-Soyuz* mission, 261, *262*
and Cobb's record-beating flight, 77
Cold War with, 77, 126
and first human to fly in space, 155–57, *156*
and first woman in space, 231, 233, 239, *255*, 255–56, *256*
and Korean War, 38–39, 40–41
MiG fighter jets of, 38–39, 40–41, 42–43, 63
satellite launch of, 82

Soviet Union (*Cont.*)

    test flights with animals, 149

    and urgent pace of NASA, 100, 154, 200

    and *Vostok 2* mission, 200

Space Race

    and Americans' *Freedom 7* mission, 170–75

    and Americans' *Friendship 7* mission, 222–23, *224*

    and Americans' partying in Cocoa Beach, 180

    end of, 261

    and first American in orbit, 222–25

    and first Soviet in orbit, 155–57, *156*

    and first woman in space, 231, 233, 239, *255*, 255–56, *256*

    NASA's revised stance on, 234–35

    and Soviets' orbiting missions, 155–57, *156*, 200

    and Soviets' *Sputnik* launch, 82

SpaceX, 282

speed, records for, 76

Spidle, Jake Jr., 284

spin recovery training, 122–23, 127–30, *128*, 173

Sputnik, 82

Sputnik II, 149

Starfire (F-94 C), 79–80

Steadman, Bea, *33*, *51*

    air racing of, 32

    and astronaut testing, Phase I, 162, 163

    and astronaut testing, results of, 283

    aviation experience of, 11

    and first American woman pilot in space, *279*

    flight hours of, 244

    as flight instructor, 50–51

    and gender discrimination, 59

    and NASA's requirements for astronauts, 266

post–space program life of, 271–72

qualifications of, 50–51

and starting her Fairchild, 49–50

stereotypes of women, 185, 203

stewardesses, 11

Stratofortresses, 81

Stratotankers, 82

stress tests, 162

Stumbough, Gene Nora

air racing of, 11, 35

background of, 34–35

employment in aircraft industry, 186–87

and first American woman pilot in space, 279

flight hours of, 245

and NASA's requirements for astronauts, 266

post–space program life of, 270

quitting job to stay in program, 218, 270

stunt flying and showboating

of Carpenter, 66

of Glenn, 15

of Schirra, 43

of Schirra's parents, 18

of Shepard, 62

survival skills training, 123–25, 124

Tereshkova, Valentina, 255, 255–56

Terrain Following Radar (TFR), 185

test pilots

about, 61–62

and advances in Soviet aircraft, 63

and attitudes about women's abilities, 189

dangers faced by, 61, 70, 71–72, 88

test pilots (*Cont.*)
  expectations of errors in, 73
  expertise of, 61–62
  and flight hours, 192
  and gender barriers, 64, 73, 74, 102, 184
  grip and rip approach of, 63–64
  Hart, 189
  as male dominated job, 64
  and Mercury 7 astronauts, 146–47, 152
  and NASA's requirements for astronauts, 89, 102, 221, 246,
    248–49
  at Naval Ordnance Test Station at China Lake,
    California, 66–67
  racial exclusivity in, 64
  recruited to space program, 88–89
  Shepard, 60–62, *63*
  Sloan, 183–85
  status of, 61
  test pilot school, 46, 61, 64, 66, 73
  training of, 60–61
Texas Instruments, 183
Thaden, Louise, 30
Thunderchief F-105 (*Thud*), 68–70
Thunderjet (F-84), 40, 42
Tiger (F11F), 60, 61
tilt table testing, 109, *110*
training of astronauts
  centrifuge training, 114–16, *115*, 122
  and lecture program, 117, *118*
  in procedures trainer, 125
  spin recovery training, 122–23, 173
  survival skills training, 123–25, *124*
  and unknowns of spaceflight, 115–16

water landings training, 211
weightlessness training, 120
Truhill, Jerri Sloan. *See* Sloan, Jerri
Truhill, Joe, 184, 272

urination in flight suits, 125
U.S. Air Force, 105–6, 206–7
U.S. House of Representatives' Committee on Science and Astronautics, 242, 252, 258
U.S. Naval Aviation School of Medicine, 206–12
U.S. Navy, 83, 219, 220
USS *Oriskany*, 47, 61

Vanguard missile explosion, 83, *84*
vertigo testing, 109, 111, 162
Voas, Robert, 258
Vomit Comet, 120
Vooyka, James, 27

water landings, training for, 211
Webb, James, 213, 235–36, 239
weight considerations in capsule design, 101
weightlessness training, 120
White, Ed, 260
Women Airforce Service Pilots (WASP), *10*
  about, 9
  dangers of, 52
  expertise achieved by women in, 54
  and flight-testing planes, 52–54
  and gunnery practice missions, 52
  Hixson's service with, 52–53
  sabotaged by male pilots, 54–55
women astronaut candidates. *See* Mercury 13

women pilots
  community of, 31
  diversity in, 6–7
  expertise achieved by, 52–54, 56, 57, 59
  focus on appearances of, 30–31, 77
  and gender barriers, 57, 58
  general attitudes about, 57, 58
  job opportunities of, 26, 187, 189, 190, 218
  male pilots' treatment of, 52
  number of licensed women fliers, 7–8
  and pressure to be perfect, 73
  racing airplanes (*see* air races)
  sabotage of, 54–55
Wood, Betty Taylor, 55
World War II
  American life after, 22
  and Civilian Air Patrol, 8–9
  flight training of male pilots in, 14
  opportunities for male veterans of, 9–10, 13–14, 16–17
  and Women Airforce Service Pilots (WASP), 9, *10*, 52–55
Wright-Patterson Air Force Base in Ohio, 91–92, 105, 132, 206–7

Yeager, Chuck, 68, 147, 152

ACKNOWLEDGMENTS

Gus Grissom once said, "Spaceflights are only a part of any space program—the final proof, the period at the end of a sentence." He was referring to the endless hours of work that led up to each flight, the enormous support crews, and the sleep-deprived scientists, engineers, and mathematicians who put their heads together in order to accomplish something as impossibly difficult as shoving a guy inside a cone and then blasting him into outer space.

While writing this book wasn't quite as involved as pioneering American spaceflight, it sometimes felt that way. And the "final proof" you're holding in your hands right now would never have been possible without an incredible pool of people who went out of their way to help me.

First, I want to thank my husband, Matt, who always believed in this project. His unflinching support was invaluable and it's something I hope my daughters will remember when they're ready to find life partners of their own. Zoe and Lena deserve their own thanks as well, for listening to their exhausted mother talk about airplanes and spaceships throughout their toddler years.

I also want to express my gratitude to the many aviators who helped me tell flight stories the way a pilot would. Special thanks go to my very favorite air force pilot, Tyler Sanborn, for walking me through the basics of jet flight, reading chapter after chapter, and helping me with pilot lingo. I'd also like to thank him for making me feel a little better about almost puking during my first flight lesson.

While I'm on the topic, I want to thank my flight instructor, Pete Subtelny, and A&M Aviation for the unforgettable lessons. Without the experience of piloting a Cessna 172, I don't think I could have truly grasped the magnitude of what these women did every day. And, Pete, I still can't believe you let me do a takeoff.

More thanks go to naval aviation instructor Stacy Kulczewski for explaining high-altitude flight, the difference between pressure suits and g-suits, and exactly *how* a pilot can get out of an inverted spin. Her patience was a gift and her insight was key.

Some very special, love-soaked thanks go to my kind, funny, and brilliant agent, Jennifer Unter, who understood that this story deserved to be read and shared. I am also so very grateful for my editors Lisa Sandell, who graciously answered emails late into the night and who bravely allowed me to follow my instincts, and Amanda Shih, whose brilliant work shaped a rough collection of stories into something much better. Amanda, you're an actual genius.

I must give proper due to the world's funniest space expert, Dave Hawksett, who gave expert advice while also making me laugh. He made fact-checking the nitty-gritty of space history unbelievably entertaining.

I am not the first person to narrate this tale. I want to thank three writers for their work documenting this story: Margaret Weitekamp (*Right Stuff, Wrong Sex*), Martha Ackmann (*The Mercury 13*), and Stephanie Nolen (*Promised the Moon*). Each of their books was an inspiration and guide for me as I navigated this complex, multifaceted story. And as most of the key players in this story have since passed, I relied heavily upon the magnificent stories and quotes these talented writers were able to capture in their own books as source material for mine.

This book is the result of two years of research. Much of the information included within its pages would not have been available to me without the thorough work of various librarians, archivists, and historians. My deepest gratitude goes to the Bentley Historical Library, the 99s Museum of Women Pilots, and the International Women's Air and Space Museum.

Finally, I want express my thanks to the women who lived through this time and shared their stories with me. Wally Funk; Gene Nora Jessen; Sarah Gorelick Ratley; and Dr. Lovelace's daughter, Jackie Lovelace, were all incredibly generous with their time and memories. During one phone call with Wally, I asked a question about the rudders on a single-engine airplane. When she realized that I didn't understand how they worked, she gasped and then exclaimed, "Oh, honey! Go get yourself into a cockpit and call me back."

So I did.

Thank you, Wally, for that gentle shove. You were right. Flying *is* amazing.

ABOUT THE AUTHOR

REBECCA SIEGEL is a children's author and editor who lives outside Chicago, Illinois, with her husband and two daughters. For more information, visit rebeccasiegel.org.